8.95
sch

DATE DUE

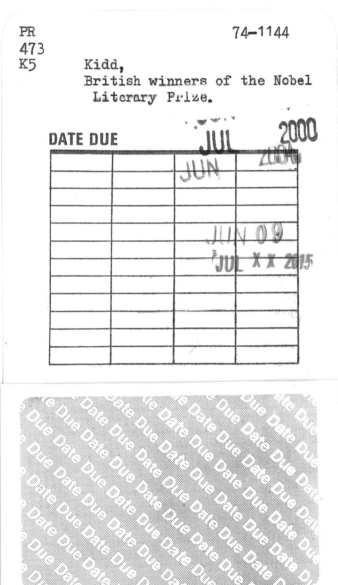

		JUL	2000
		JUN	
		JUN 09	
		JUL X X 2015	

British Winners of the Nobel Literary Prize

★ ★ ★

by Walter E. Kidd

UNIVERSITY OF OKLAHOMA PRESS
NORMAN

The paper on which this book is printed bears the watermark of the University of Oklahoma Press and has an effective life of at least three hundred years.

Also by Walter E. Kidd

> British Winners of the Nobel Literary Prize (editor, Norman, 1973)
> Oregon Odyssey of Wheels (Fort Smith, 1973)
> American Winners of the Nobel Literary Prize (editor, with Warren G. French, Norman, 1968)
> West: Manhattan to Oregon (Chicago, 1966)
> Adventures of Frelf (Racine, 1963)
> Time Turns West (Cleveland, 1961)
> Slow Fire of Time (Chicago, 1956)

Library of Congress Cataloging in Publication Data

Kidd, Walter E.
  British winners of the Nobel Literary Prize.
  Bibliography: p.
  1. English literature—20th century—History and criticism. 2. Nobel prizes. 3. Authors, English—20th century—Biography. I. Title.
PR473.K5   820'.9'0091   72–9270
ISBN 0–8061–1075–9

To the memory of
DR. THOMAS E. FERGUSON
a dynamic educator
who helped to vitalize
the aspiration of democracy
toward a humanized world

CONTENTS

BRITISH WINNERS OF THE
NOBEL LITERARY PRIZE

BRITISH WINNERS OF THE
NOBEL LITERARY PRIZE
INTRODUCTION

by *Walter E. Kidd*

O F THE FIVE INTERNATIONAL awards prescribed by the Swedish
industrialist Alfred Nobel in his will of 1895, the Nobel Literary Prize
has caused the most difficulties for the awards committee. Nobel's will
directs that the prize is to be awarded "to the person who shall have
produced in the field of literature the most outstanding work of an
idealistic tendency" and that it be administered by "the Academy in
Stockholm"—the Swedish Academy.

While the monetary award is substantial, the resulting international
prestige is enormous. Whether or not each honoree has been unquestionably worthy according to literary criteria has often been debatable.
It can probably be argued that in certain cases dissension within the
Swedish Academy has made compromises necessary, as in 1908, when
the German philosopher Rudolf Eucken was selected over Algernon
Charles Swinburne, Count Leo Tolstoi, and Selma Lagerlöf. Even the
committee members' interpretations of "work of an idealistic tendency"
have involved debate about whether or not an author should be
appraised for a single work or for all his works up to the time of
judgment.

Since the first literary award in 1901, seven British writers have been
honored by the Swedish Academy. *British Winners of the Nobel
Literary Prize* is concerned with these seven writers, an assessment of
the literary merits of their writings both before and after they received

3

the prizes, and brief considerations of other close contenders. The qualities primarily responsible for the award to each of the seven British writers honored from 1907 to 1969 are appraised, and attention is focused on the qualities in British writings that are regarded as most important in contemporary culture.

The approach and format of this book largely follows that of the earlier *American Winners of the Nobel Literary Prize*. The selections evaluating the honorees are arranged chronologically according to the year of each award:

Rudyard Kipling (1865–1936)	1907
William Butler Yeats (1865–1939)	1923
George Bernard Shaw (1856–1950)	1925
John Galsworthy (1867–1933)	1932
Bertrand Russell (1872–1970)	1950
Winston Churchill (1874–1965)	1953
Samuel Beckett (1906–)	1969

Each author's technical, psychological, and ideological kinships with and differences from the other honorees and the runners-up, as well as his part in the literary continuity in Great Britain, are not necessarily discussed according to such chronology. His significance and writings are analyzed and evaluated but are not dissected; such analyses are more appropriate to a history of literature. Each selection does, however, explore the extent of the winner's pertinent contribution to and exemplification of the main literary trends of this century, from 1900 to 1970.

Biographical data are included only when such details are essential to validate or illuminate the appraisal. Each honoree's literary career up to the time of the Nobel recognition and the probable reasons for the international salute are critically examined. His writing career subsequent to the honor is also sketched, with comments on whether or not he has appeared to decline or progress in his writing. Whenever feasible, the author analyzes the winner's qualifications for the tribute, comparing them with the merits of the runners-up—such as Rudyard Kipling versus George Meredith, Swinburne, and Thomas Hardy; John Galsworthy versus James Joyce and H. G. Wells; Bertrand Russell versus W. Somerset Maugham, E. M. Forster, and Aldous Huxley;

Winston Churchill versus Edith Sitwell and Dylan Thomas; and Samuel Beckett versus W. H. Auden and Stephen Spender.

The winners representing the literary trends in twentieth-century Great Britain and the force of change through the vitalized extention of traditional technique and thought, or through dynamics of revolt in these times of increasing cynicism, pessimism, and technological lustiness, are Kipling (to a limited degree), Yeats, Shaw, Galsworthy, and Beckett. T. S. Eliot, honored in 1948 by the Swedish Academy, is evaluated in *American Winners of the Nobel Literary Prize*.

These authors Kipling, a post-Victorian, partly excepted—imply the dominating disillusionment and pessimism of this century. Disenchantment, shifting behavior patterns, and the psychological ruthlessness of an industrializing era particularly mark the writings of Shaw, Galsworthy, Russell, and Beckett. The works of Beckett especially, with their nihilistic view of mankind's increasing futility, their stress on the irrationality of human behavior, their depiction of the lack of human communication, their ultimate despair at human emptiness and impotency, are the epitome of the prevailing existentialist-absurdism of this age. Beckett moves beyond T. S. Eliot's dehumanized wasteland determinism in the commercialized condition of man.

Although his fellow British authors and critics did not rank Rudyard Kipling as the leading candidate for the Nobel Literary Prize in 1907, the Swedish Academy selected him nonetheless, praising him as a sterling idealist and a prolific creative writer. Furthermore, the Academy stated that he had exhibited a profound knowledge of India and Indian customs, as well as the sociology of Anglo-Indians.

Since the award to Kipling, many critics have considered his "idealism" as "imperialism" and his knowledge of Indians and Anglo-Indians as shallow. A few critics have labeled his verse and fiction as merely popular and undistinguished. A perceptive evaluation of Kipling, however, reveals much sound idealism and functional artistry in the best of his short stories, novels, and poems. Beyond doubt, *Kim*, a novel about India, is a masterpiece. By the literary criteria of the early twentieth century Kipling deserved the prize. In fact, had not the glamor of the Nobel award ironically made him profligate of his creative talent, he might have extended his literary best beyond 1907.

5

From the publication of William Butler Yeats's early poems in 1882 to his reception of the Nobel salute in 1923, the character of his writings changed radically. The dreamy romanticism of his early poetry gave way to firm, varied, and vigorous creative expression exemplified by "The Second Coming," composed before the Nobel honor came to him. Fortunately this recognition did not mislead Yeats into assuming a messianic role of self-importance resulting in paradigmatic decline, as was the ironic outcome for many other Nobel honorees, including Kipling, Shaw to some degree, Russell, and all seven American winners.

Yeats continued to grow poetically, surpassing even his books *The Tower* (1928) and *The Winding Stair* (1933). In his final phase the "late Yeats" created such memorable poems as "Lapis Lazuli" and "Long-Legged Fly." His later poems "are weighted with a sense of isolation, with the disillusionments of the age—and of old age—with defeated dreams, with the decay of beauty, . . . and the degeneration of the contemporary world. Yet, though Yeats voiced horror, . . . he did not despair."[1] In his best mature poems he is realistic, symbolic, metaphysical, and glowingly epigrammatic.

Paralleling his remarkable poetic career, William Butler Yeats wrote plays, a few of them farces but most of them poetic tragedies. Like his early poems, his early plays were dreamily romantic, but at the beginning of the 1900's, he wrote such lively acting plays as *Deirdre* and *On Baile's Strand*. In 1914, under the influence of Ezra Pound, Yeats's interest included the Nō drama of Japan. Although he continued to utilize the heroic folklore and the living substance of Ireland, he discovered that the Nō techniques were artistically suitable to his playwriting. Mainly as a result of the Nō influence, he wrote such memorable dramas as *The Words upon the Window-Pane, Resurrection,* and *Purgatory.* Yeats contributed to the reshaping of Irish drama not only by helping to foster the splendid talents of John M. Synge, by his dynamic leadership in organizing the Abbey Theatre, and by directing the Celtic dramatic movement toward essential reality but also by fusing poetry and drama in his plays about medieval Irish cycles and about the Irish actualities of his age. He is a master of modern literature.

[1] Louis Untermeyer, *Modern British Poetry,* 110.

6

George Bernard Shaw believed in Creative Evolution—the "meta-biology of the Life Force"—which consistently permeated his writings and his life. As a result, it is very difficult to analyze him as a creative artist. Shaw provocatively influenced a few of his contemporaries and unfailingly needled or upset others with his startling innovations in the theater and with his unorthodox moral and social credo. Without catering, Shaw was versatile enough to stimulate, pro or con, all kinds of persons and organizations, ranging from the neo-Darwinist to the anti-Darwinist, from the Marxist to the anti-Marxist, from the re-ligionist to the rationalist and atheist. Shaw seemed to favor each in some instances but in time failed each because he refused to finalize or validate such support. Being basically honest and too reasonable not to perceive the qualifications, pro or con, of any outstanding creed or belief or movement, Shaw was rejected by the dogmatic believers either resentfully or condescendingly. He, of course, was flattered rather than discouraged by such reactions.

Some critics judged his views as extreme and his prose as confusion between forcefulness and fanaticism. The fact is that his middling beliefs were not aggressive enough for men of action and too subjective and self-demanding to attract disciples. Although Shaw assimilated much from a number of doctrines, he promoted no doctrine in its entirety; although he regarded with favor a number of factions, always as an onlooker, he did not become a member of any faction. Eventually he withdrew from his involvement with the Fabian Society when that party initiated the Labour Party, which he considered another pressure movement. He consistently adhered to his refusal to found a movement or to lead one.

After having written five novels, all of which failed to win critical approval and reader popularity, Shaw eventually revealed his dra-matic talent and theatrical flair by writing plays which indicted social ills and evils. In 1892 his *Widowers' Houses* initiated modern British drama. "Shaw's 'intellectual' theater is set in a framework of hi-jinx and hokum, characteristic of 'unintellectual' theater. Shavian dialogue is rhetorical, and at times operatic. One of its most distinctive features is its humor: the impudent placing of familiar phrases in unfamiliar con-texts, paradox, comic irony, inversions as well as low-comedy devices."[2]

[2] Ruby Cohn and Bernard Dukore, *Twentieth Century Drama*, 4.

With incisive wit equal to Oscar Wilde's and a consistency of creative purpose and intellectual perspicuity much better than Wilde's, Shaw was powerful in refining prose drama to literary quality.

With the realistic perceptiveness of Samuel Butler, Jonathan Swift, and Hendrik Ibsen, Shaw challenged and brilliantly satirized the pat shams, prudery, professional humbug, romantic morality, spiritual bankruptcy, and poverty in his revolutionary and technically exciting plays and ideas. He used traditional dramatic structure and familiar themes, enlivened by probing wit, for the purpose of provoking the audience out of daily pretenses, outworn morality, absurd conventions, and blind acceptance of social evils. Instead of expressing indignation, he highlighted the causes for and results of social, political, and religious absurdities and implied natural morality and natural reform. "He is at his best when he uses effective dramatic and brilliantly entertaining dialogue in order to expose contradictions, inconsistencies, gaps between the pretended and the real, in contemporary attitudes and behavior."[3]

Unquestionably George Bernard Shaw is a major dramatist of this century, but paradoxically he has been so vitally unique and so discouragingly inimitable that concrete evidence of his influence on modern plays and playwrights has not yet been authentically traced. Most of the plays of Samuel Beckett give the implications obscurely, but Shaw's complex plays clearly present the meaning and importance beneath the external action. Shaw stated, "Great dramatists help their fellow-citizens to a purifying consciousness of the deepest struggles of the human soul with itself." This statement illuminates why—despite the modern revolutionary and often violent changes in the social process—Shaw, a Life Force believer, adhered firmly, with basic optimism, to his vitalist creed.

When the Nobel Literary Award was conferred upon John Galsworthy in 1932, it seemed, very late in his life (he was sixty-five), to be a suitable climax to his literary career, which had been fabulously successful. As a novelist, playwright, story writer, and essayist, he was

[3] M. H. Abrams (ed.), *The Norton Anthology of English Literature*, II, 1286–87.

8

judged by a number of the best critics of his time to be an international literary master.

Influenced more by the realism of Honoré de Balzac and Guy de Maupassant than by the Victorian realism of George Eliot, Charles Kingsley, and Charles Reade, Galsworthy extended objective realism to social documentation of the era and to a frank criticism of Victorian shortcomings and social ills. Galsworthy, a minute and sensitive realist, often superimposed on reality a social and spiritual symbolism. His pessimistic conclusion that man is incapable of coping with social and moral dilemmas contrasted sharply with the optimistic belief of H. G. Wells that man can solve his problems and create a utopian civilization.

Galsworthy's limited attainments and his clichéd style do not prove that his creative productions lack merit. A product of his time, he capably handled the materials within the literary tradition of the age. In fact, he is unsurpassed among English writers as a social historian, especially of the upper middle class toward the end of the Victorian era.

It is true that Galsworthy's objective and documented realism seems old-fashioned in contrast to the innovative subjective and psychological realism of such writers as Virginia Woolf, D. H. Lawrence, Aldous Huxley, James Joyce, William Golding, and Samuel Beckett. At present the Victorian and post-Victorian ages, as well as the interpreters of them, are again beginning to be considered by current scholars and critics as worthy of reappraisal. As a result, John Galsworthy may yet be recognized as an author whose most important novels should win for him a secure place as a novelist of at least a lesser rank.

The Swedish Academy awarded the 1950 Nobel Literary Prize to Bertrand Russell "in recognition of his many-sided and important work in which he has constantly stood forth as a champion of humanity and freedom of thought." The award in this category surprised the critics and scholars because Russell had been widely favored as a candidate for the Nobel Peace Prize. The literary award seems somewhat appropriate, however, because Russell kept alive in his elegantly clear writings the Voltairian tradition of philosophy as literature. Most of his productions were readable and entertaining, as well as instructive. Even during the last twenty-five years of his long life, he remained a colorful publicist, youthful in spirit, witty, and energetic.

In honoring this controversial figure, condemned as heatedly as he was praised for his public activities and essays, the Nobel jury did not follow its pattern of previous choices of out-and-out "literary" authors, such as Kipling, Yeats, Shaw, and Galsworthy. Instead, its judgment focused on the ideals specified by Alfred Nobel in his will—ideals that Russell consistently expressed in his activities, which contributed strongly to human awareness among a broad range of people. The honor was not restricted to a single book or to his dissertations on logic and mathematics. It applied to his versatile, precise, clear, and vivid writings and thinking up to 1950 and to the impact of his logical empiricism, through his philosophic and often witty propounding upon doctrines which have permeated much of creative thinking during the last forty years.

Early in the twentieth century Bertrand Russell mulled existential questions but was only casual about subsistent ones. "This bias explains his glee over eliminating classes, and his indifference over the status of the surviving propositional functions; for we noted in *Principles* the classes occupied . . . the existential zone of being."[4]

Despite being a rationalist in his philosophy and view of life, Russell had some sympathy for romanticism in the arts, though little for metaphysical idealism and none for mysticism and orthodox religion. His approach to philosophy was mathematically formal, rigorous, and logical as opposed to common sense "with its imperfections." His aim was to unite philosophy and science. Scientific reason, he maintained, can solve all problems of men by guiding them to rational solutions and eventually to world peace and global government, thereby saving mankind from self-annihilation.

Because Sir Winston Churchill was judged distinctive as a writer and a national leader by many leading critics of his time, it seems ironic that most of them considered him not quite entitled to the Nobel

4 W. V. Quine, "Russell's Ontological Development," *Journal of Philosophy,* November 10, 1966, p. 660.

Literary Prize. They pointed out that his literary expression and his view of the social and political changes did not exemplify the fundamental trends of the twentieth century. They further reasoned that other winners of the award after 1918—Yeats, Shaw, Galsworthy, and Russell—achieved significantly as appraisers and interpreters of a post-war generation disturbed increasingly with disillusion, frustration, and futility.

As a writer and public leader Churchill embodied the seemingly indestructible self-reliance of the Victorian era, so drastically diminished by World War I. His writings and speeches supported attitudes and values which were ignored or rejected by post–World War II writers in Great Britain. Scorning the deterministic theory and all its despair, Churchill believed that individual man, by wise self-discipline and orderly initiative, could creatively alter environment for the benefit of mankind. He affirmed that there are universal moral orders, such as honor, loyalty, valor, and unflagging devotion to duty—all necessary for a people and a nation to remain dynamic and enduring. Although he championed the principles of individual freedom and constitutional government, according to Amos C. Miller, he was fundamentally an aristocratic conservative who adhered to the idea of a hierarchical order of society in which tradition was respected and in which leadership was exercised by a gifted and cultured elite.

As an author Churchill was traditional, shaping his style after the masterful craftsmanship and oratory of Edward Gibbon, Edmund Burke, and Thomas Macaulay. Churchill became a clear, vivid, and pungent narrator and an eloquent orator. At times he was rhetorical, but seldom pedantic. Furthermore, he deepened his insight into the psychology of leaders by drawing upon his experiences as a soldier and as a director of historic events.

Despite some faults of expression and the eventual obsoleteness of some of his ideas, Churchill had a dynamic sense of the enduring virtues of the past. The historic heritage and greatness of Great Britain and the bravery and stamina of the British people at times enhanced his vision to epic proportions. Thus, through his finest oratory and writings, he inspired Great Britain to heroic action during World War II. Those contributions are enshrined in the literary heritage of the nation.

Early in his career Samuel Beckett transcended such models as James Joyce, Yeats, Anton Chekhov, Feodor Dostoevski, and Marcel Proust, and he has helped shape the technique of Edward Albee, Harold Pinter, and other modern writers.

In the plays, novels, and stories of Samuel Beckett, Russell's casual interest in existentialism has been distorted from its humane wit and orderly philosophy to the irrationality of human behavior, to the futile decline of man into nihilism. Because Beckett believes that there can be little if any communication between individuals and among peoples, he regards the utter frustration, chaos, and emptiness of existence with despair in his existential-absurdist writings, which have a suitably bareboned style. Invariably he writes with painful honesty and a staccato terror of vision.

Beckett expects the spectators of his staged plays to discard any illusions that they have tangible identity. This is his "price of admission" into his private world of avant-garde iconoclasm, anti-intellectualism, and terrifyingly real symbolic abstractions of existence.

Although Beckett insists that he has no profound interest in playwriting he has become an internationally popular master of the symbolic drama of the absurd—of the inarticulate beings of the Western world. Usually the dialogue or monologue is fragmentary and mechanical, often passing into moments of silence and touching pantomime, while the characters merely exist in a limbo of despair, monotony, frustration, and physical discomfort. "Beckett, like Ionesco, is a prose-poet of the ultimate unintelligibility of the seemingly intelligible. Their universe, conceived as constantly flying away from any center—and this *ab surd*, is a wasteland of words."[5]

Beckett's novels and short stories, as well as his plays, depict the tragicomedy of human beings, most of them Irish, in their absurdity and ludicrous commonplace. His untraditionally plotless writings present disintegrated characters with little identity—some with none at all—in a dislocated and dying world. Through the spare dialogue or seemingly disconnected monologues, stripped settings, and almost static situations, Beckett implies mankind's floundering and futile search for communication and for at least an iota of meaning in the

[5] Haskell M. Block and Robert A. Shedd (eds.), *Masters of Modern Drama*, 1102.

desolate terror and grotesque vulgarity of outrageous life. Beckett, self-exiled from the repressive censorship of his native Ireland since 1932, regards the human dilemmas without hope or faith.

Seemingly contrary to Alfred Nobel's will that the award should honor the author "who shall have produced in the field of literature the most outstanding work of an idealistic tendency," the prize to Samuel Beckett in 1969 was a salute of the Establishment to contemporary avant-garde literature.

RUDYARD KIPLING

by Faith G. Norris

E VEN IN 1907 THERE WERE those in England and the United States who cast upon Rudyard Kipling a cold and critical eye and who obviously felt no enthusiasm about the announcement that the Swedish Academy had selected him as that year's recipient of the Nobel Prize in Literature. There were outspoken detractors like the Scots literary critic Robert Buchanan, and there were silent denigrators like the editor of the *London Times*, who confined himself to the bare news announcement that Kipling was the choice for the award.

In part, perhaps, the lack of enthusiasm displayed in England and the United States was due to the knowledge that peculiar political pressures had been exerted on the committee awarding that year's prize. For although Alfred Nobel had stipulated in his will that politics was to have no part in the granting of the various awards, the donor's wishes were soon ignored. To be more precise, the Swedish Academy had often bowed to force from other lands. The force most irresistible in 1907 in connection with the literary award was that of the United Kingdom. Patriotically eager to see an English author at last a recipient of part of Nobel's bequest, a group of authors who called themselves the Society of London had worked diligently to that end and, in 1906, had sought intercession for such an honor from a Swedish diplomat in London, one Baron Bildt. In addition, by the beginning of 1907 the society had submitted to the Nobel committee letters from twenty-

14

seven prominent British writers. All twenty-seven letters, however, plus the words of Baron Bildt, were in support of the poet Algernon Swinburne, long famous for his republican idealism. As a result of this campaign, in the summer of 1907 the British and American presses were spreading the rumor that Swinburne was to be the first Englishman to receive the world-famous award. When the Swedish Academy announced its decision in the autumn, however, the first English recipient proved to be not Swinburne but Rudyard Kipling, protégé of the society's secretary, the literary critic Edmund Gosse.

The official reason for the change in the candidate at first so eagerly promoted by the Society of London was Swinburne's age: he was seventy, too old. This consideration may indeed have carried weight, since the 1906 winner, the Italian poet Giosuè Carducci, a man of seventy-two, had died only a few weeks after receiving the award. The unofficial reason why Swinburne did not receive the honor may have been that a considerable amount of his work was known for its "sensual paganism" rather than for its "idealism." The same prudish objection was applicable to the sixty-seven-year-old Thomas Hardy. No such criticism could be leveled at George Meredith; but since he, too, was old—seventy-nine in 1907—he also was unsuitable. Thus it came about, to the disappointment of certain liberal British and American intellectuals, that a forty-two-year-old Englishman was handed the Nobel Prize for Literature on December 10, 1907.

Interestingly enough, however, the citation which accompanied the award suggests that the Swedish Academy thought their choice a good one, despite the pressure that had originally been exerted upon them by patriotic Englishmen to reward a very different subject. In the view of the spokesman for the Nobel committee, Rudyard Kipling was not only a talented poet, story writer, and novelist but also a man who "had acquired a complete knowledge of the ideas and mentality of the Hindus," with the result that his account of their "customs and institutions" had done more to contribute to a knowledge of the India of England than had "the construction of the Suez Canal."

In addition, the giver of the speech which went with the award praised Kipling as an "idealist" of the concept of empire. Though before 1907 certain British and American liberals had attacked Kipling as a spokesman for "vicious jingoism," the speechmaker expressed the view that Kipling deserved praise for having done more than any other writer of "pure literature" to make tighter "the bonds" uniting England to its colonies.

When one considers that the decision to give Kipling the Nobel Prize was in large part due to the pressure exerted upon the committee by a small band of Englishmen, one is at first skeptical of the above quotation and of even more extreme, flowery tributes to Kipling. At the same time, one has to recall that he had been both a critical and a popular success in France, Germany, and Scandinavia since the late 1890's. At the time he won the award, for example, Sweden's distinguished woman novelist, Selma Lagerlöf, who was herself to receive the medal in 1909, announced that her most recent work, *The Marvelous Voyage of Nils Hölgersson*, owed a great debt to Kipling.

By English and American critical standards did the man who received the award in 1907 deserve to be so honored? The answer is yes, especially if one takes into account both the aesthetic and the political ideals of 1907. Much of his work still has value in our own time, but the rest deserves a far less harsh judgment than it usually receives, if one examines it from the standards of his world, not ours.

First, let us consider the poetry which Kipling had produced by 1907. During or a short time before that year four British contemporaries of Kipling had produced notable poetry: Hopkins, Housman, Hardy, and Yeats. None of this quartet, however, was then known beyond a small circle. There were also Meredith and Swinburne, who undeniably had produced more genuine poetry by 1907 than had Kipling. Meredith and Swinburne, however, had not contributed to the English language such rhythmic statements of "international morality" as "East is East and West is West/And never the Twain shall meet"; such neatly turned phrases as "the White Man's Burden," or "Our Lady of the Snows" as a name for Canada; the interesting, if arguable, thesis that "East o' Suez, . . . the best is like the worst"; or the oft-quoted rhetorical question, "What can they know of England who only England know?" Furthermore, since the death of Robert Browning, what "weaver of verse" had produced rhymed tales containing such a varied gallery of characters as Gunga Din, "Fuzzy Wuzzy," Tommy Atkins, and McAndrew or had painted as sardonic a rhymed portrait as that of Queen Victoria in the "Widow o' Windsor"?

16

When it came to word pictures of natural scenes, aside from the as-yet-unknown quartet, no one else in the United Kingdom had written anything with imagery as clear or as moving as that to be found in "The Way Through the Woods," "By the Hoof of the Wild Goat," or "Christmas in India," only three of the most moving of Kipling's dozens of nature poems.

Finally, though the average contemporary reader tends to think of Kipling as *the* writer of galloping rhymed tales but little else, by 1907 he had proved his ability to master various other forms and techniques· the regular hexameter couplets of "McAndrew's Hymn" the Browningesque blank-verse dramatic monologue of "One Viceroy Resigns," his many "songs," his technically perfect example of that most intricate of all poetic forms, the ballad, in "The Ballad of Jakko Hill."

Before we consider in detail one of the best of the many hundred pieces of verse which Kipling wrote before 1907, we should also consider the variety and general nature of his production in other fields. Between 1882 (when he became a reporter in India at the age of seventeen) and 1907 he had also published thirteen volumes of short stories; four novels; three books of tales for children; several collections of lively, informative travel sketches dealing with his wanderings in India, China, Japan, and the United States; several sociological essays and pamphlets, including a dated but thorough proposal for "Railway Reform in Great Britain"; and, finally, to the despair of would-be "definitive" bibliographers of his work, a number of unsigned pieces of reporting for two Anglo-Indian newspapers, along with many journalistic efforts under his signature.

In short, during the quarter century between his seventeenth birthday and his winning of the Nobel Prize, the man who had once been called a "precocious pup" had written far more, and in a wider variety of genres, than many another author does in a period twice as long. Readers may at once object that quantity is no substitute for quality—that Flaubert's literary heritage was minuscule when compared to that of Dumas. One can also argue that much of the early Kipling is imitative: his rhythms and alliteration are often those of Swinburne; his horror stories echo the manner of Edgar Allan Poe.

At the same time, though one may condemn as lacking in quality much that Kipling wrote before 1907 or dismiss it as "imitative" in style, any fair-minded reader should realize that, to every form he attempted, he brought originality of subject matter. Indeed, because of that last aesthetic fact alone he deserved the Nobel Prize. For much of Kipling's fresh subject matter exhibited, in terms of 1907, the "idealistic" character which Alfred Nobel had hoped the winners of the literary prize would possess. Some general observations about this originality of content seem worthy of inclusion before a detailed analysis of certain specific works.

Perhaps the best way to see Kipling's pre-1907 originality of subject matter in the clearest light is to begin with an examination of his early short stories, the works which first won him a public when they were originally published in that long-dead Lahore newspaper, the *Civil and Military Gazette* and which were later issued in collected form as the volume *Plain Tales from the Hills* (1888), when their author was twenty-three. In considering these stories, however, we must look also at samples from the six other collected volumes issued by an obscure Indian publishing house in that same year: *Soldiers Three*; *The Story of the Gadsbys*; *In Black and White*; *Under the Deodars*; *Phantom Rickshaw*; and *Wee Willie Winkle*. Aside from the last-mentioned work, which contains for its era a special kind of originality in that it includes stories about small children for grownups to ponder, all these volumes are a series of "tales" about adult Anglo-Indians,[1] Indian Hindus and Moslems, Eurasians, and sundry other nationals who, for one reason or another, had resided for a greater or lesser time in either the British Raj (the territory directly controlled by Great Britain) or the Native States (the territory ruled by Indian princes "advised" by British civil servants).

That a number of the pieces in all seven volumes are as meretricious as the tales ground out by the young Chekov and by O. Henry, no one can deny. Many have endings which involve cheap, obvious tricks, as in "His Wedded Wife," where the reader guesses the end only a few paragraphs after starting the piece. Many contain passages marred by excessive and explicit sentimentality, as in "Thrown Away," which almost demands that we weep on behalf of the improbably noble

---

[1] An Anglo-Indian here means an Englishman who was born in or lived a good part of his adult life in India.

young English subaltern who during a cholera epidemic gives up his life for the men he commands.

There are also the horror tales, in which suspense leads one on and on, which seem in no way to trick the reader at the end, and which leave one with a feeling of having had a nightmare so grisly that the coming of day cannot dispel it. In this category are "The Gate of the Hundred Sorrows," "Phantom 'Rickshaw," "The Strange Ride of Morrowbie Jukes," and "The Man Who Would Be King." The tales in this category have the powerful effect that they do because they show us more or less "normal" Anglo-Indians driven to insanity or death because of some clash with Hindu or Moslem beliefs.

In another group of stories Kipling again leaves us emotionally exhausted as he depicts the futility of trying to establish lasting human relationships in a land where floods and cholera are annual visitors, sunstroke is a daily threat, and the average Englishman and Indian have nothing but loathing for both the Eurasian and any "white" who has "gone native." To this group belong the ghastly yet moving "Beyond the Pale," with its pathetic Indian girl singing to her British officer-lover the lament "Come Back to Me, Beloved, or I Die," a song which proves only too gruesomely true; "Without Benefit of Clergy," with its understated account of another British officer's passionate attachment to his teen-age Moslem mistress and the child she bears him, a relationship ended by cholera; "In Flood Time," an Indian version of "Hero and Leander," except that Kipling's Leander lives on to become a withered old Hindu possessing nothing save memories of his passion for his erstwhile Moslem mistress.

Then there are the stories far worse than the ones dependent on cheap tricks, pieces so bad that one almost wonders how a man who could write "The Man Who Would Be King" and "Without Benefit of Clergy" could stoop to produce such vulgar expressions of contempt for the "native." Typical of these is "His Chance in Life." In this incredible creation, a "native" with a faint trace of English blood far back in his ancestry achieves a brief rise in the world because of that faint trace but falls back into nothingness when a "true-born Englishman" appears on the scene. The protagonist's failure in exhibiting the bravery and determination of his successor, Kipling makes clear, is due simply to the "fact" that the blood that flows in his veins is not all "white." This tale is incredible not just because it, and others of the same ilk, are invalid anthropologically but also because Kipling abandons his function as a teller of tales to become a propagandist for his race theories.

Even though the seven collections published in 1888 have flaws, artistic and racial, the stories about various facets of Indian life deserved the warm reception which they won in many lands. They offered to Europeans, Americans, and Englishmen who knew nothing of India something new and strange in the way of subject matter. Furthermore, many contemporary readers enjoy the tales because they *still* offer an entry into a world about which millions know nothing.

Kipling's early short stories deserve praise for their freshness of locale and subject matter, although their content has been attacked by both Indian and Anglo-Indian critics. It has become almost a cliché to say that Kipling did not know well either the India of the Indians or that of his fellow Englishmen. The point is valid; but the person making the criticism is also revealing his ignorance of British and Indian mores of the 1880's and of half a century thereafter. If the Swedish academician erred in 1907 in attributing to Kipling "a complete knowledge . . . of the Hindus," the author's foes have been just as unthinking in their denial to him of much knowledge of the subcontinent.

Let us first consider the accusation that he did not have a proper appreciation of the world of the Anglo-Indians. Accurate though the charge is, there are three good reasons which explain his failure to achieve true intimacy with many Englishmen in India. The first and most obvious explanation is his age. What his foes forget, or overlook, is that though Kipling lived in India for thirteen years, the first six were the years from his birth to his voyage back to England for schooling; the others elapsed between his return to India at age seventeen and his departure for London in his twenty-fourth year. During the first six years he learned to speak Punjabi fluently—or as fluently as a six-year-old speaks any language—but it seems almost needless to point out that he would not have learned much if anything about the mores of adult Indians and Anglo-Indians—except, perhaps, that both groups scorned Eurasians. How much better off, however, was he at

age seventeen upon his arrival in Lahore from schooling "at home"? In
Plain Tales he speaks often with a confident air about incidents involving senior British officers in the Indian hill town of Simla. He is
also most assured in manner when he describes fictitious episodes involving middle-aged British engineers, health officers, foresters, and
jurists. Once more, however, he "doth protest too much" about his
confidence in his knowledge. Rather, "confidence" is the wrong word:
what he is displaying is the bravado of a youth who does all the observing that he can but who is unable to be truly "at one" with the
middle-aged protagonists of many of his tales.

For his years, Kipling seems to have been precociously observant of
all that he saw. But how much did Anglo-Indian colonels or mature
civil servants permit him to see? The answer, perhaps, is only as much
as a person in middle age is willing to reveal to a bright boy of
eighteen or nineteen. No doubt there were moments of indiscreet
revelations, the results of fatigue and alcohol, and these "unconsidered
trifles" the prodigy used in his stories. But the point still remains: his
youth was a barrier between him and many of the kinds of people
about whom he wrote.

Age differences aside, Rudyard Kipling could not become intimate
with most Anglo-Indians for a second and more important reason: he
did not "belong." He had no pigeonhole into which he could be in-
serted in a British society organized with a rigidity almost as fixed as
the much-condemned Indian system. On the one hand was the hierarchy of officers and men who made up the British army. Though
Kipling was to inform the world that the "Colonel's Lady and Judy
O'Grady" were "sisters under the skin," he knew full well that that skin
was too deep to be penetrable and that "East" would meet "West"
sooner than Tommy Atkins would be invited to play polo with the
colonel, or even with the newest young subaltern. Into a military
world as snobbish and ordered as the British army in India, a youthful
civilian could find no passage. Because of his few attempts to discover
such an entry, he won the unpleasant distinction of being dismissed as
an "incredible young bounder."

At the same time, Kipling could not fit into that other British world,
that of the Indian Civil Service, made up of police superintendents,
health officers, civil engineers, foresters, magistrates, and government

21

officials. These individuals were specialists, many of them brilliant university graduates who had had to pass stiff competitive examinations to win their posts in India. To such individuals the youthful writer was beyond the pale. After all, he had had no visible training for anything. He had come straight from an English boarding school to a job which involved doing a variety of "chores" (Kipling's own word) in a small newspaper office in Lahore, India (now West Pakistan).

At this point we come to the third reason why most Anglo-Indians would have looked askance at Kipling and why, with each passing year, they would have held him at a greater and greater distance. Though both army officers and civil servants may have had little understanding of or respect for the complex tasks involved in putting a newspaper to press, they must soon have come to comprehend that this particular young practitioner of the journalism trade had a way of turning out for the *Civil and Military Gazette* pieces of which they did not approve. True, the protagonists and content of certain of his tales would have seemed to them unobjectionable; but both army officers and members of the Civil Service would have deemed contemptible those of Kipling's tales which dealt in sympathetic fashion with Eurasians and with British soldiers who felt love, not lust, for Indian women.

Here lies the unhappy paradox of Kipling as writer about Anglo-Indians. In the sometimes irritating "knowingness" of style, especially in his earliest work, he unconsciously made clear his wish to be accepted, to belong. Others of his tales, however, are by their very content works almost guaranteed to keep him beyond the pale. That British army officers and members of the Indian Civil Service did, in large numbers, read his verses and short stories is a matter of fact. Yet, though this wide reading of his creative work made him well known, it led to rejection rather than acceptance, for many of his earliest readers began to follow his work because of the rumor that certain of his "plain tales" and "ditties" were little more than embellished accounts of scandals at Simla. What those who were within the pale found more objectionable—the works based on themselves or those sympathetic to "outsiders"—we cannot know. All we can be sure of is that many of his efforts evoked from his fellow Anglo-Indians the charge that he was

22

"superficial" or "inaccurate." But, given Kipling's age, occupation, and attitudes, what else could certain of his Anglo-Indian stories have been?

The other charge—that he did not fully understand the India of the Indians—is one that has been advanced often in the last fifty years by both liberal Anglo-Indians like George Orwell and John Masters and also by Indians and Pakistanis. On the occasion in March, 1969, when wreckers began to tear down Kipling's one-time editorial office in Lahore, the last editor of the *Civil and Military Gazette*, Abdul Hamid Shcik, told an Associated Press interviewer that Kipling "has never been very popular with the people he wrote about." To this comment the Associated Press reporter added the remark that "Many Pakistanis —and Indians too—feel that Kipling merely reflected the views of the ruling British and treated the locals in a patronizing way."

But here, too, Kipling is not altogether blameworthy, given his world and time. He regained his perfect Punjabi accent when he returned from England to work in Lahore. He was able to talk with ease to servants, shopkeepers, and other members of the poorer classes who performed tasks for him. Furthermore, the generosity of several rajahs, or their desire for favorable publicity, led to invitations to visit and even stay in the palaces of Indian princes. Hence he received a glimpse of life among the rich. Similarly, his dealings with servants, camel drivers, and beggars gave him only snapshots of actual life among the poor. To put it another way, the rich patronized him, and he patronized the poor. In both cases true "understanding" was impossible. But in the 1880's would the talented son of a not-too-affluent art historian have had any more opportunity to know well the rich or the poor of England itself?

Ironically, the segment of Indian society which he knew least—and wrote almost nothing about—was the one that has been most vociferous in attacking him: his own, the middle and upper middle class, the lawyers, writers, and teachers. These were the people, of course, whose sons were to furnish aid and comfort to Gandhi in leading the subcontinent to freedom from England in 1947. In his failure to come to know them—especially, since many were literary figures—Kipling seems to have been guilty of a stupid aloofness. However, two formidable barriers lay in the path of any Englishman who sought an intimate understanding of this important group in India. On the one hand, the Indians might well have rejected him. Throughout the last twenty years of the nineteenth century hostility to the British Raj grew so steadily that many of Gandhi's earliest followers refused any social advances from their rulers. On the other side, Kipling would have faced ostracism from all "right-minded" Englishmen if he had had the persistence to seek out an Indian of his own class with whom he could be friends. Rejection by Anglo-Indians he did not dare court. Aside from depriving himself of such companionship as he received from the army officers and civil servants he did know, he would also have lost the audience necessary for publication of his tales. Any reader skeptical about the hostility friendship with an Indian would have brought to Kipling from his own countrymen need only turn to the work of E. M. Forster, George Orwell, or John Masters to learn of the anger customarily unleashed by Anglo-Indians against the handful of their "own" who had achieved genuine friendships with middle-class Indians—and Forster, Orwell, and Masters deal with twentieth-century Anglo-Indians, individuals somewhat less rigid than those Kipling knew in the tense decade of the 1880's.

It is possible, of course, that Kipling would not have sought friends among the Indians even had politics permitted. With the reticence characteristic of his autobiography he does not say. But whatever the state of his personal feelings, fanatics among both the rulers and the ruled prevented him from doing any more than leave to the world a series of what might be termed charcoal sketches of the people, brown and white, of India. The country's deserts, its jungles, its cities, and its villages he depicted, on the other hand, in three-dimensional color. The *things* of India he came to know well; its people, never.

Yet if the Nobel citation which praised him for his "complete knowledge" of the Hindus was in error, the mistake was understandable—and one shared by Kipling's French admirers of the first decade of this century. From his start, in the years when he was a "precocious pup" of a reporter, Kipling had worked in a manner comparable to that of Daniel Defoe. Like the creator of *Robinson Crusoe*, the teller of *Plain Tales* makes you think that we can believe in his people because of the careful detail with which he describes *things*. Because he sounds, and well may be, accurate in depicting hills and houses, we tend to conclude that he is as reliable in reporting on their habitants. The deduction is false, but natural. It is, therefore, no wonder that so many thousands in 1907—and in later years—unthinkingly accepted the verdict of the Nobel committee, and that of the French critics, in regard to the realism of his fiction and verse. Despite the false notes in the work Kipling produced in his adult years in India (1882 to 1889)—and in his "Indian stories and poems" written between 1888 and 1907—what he turned out in the first quarter century of his adult life represented the most vivid and the largest verbal panorama of India that the European world of 1907 had ever seen.

Furthermore, though the characterization might at times be faulty, his early tales and verse offered three categories of protagonist original in both genres: the Eurasian, the British common soldier (plus his Indian and Boer counterpart), and the idealistic, rather than the dishonest, civil servant.

Let us first consider the Eurasian. Most children of a European-Asiatic marriage or affair grew up to join a desperate legion—at best ignored, at worst damned. In certain of Kipling's tales, however, we find for these lost souls a sense of compassion, notably in three of his most emotional tales: "The Gate of the Hundred Sorrows" (in *Plain Tales*); "Namgay Doola" (in *Mine Own People*); and "Without Benefit of Clergy" (in *Mine Own People*).

Although the compassion in these tales is somewhat lessened by a condescension which a Eurasian finds infuriating, Kipling's patronizing tone is not much worse than what one encounters in portraits of "half-castes" painted by Conrad, Somerset Maugham, and André Malraux. Thanks to the trio of writers just mentioned, and to others less well known, Eurasians with problems of identity have become stereotypes in a great deal of fiction about lands "East o' Suez." But in Kipling's early years he was a pioneer in the area. Despite his condescension, he does at times show a compassion greater than what one finds in Conrad or Maugham.

This same divided attitude we find in his portraits of British and Indian privates in the Indian army and in his pictures of common soldiers in other fighting forces. The world had been well aware, long before the Nobel Committee praised him for having done so, that Kipling had been the first author to bring vividly to his readers' atten-

25

tion the troubles of British and other common soldiers. That he felt a large measure of sympathy and admiration for the members of the lowest ranks in any army is the conclusion that we draw from such famous dialect ballads as "Tommy," "The Widow of Windsor," "Fuzzy-Wuzzy," and "Gunga Din." Even more proof of Kipling's affection and regard for the common soldier—"Thomas Atkins"—is to be found in the "Prelude" to *Barrack-Room Ballads*, that tribute in "standard" English:

> O there'll surely come a day
> When they'll give you all your pay,
> And treat you as a Christian ought to do,
> So, until that day comes round,
> Heaven keep you safe and sound,
> And, Thomas here's my best respects to you.

Despite the affectionate admiration and sympathy expressed in these lines, George Orwell argued that Kipling's "distorted class-consciousness" not only makes one suspect the depth of the poet's compassion when he characterizes Thomas Atkins as a "music hall cockney" incapable of using the letter "h" properly but also lessens the sound effects of certain of the *Barrack-Room Ballads*. Or to put it another way, one might well argue that Kipling's affection for Tommy, and for the Boer Piet, is so mixed with condescension that it is hard to say where one stops and the other begins. It is hard to judge exactly, for example, what we are to make of Kipling's tribute to the British common soldier for having provided Queen Victoria with ownership of "'alf of creation":

> We 'ave bought 'er the same with the
> Sword an' the flame
> An' we've salted it down with our bones,
> (Poor beggars!—it's blue with our bones!)

The verb "bought" is the choice of a true craftsman, of someone most compassionate for Thomas' wretched pay, but is it also a word which would be used by someone who had real respect for this fictional figure's living counterpart who regarded him as an equal?

Ironically, it is certain of Kipling's other pictures of the British

26

common soldier that have earned for him vicious attacks as a writer given to "hymning" the praises of "brute force" and "the worst excesses of British Imperialism." For men very like those who win from him the compassion shown in the "Prelude" to *Barrack-Room Ballads* behave in other poems and in certain stories in a fashion that he himself termed "barbarious." Probably no two of his works have aroused more disgusted comment than "Loot" in *Barrack-Room Ballads* and the tale "The Taking of Lungtungpen" in *Soldiers Three*. In the ballad the Cockney narrator wallows in his description of the joy that he experienced robbing jewels and gold from a Buddhist temple and of the fun that he had being sadistic to the natives who had attempted to keep the structure from being robbed. In the short story "The Taking of Lungtungpen," Private Mulvaney exults in the clever piece of trickery he employed to capture with a handful of soldiers a Burmese town "dhrippin' wid . . . elephints and jingles." And the story is preceded by its own "Barrack Room Ballad" tailored to fit the content of the plot:

> So we loosed a bloomin' volley
> An' we made the beggars cut,
> An' when our pouch was emptied out,
> We used the bloomin' butt,
>   Ho! My!
>   Don't yer come anight
> When Tommy is a playin' with the baynit an' the butt.

Upon reading lines like the above, one can well understand why many present-day Burmese, Indians, and Pakistanis still loathe Kipling. One can also comprehend why his winning of the Nobel Prize evoked indignant protests from certain American newspapers and journals of the time. What seems at first baffling, in fact, is not only how the Swedish committee could praise him for his "idealism" and "ethico-religious strain" but also how, in 1907, a certain W. B. Parker could write in the defunct American magazine *World's Work* that Kipling was not only a creative artist but also a man who had performed the task of a "preacher, patriot, moralist."

His admirers, however, had a point, and it may well be that his detractors were unfair. The brutal sentiments of his private soldiers may not have been his any more than were their pronunciation and idioms. It is possible that he tried only to do two seemingly incompatible things: to exhibit Tommy Atkins as an object of compassion, while at the same time showing that the ill-paid British privates of his day were often little more than greedy brutes when it came to dealing with natives unfortunate enough to possess articles of value. Though the brutal ballads are forever a part of Kipling's achievement, one can find other materials which show a Kipling compassionate to the Indians and critical of his fellow Englishman. For example, were one to judge him solely on the basis of "The Story of Muhammed Din," one would conclude that he felt a deep pity for four-year-old Moslem victims of cholera and nothing but scorn for the white doctors who tended such pathetic innocents in a manner both careless and callous. All one can conclude is that his attitude to Tommy Atkins was a split one; he felt sorry for the common soldier's sufferings, but at the same time he recognized that such a man in the heat of combat could become a beast. That he approved of such bestial conduct, however, seems refuted by his sympathetic view of the native as expressed in "Muhammed Din" and elsewhere.

The one possible clue we have to his feelings about cruelty to the Indians and Burmese may be found in his stories with a third kind of protagonist, whom he represents as honest, hard-working, and admirable: the members of the Indian Civil Service. As Kipling saw India, it was the work of British foresters, civil engineers, health officers, and magistrates that had made the subcontinent the least wretched part of Asia. In his story "The Bridge Builders" (in *The Day's Work*) he shows us the struggles of the civil engineer Findlayson, a fictional representative of the many men who gave to India a network of railroads much more far-flung, and much better operated, than the systems possessed by any other Oriental country in 1900. Although Kipling is silent about the profits these railroads brought to the mother country, he shows how the trains made possible the rushing of food to stricken thousands during famine and drugs during epidemics. Kipling's tales make clear that the task of laying railroads and performing such tasks as fighting famine was not only unglamorous but also both physically and emotionally exhausting for the men who performed them. With slightly modified phrasing, Kipling's account of Findlayson's struggle

28

to build a bridge over the Ganges might apply to a British health officer or a forester: "For three years he had endured heat and cold, disappointment, discomfort, danger, and disease, with responsibility almost too heavy for one pair of shoulders." With all the imperfections that it has, life in British India seems to Kipling far better for the poor than that in the Native States—thanks to the labors of the I.C.S. Of course, he forgets—or ignores—the point that the Indian poor, as well as the middle class, might well have preferred freedom to well-meant paternalism. At the same time, we must not forget that the India of which he wrote was one of the 1880's and 1890's, a land which he could not conceive of as being free. And we must further recall that his Swedish and French admirers of 1907 would have had the same view—would have agreed that it was "idealistic" to aid the Indians, that Kipling's members of the I.C.S. were shouldering nobly "the white man's burden." I would, in fact, judge that the Nobel committee found Kipling's imperialism "not intransigent" because of the considerable body of his stories which deal with men struggling to improve India, the kinds of high-minded individuals we find often in his collection entitled *The Day's Work*, perhaps most notably in his picture of the British famine fighters in the tale entitled "William the Conqueror."

Only one more general point needs to be made about why his fiction and his verse seemed to some, if not to all, "idealistic" in 1907. By that year Kipling had turned out a number of stories hymning praises to machines and technologists, most notably in his collection *Many Inventions*. Though early-twentieth-century faith in the good to come of airplanes and automobiles may now seem tragically myopic, one has to recall that Kipling's initial optimism would probably have been shared by that idealistic technologist Alfred Nobel himself. In Nobel's original will of 1893 he had restricted the donation of the awards to a thirty-year period—on the grounds that "barbarism" would result if in three decades scientists and writers had failed to improve the world. Had not Rudyard Kipling foreseen a future age when "the Captains and the Kings" would "depart," to have their ruling places taken by technologists working for nothing save the good of mankind? Though the view seems naïve now, it was new then.

Before turning to the story of the author's productions in the last twenty-nine years of Kipling's life, we need to examine in detail three

29

of his carefully wrought works which should endure as long as his great fairy tales in *The Jungle Books*. Although he produced a veritable horde of full-length poems, together with snatches of stanzas to precede his tales, of the years before he received the Nobel honor, his best-known single collection is *Barrack-Room Ballads*. Aside from certain lines in "Recessional" and "If" and the opening of "The Ballad of East and West" it is in this group that are found his most-quoted poems. Although there seems to be no gainsaying the long life of "Danny Deever," "Mandalay," and "Gunga Din," it seems suitable to evaluate a poem which is much less known but which deserves far more praise for both form and content than the three just cited; it is "Soldier, Soldier" in *Barrack-Room Ballads*.

From the technical point of view this poem is like "Danny Deever" in that it is written in the fashion employed in many medieval rhymed horror tales; that is, the events are unfolded to us in the form of a genuine dialogue, a manner not employed in the other pieces in the collection. Like "Danny Deever" and its ancient prototypes it builds to a climax through a series of questions and answers. Unlike "Danny Deever," however, but like the medieval "Edward, Edward," it has a respondent whose answers to the woman with whom he is talking are at first vague but which conclude with a cynically brutal suggestion which implicates the innocent-appearing questioner. Until the very end the woman asking questions of the "Soldier, come from the wars" seems to desire nothing save news of her "true love," the comrade-in-arms of the man being questioned. At the end, however, when the "Soldier, come from the wars" suggests that she take him for a "True love! New love," since her former sweetheart lies dead in a pit with twenty other men, Kipling allows the woman not one line in which to reject this offer. Hence the conclusion implied seems obvious: she will forget her old love and at once accept her former sweetheart's friend. Only a few lines earlier, of course, she has said, "I'll down an' die with my true love." But the utter impossibility of her performing the act is denied her by the speaker's grisly account of the fullness of the pit where lies her once-beloved.

To complement a tale told in the manner of, and as gruesome as, "Edward, Edward" Kipling employs a rhythm, a stanzaic and rhyme form far simpler than the techniques he employs in "Mandalay" and

"Gunga Din"; but the style he uses here seems perfectly adjusted to the content. Each of the eight stanzas of dialogue begins with the same line—"Soldier, soldier come from the wars"—and follows it with a question or statement about the "true love," each second line containing a small but important variation. "Why don't you *march* with my true love?" (italics added) is the first second line. A later one is, "Did aught take 'arm to my true love?" The final one is, "O then I know it's true I've lost my true love." The remaining two lines in each stanza represent the man's reply; the third line contains an internal rhyme and varies in what it says; the fourth and concluding line resembles the first in being unvaried in wording but serves to form a perfect rhyme for the woman's question or statement about her "true love." The concluding line is "An' you'd best go look for a new love." The beginning and the end of each stanza, then, are constants; the variables lie in the woman's question or statement about her "true love" and the soldier's third-line reply with its internal rhymes. The lack of word and sound change in the opening and close of each stanza of dialogue, as opposed to the neatly subtle shifting in the middle, makes for a beautifully ironic contrast between form and content such as one does not find in any of the other *Barrack-Room Ballads*.

Whatever their merits the other poems in *Barrack-Room Ballads* are verses pertinent to the British army when the Empire was at its height. In a way, of course, to any white reader it is this fact that gives the pieces much of their appeal. They seem to reflect a simpler, less threatened world. On the other hand, the fact that "Mandalay," "Gunga Din," and "Danny Deever" belong to a dead era makes them "period pieces" just as much as "Recessional" with its British "dominion over palm and pine."

To some readers the gray universality of the subject matter in "Soldier, Soldier" may make it less appealing than a work as colorful, though temporally limited, as "Mandalay" or "The Ballad of East and West." In its simple way "Soldier, Soldier" is an assessment of the human plight in all wars. A man lays down his life for his country and receives a burial fit only for diseased cattle and forgetfulness from one who had loved him greatly. Yet to weep over, or condemn, such quick dismissal is foolish. So that human life may go on, it *is* better, perhaps, to take a living "new love" at once than to mourn a dead "true love."

However one judges the content of "Soldier, Soldier," technically it is a first-rate ballad and also a work which should appeal to young readers today on grounds very different from those which once made young Englishmen react with a romantic longing to be "Somewhere East o' Suez" when they heard "Mandalay" or "Gunga Din."

Of the dozens of short stories that Kipling published before receiving the Nobel Prize, it is impossible to single out one as the "best." For despite the fact that he produced many tales that are cheap, contrived anecdotes, he also wrote many that are admirable in both form and content. A less well honored but very fine story "At the End of the Passage" from the collection *Mine Own People* best exemplifies three qualities which one finds scattered here and there in Kipling's other short stories but which in this instance are brought together in the compass of a few pages. In this story we find Kipling's lifelong concern with men's loneliness and their desperate attempt to escape from that particular human misery through work or social meetings with others trained to earn their living in a similar manner; his concern with the horror of hallucinations born of the exhaustion of insomnia (an interest derived, one assumes, from his own not-infrequent experience with that form of emotional disturbance); and, finally, his skill in suggesting atmosphere with a minimum of description.

The plot of "At the End of the Passage" is simple enough to be summed up in one sentence; what matters is the feelings of its four characters. It is the story of the reactions by three members of the Indian Civil Service to the behavior of a fourth, a civil engineer named Hummil, on the Sunday before Hummil dies in the bungalow where he entertains them each weekend, and of their feelings on the following Sunday when they discover him dead. Two of the surviving trio are not aware on the first Sunday that the man so soon to die is seriously ill, physically and emotionally. Involved in problems relating to their jobs and oppressed by the 104-degree heat, they regard Hummil only as a fellow whist player and disagreeable host. Those two have traveled 130 miles by horse and rail to rid him and themselves of loneliness for a few hours at cards. The third survivor, Spurstow, is a health officer in the Indian Civil Service. As a doctor he recognizes that Hummil is deathly ill and, when the other two have left, yields to the sick man's plea for morphia which will allow him sleep without nightmares and perhaps thus induce a freedom from the hallucinations he has been experiencing as a result of trying *not* to sleep from fear of these very nightmares. Although Kipling never says so, it seems clear that the doctor is far less shocked the following week than are the two others when the three find Hummil lying dead. On the other hand, Spurstow seems more shaken than his two companions by the look of horror in the eyes of the corpse. This intense reaction presumably is due to the doctor's last conversation with Hummil and the full realization of the strength of the hallucinations experienced by the invalid

Aside from the grisly nature of Hummil's death from heat and exhaustion in an isolated ugly bungalow on the Indian plains, the power of the story lies in its economical presentation of simple but horrifying details about the lonely lives of the three other whist players. Even at the best of times, when their host is amiable, the trio who go weekly to play whist at Hummil's do not like the game, their host, or one another. Yet two of them are described in one brief sentence as traveling vast distances to escape for a few hours the hell which is their life among sick or hostile Hindus and Moslems. Of their attitude toward whist, Kipling says simply that they "played . . . crossly with wranglings as to leads and returns." The superficiality of their "friendship" emerges in brief but horrible clarity when the heat makes them abandon the game and one of the visitors seats himself at the host's out-of-tune piano. The man has some musical talent and is able to evoke from the wretched instrument quite a repertory of tunes, is a fact of which the three others have been unaware. That the trio of listeners have incompatible tastes Kipling reveals by the simple device of having them request or condemn widely different melodies. They are, in short, four reserved men who would not under other circumstances associate with one another but who indulge in these card sessions as a weekly sedative for loneliness. Hummil, it is true, is less reserved than the others in that he reveals to the doctor the fact that he has been experiencing hallucinations. But this intimate disclosure comes only after he is alone with Spurstow and because he hopes that the doctor may give him a drug which will render possible sleep devoid of nightmares. The intensity of the horror which Hummil feels in regard to falling into an undrugged sleep Kipling makes clear through reference to one simple but ghastly detail. The wretched engineer confesses to the fact that he keeps in his bed a horse's spur: if he relaxes enough to fall asleep, he will at once be "rowelled" awake. His decision has apparently been that it is better to suffer hallucinations from exhaustion than to endure a sleep so bedeviled.

When, a week later, Spurstow is the first to find Hummil dead, there is only a brief exchange of comments about the look of terror in his eyes and about who should read the burial service. Then, Kipling writes:

> There was no further speech for a long time. The hot wind whistled without, and the dry trees sobbed. Presently the daily train, winking brass, burnished steel, and spouting steam, pulled up panting in the intense glare. "We'd better go on that," said Spurstow. "Go back to work. I've written my certificate. We can't do any more good here, and work'll keep our wits together. Come on."

For a moment no one moves since, as Kipling comments, "it is not pleasant to face railway journeys at mid-day in June." But the men must go, and go they do, leaving in silence the heat of the bungalow where they have so often played whist "with wrangles." Like their dead companion, they too are "at the end of the passage." Never again can they form the particular quartet of which Kipling can say, as he does in the story's opening sentence: "Four men, each entitled to 'life, liberty, and the pursuit of happiness,' sat at a table playing whist."

Into eleven pages Kipling packs all the horror of a man's going to his death from apoplexy caused by heat and exhaustion while no one is aware of the fact save a doctor too fatalistic to care greatly. At the same time Kipling injects into the account a grim kind of humor through inclusion of the childish squabbles over the whist table, during the piano recital and the meal following it, and, finally, over the matter of whether a chaplain should be found somewhere or whether Spurstow, as doctor, is adequate to read the service for the burial of the dead. There is also a certain black humor in the way each man tries to "prove" to the others that his job and living conditions are worse than those experienced by the others.

From start to finish the story rings true—seems a valid slice of life among young Anglo-Indian civil servants, unlike many of the brittle anecdotal tales in his first volume. Despite, or because of, the elements of black comedy, it is far more powerful than his Poelike tales of terror. For here Kipling worked with material about which he knew, experiences he himself must have had.

On first reading, certain of Kipling's pre-1907 short stories may create more of an impression because of the grotesque nature of their horror—"The Man Who Would Be King," for example—or the terrible strength of their emotional impact, especially "Baa Baa Black Sheep," which seems especially ghastly since it is mostly autobiographical. Nonetheless, though there are these two and a dozen other candidates for the award of "excellent," "At the End of the Passage" stands out as a work to be read and reread for its economical inclusion of simple but horrible details and, finally, for its economy of style. Even the first paragraph, a brief descriptive piece, is so simple and yet so complex that one comes at last to the realization that it is perfect. Each of its seven short sentences adds one extra little stroke to a needed background. There are the four whist players of the above-quoted opening sentence. The second sentence tells us that the inside thermometer marked over a hundred degrees and that the room was darkened. From this appalling interior Kipling takes us outside briefly to tell us that "there was neither sky, sun, nor horizon—nothing but a brown purple haze of heat. It was as though the earth were dying of apoplexy." The earth, of course, is not dying. It is the wretched Englishmen who have to live on this one particular part of it who are dying, as the story relentlessly goes on to show. Had Rudyard Kipling never written another tale than "At the End of the Passage," he would still deserve a place as a man who could, when he wished, prove himself a true master of short fiction.

In the field of the novel he was less successful. Of his four long works only one met with both popular and critical acclaim in its own time (before 1907); That book, *Kim*, is the only one still widely read.[2] Even *Kim* (1901), has suffered the fate of often being lodged in children's libraries and considered a book for boys because its protagonist is a lad in his early adolescence. Yet it no more deserves such a lot than does that other great work about a boy of approximately the same

[2] The other three are Captains Courageous, The Light That Failed, and Stalky and Co. Though the last has been a popular story among adolescent boys, it is not so much a work of art as a rollicking account of the perennial war between boys and teachers.

age, *Huckleberry Finn.* Like Twain's novel, the color and excitement of the story, together with the simplicity of style, render *Kim* a book which an adolescent can enjoy. But just as Huck Finn's wanderings down the Mississippi are more appreciated by adults than by the young, so should be Kim's journeyings from city to city in India and the passes of the lower Himalayas.

For *Kim,* like *Huckleberry Finn,* is far more than an adventure tale. It is the story of a precocious lad's search for his identity and also a study of how the conventional mores of a number of societies appear to a youthful observer who violates the "accepted" morality of adults and yet at the same time is far more ethical than they are. Like Huck, Kim lies, cheats, steals, smokes by the time he is twelve, and has for school and its discipline nothing but contempt. At the same time, Kim, like Huck, is a loyal and even tender protector of an elderly man of a different race, a dignified but simple soul to whom the conniving of the earth would do harm were it not for the protagonist's intervention. Although both Huck and Kim find much in their respective older companions that baffles them, neither boy mocks the customs or superstitions of the mature innocent whose search for freedom they seek to aid. True, Kim feels a certain condescension toward the lama he befriends because the boy is white and the old man is Tibetan. In just the same way, of course, Huck exhibits toward Nigger Jim a certain condescension. But in both cases the boys' superiority seems based not so much on racist feeling as on the fact that the two young rogues have learned more of the evil ways of the whites, because they themselves are white, than have their nonwhite companions. Even if there are a few instances in which the two lads lord it over their companions simply by dint of belonging to the white race, one has to take into account the era which each work was describing. For the United States in which Huck is supposed to grow up, he is remarkable in his acceptance of a runaway slave; for the 1880's in which Kim is supposed to dwell, he is just as remarkable in his preference for the ways of nonwhites to those of the race to which by birth he belongs.

It has often been argued that Kim plays a double-dealing game with the lama in that the supposed "disciple" uses his old Buddhist "master's" search for a mystic river of "soul freedom" as a means to work at the same time for the British Intelligence Service. Valid though

36

this objection is, Kim's actions in regard to the lama are consistent with the boy's devious character, as consistent as Huck's in regard to Nigger Jim. Like Huck, Kim is a picaro with a strong urge for excitement. Is it not natural, then, that such a fictional character combine altruism with self-seeking? In both cases is it not obvious, considering the protagonist's race, that ultimately he must abandon the way of life which has formed the novel's heart, that a day *must* come when free and easy association with one of another color will no longer be possible? Given this fact, plus the precocious shrewdness with which Kipling endows Kim, it seems only natural that the boy should early render service and loyalty to British Intelligence, since a day has to come when he must abandon his "Indian" way of life so that he may win full acceptance by his "own kind."

The simplicity of style in *Kim* resembles Twain's masterpiece. Intrusions of the author's own opinions are few, and the descriptions of towns or countryside are no longer than necessary to convey atmosphere and information essential to events in the plot. Typical of Kipling's word pictures is the following account of the spot in the Himalayan foothills where they meet the two Russian spies, one of whom brutally attacks the weakened lama and so hastens the old man's near approach to death in the novel's last pages:

At last they entered a world within a world—a valley of leagues where the high hills were fashioned of the mere rubble and refuse from off the knees of the mountains. Here one day's march carried them no farther, it seemed, than a dreamer's clogged pace bears him in a nightmare.

Thanks to these two sentences we find believable the exhaustion which overtakes Kim, as well as the lama, following the encounter with the Russians, an exhaustion which drives them out of the mountains and once more into the plains, a move essential to the novel's close. Such a piece of writing compares well with Twain's paintings of scenes along the Mississippi. Like Twain's writing it presents no barriers to a reader who has grown up on Hemingway and Steinbeck but who finds wearisome the involuted word paintings of Dickens. Nor is this passage atypical. At no time does Kipling become so lost in painting his myriad pictures of the India of the mountains and the plains that he forgets his first task—to tell us of Kim's adventures with the lama.

Kim also stands comparison with another widely read example of the picaresque novel, Don Quixote. Granted that Kim is a mere lad and Sancho Panza an adult, the fact remains that the old man whom each rogue both serves and uses for his own ends is a seeker after an ideal of perfection in a way that Nigger Jim is not. In contrast to the unearthly moral purity of the old man in each story are the misdemeanors of the younger companion. Furthermore, in a world as corrupt as it is, there is something pathetic about the nobility of both Don Quixote and Kim's lama. It is this very pathos of the two old visionaries that brings out the best in their earth-bound companions. Throughout Kim the young rogue is content to achieve his ends by trickery and lying—until the lama is struck by the Russian spy. Then at once the lad's reaction is a spontaneous leap to the old man's defense, a physical attack upon an assailant both bigger and better armed than he. Furthermore, despite the many notes of ludicrous comedy in both Don Quixote and Kim, the conclusion of both these works lacks the happy quality of Huckleberry Finn. To say this is not to imply that any novel with a happy ending must perforce be less admirable than one with a conclusion that leaves one troubled and puzzled.

Although Kipling does not actually show us the lama at the moment of death or Kim turning his back forever on the carefree days of playing Hindu or Moslem beggar boy, the conclusion does suggest that the old Tibetan is nearing his last days on earth; and Kim has been so successful in his final espionage mission for Colonel Strickland that, once the "master" is dead, the lad will dissociate himself from the Buddhist way and will soon become a full-time agent of the British Intelligence Service. The old man, though, knows nothing of Kim's other life and thinks only that the discovery of what the lama believes is the mystic river will enable both master and disciple to be baptized in its waters and thus freed forever of the evils of lust, anger, and ignorance. With Kim baptized, as well as himself, the dying old man is content. But knowing the boy as we do, we cannot believe that either the "master's" teachings or the washing in the river will make the young rogue pure. Hence the final sentence of the book is as poignant in its way as is the end of Don Quixote: "He [the lama] crossed his hands on his lap and smiled, as a man may who has won salvation for himself and his beloved."

There is one more interesting facet of *Kim* which seems worthy of tribute, though it has not received it. This is the fact that the novel is also the story of a youth involved in an identity crisis, groping for values. Although Kipling gives us none of the long introspective passages that we find in *Portrait of the Artist as a Young Man* or *Tonio Kröger*, he nonetheless implies several times that, as he grows older, Kim is deeply troubled about who and what he is. From the opening page he and we know that both his dead parents were white, despite the fact that he lives with a slatternly Hindu, dresses in Indian clothes, has dark skin, and can speak in various Indian dialects better than he can in English. As the years pass, Kipling depicts his young protagonist asking himself, "Who *is* Kim?" On one occasion the author even intrudes into the story with the comment, [Kim] considered his own identity, a thing he had never done before, till his head swam." Although loyalty and affection draw him to follow the wanderings of the pure old lama as he seeks the river, Kim knows full well that he is no true *chela* ("disciple"). Even the lama's financial sacrifices only serve to confuse Kim further: by paying for Kim's education in a Catholic boarding school, the lama introduces him to a world of British clothes and values, one where Kim looks down with the same contempt on his half-caste fellow pupils while certain of his other classmates sneer at him for knowledge of Indian ways and a preference for Indian over British clothing.

Yet even as Kim rebels at the school against British dress and standards, he knows that he *is* a sahib, that his future lies with the rulers, not the ruled, and that the lama's hard-sought "salvation" from the "wheel of life" can never be his. The cheerful street urchin, the illiterate orphan of the first page has changed by the end: shadows of the prison house of adult Western life are falling upon him even as the shade of death is stealing over the lama. Never again will the boy earn his living in the same free manner that he enjoys while begging for his Tibetan "master."

Also like *Don Quixote*, *Kim* is not faultless. The order of many of its episodes grows out of no logical necessity; an event that occurs in Chapter VIII could take place just as easily in Chapter III. Certain of

39

its characters are nonessential, and so are certain of its scenes; their sole function seems to be to fulfill a wish on Kipling's part to paint as many Indian cities and rural areas as possible. Such qualities, however, are standard ingredients in any picaresque novel, and to condemn them as faults may perhaps be as foolish as to complain that an orange does not have the texture and flavor of a pear.

It may be that the presence of such faults is the reason for the relatively low critical esteem in which the picaresque novel as a genre tends to be held. Yet it remains a literary form which has produced three works that are likely to be read as long as men delight in books: *Huckleberry Finn, Don Quixote,* and *Tom Jones.* To this great trio I would add Kipling's *Kim.* Granted that many a contemporary reader may not approve of the British intelligence system as depicted in the work, the same kind of objection can be made to aspects of the others of the great trio. The same eternal qualities of *Huckleberry Finn* and *Don Quixote* which give pleasure in the twentieth century exist in *Kim.*

To what extent did Kipling's career after his receipt of the award resemble that of other Nobel winners in every field? Did the prize come just before a decline? Or, as in the case of Hemingway and Steinbeck, had a period of doldrums set in before the award? That he had been less productive just before he received the award, that he had published fewer works between 1900 and 1907 than he had between 1882 and 1889 is a matter of record. That after 1907 he continued to be less and less productive in the areas of fiction and verse is also undeniable. During the twenty-nine years after he received the award, he concentrated most of his energies on writing articles, speeches, and historical works. Bibliographical records make it clear that in the latter part of his life he became far more the reflective journalist than a creative artist. It is also a fact that a number of the verses he did write in the months just before and after World War I are little more than propaganda intended to generate hatred for the "Huns." (To Kipling, by the way, is usually given the questionable credit for being the first person to use that abusive word for the Germans.)

Yet, although many of his World War I verses are best dismissed as rhymed propaganda, one can also argue that, if Kipling does deserve to be called poet rather than a mere versifier, his claim to the more exalted title stems in large part from a number of the brief lyrics which he

40

composed between 1914 and 1918. There are, for instance, the elegy he wrote about his only son, John, missing at the Battle of Loos in 1915, and his poignant "A Nativity."

In the years from 1918 to 1936, when Kipling died, he wrote only a handful of new poems. Of that period perhaps the most nearly finished poem in form and the most haunting in content is the one which T. S. Eliot praised very highly; it is "Farewell," written by the publicity-shy, secretive Kipling in 1935, a year before his death.

In rhythm and language, as well as in space, it seems clear that at the end he had traveled a whole continent from "lyin' lazy" by "the old Moulmein Pagoda," watching the dawn come up "like thunder, outer China crost the Bay," or brooding over the bugles "blowin' " to signal the "hangin' " of Danny Deever "in the mornin'." By the standards of the poets of this age, and even by those well known in the 1930's—W. H. Auden, Christopher Isherwood, and E. E. Cummings—Kipling was mining a long-worked-out technical lode. At the same time, one must grant that the poetic style of his last years represents a tremendous leap from the Swinburnian alliteration and Poe-like internal rhyme he had once used.

Of the relatively few short stories which Kipling published between 1907 and 1936 (notably in the collection *A Diversity of Creatures*), two generalizations can be made. On the one hand, they are vastly different from his tales of 1882 to 1900; on the other hand, they do not seem like most of the serious short fiction published in the 1920's and 1930's. They are *sui generis*—of their day and not of their day. They allude to World War I, to automobiles, to Freud, and even to fictional science. Yet because of their involved style, complex plots, and enigmatic tone, they seem more akin to the writings of Henry James than to what one finds in the representative short story written since World War I.

Because of their involved style and elaborate plots they have been largely ignored as being "out of due time," unlike the still-often-anthologized "The Man Who Would Be King" and "Phantom 'Rickshaw." But some of them do not deserve the neglect that has been their fate. One must approach them as the work neither of the young Kipling nor of a modern writer. Above all, one must not expect the young Kipling's content. With the years went the desire—or the ability—to

41

write about such wonders of the world as the fairy-tale lands of children, the exoticism of "East o' Suez," and the marvelous potential of machines. Although it is true that India still sometimes played a part, it became a country of memory; and the best-written, best-structured, most complex of his later stories make no mention of the subcontinent. True, there were "horror tales" still; but the best among his last pieces of fiction dealt with mental and physical disease and death as those aspects of the horrors in the human condition manifested themselves in the villages and cities of England. Nor is there any romantic element to offset endings in death. Instead of stallion-spurring subalterns to rouse our urge to find a more "colorful" world, we have weary, unglamorous English physicians, surgeons, businessmen, and workmen. Instead of the flirtatious females of Simla, we encounter respectable aunts or spinsters who are both devoted and vindictive, as in "Mary Postgate"; pathetic old cleaning women, as in "The Wish House"; and a number of other remarkable ladies who combine strength with weakness, most notably the protagonist of the story "The Garden," who has successfully posed as the "aunt" of her illegitimate son until he reaches adulthood, when she loses him to death in World War I.

Before 1907, despite the remarks of some hostile critics, Kipling won not only worldwide popularity but also the remarkable encomium from William James that he was a writer as "universal" as Shakespeare. But almost from the very year in which he received the Nobel Prize, Kipling became a man whom many thoughtful English-speaking readers overlooked, condemning more and more with each decade the "idealism" which the Nobel committee had praised; the once much-admired "ditties" and ballads; the once widely read "tales"; the once-hailed travel sketches—leaving as praiseworthy only *The Jungle Books*. In the second half of the twentieth century Kipling's coeval Yeats seems to garner increased glory with each passing year; and two older novelists, Thomas Hardy and Joseph Conrad, continue to be read and widely praised. But to Yeats, Conrad, and Hardy one would never apply Kipling's line "Dayspring mishandled cometh nat agayne."

Of Kipling, on the other hand, one can say that he had a marvelous "Dayspring," but also one in which he often "mishandled" his many talents. If his work had consistently matched the quality of some of his early efforts and much of his last, there would be no need for those who admire him to take a defensive stance. Yet, perhaps, given the fatalistic note so common in his reticent autobiography, *Something of Myself*, he might have regarded the quoted imitation of a Chaucerian line an apt epitaph for the pattern of his life: too great riches of talent spent in his youth often with too little thought left him with no opportunity for a second chance.

WILLIAM BUTLER YEATS

by James V. Baker

O NE DAY IN NOVEMBER, 1923, William Butler Yeats was surprised to learn from a journalist's report that the Swedish Academy was considering Thomas Mann, the distinguished German novelist, and him for the Nobel Prize in Literature. Because Mann had many readers and was a famous novelist with a fixed place in world literature, Yeats doubted that the Swedish Academy had ever heard his name. Then, eight days later, he received a telephone message from the *Irish Times* informing him that he was the one chosen, and some ten minutes later came a confirming telegram from the Swedish ambassador.

Yeats received the diploma and the medal in Stockholm on December 10, 1923. He was at home in Stockholm, for he had long admired the Scandinavian theater. At the banquet on the evening of the day he received the prize he spoke of Swedenborg, Strindberg, and Ibsen. When it came time for him to deliver his official lecture to the Swedish Royal Academy, he chose as his topic "The Irish Theatre." In the course of his speech he said, "When your King gave me medal and diploma, two forms should have stood, one on either side of me, an old woman sinking into the infirmity of age and a young man's ghost." He was referring to Lady Augusta Gregory and John M. Synge, the two who had been his co-workers in writing plays and who had stood by him in the battles for the Abbey Theatre of Dublin. In addition to all these activities, he was honored by a performance of his play *Cathleen ni Houlihan* at the Royal Theatre.

Yeats, who was born in 1865 and died in 1939, was the son of John Butler Yeats, the portrait painter, a skeptic who probably caused Yeats, by nature strongly religious, to lose his religious belief early in life. A man of strong opinions and high intelligence, Yeats's father, until his death in 1922, continued to influence his son.

As an adolescent, Yeats divided his time between Sligo, his home in Ireland, and London. In London he felt homesick for the seaport town of Sligo, where he spent happy holidays with his mother's relatives, the Pollexfens. There, he felt, were his real roots; there he enjoyed stories of seafaring life, and there he first began to pick up those Irish folktales and the fairy lore which remained one of his leading interests.

His education was somewhat patchy, for, being quite dreamy, he did not take kindly to formal studies. At school in London at Hammersmith, because he was Irish, he had many fights with the English boys. Later he attended the Metropolitan School of Art in Dublin, where he met that remarkable mystic George Russell, who went by the pen-name A.E. Yeats did not go to Trinity College, Dublin, as his father wished, because he could not pass the stiff entrance requirements in classics and mathematics. But though Yeats never went to college and never was a formally trained scholar, he became a man of profound learning whose reading was wider and deeper than that of many pedants.

One paradox concerning Yeats was that, despite his extreme shyness, he was a gregarious man; he was forever joining organizations or founding them. He first became interested in theosophy in Dublin; in 1887 he joined the Blavatsky Lodge of the Theosophical Society in London. In 1890 he joined the Hermetic Order of the Golden Dawn, a society with a secret ritual, an offshoot of the Rosicrucians. In 1891 he was a founding member of the Rhymers' Club, London, which included such poets of the "tragic generation" as Lionel Johnson and Ernest Dowson, and also of the Irish Literary Society in London. Next year he was a founder of the Irish Literary Society in Dublin. In the latter part of the 1880's he had attended meetings of the Young Ireland Society, of which O'Leary was president, and "as a training for self-possession" made many speeches. In 1902 came the founding of the Irish National Theatre Society, with Yeats as president; in 1906 he was named a director of the Abbey Theatre, Dublin, with Lady Gregory and Synge, and the next year defended Synge in the riot over *Playboy of the Western World.*

After his experience at the Dublin art school Yeats definitely decided upon a literary career. He composed his first poems in 1882, and the *Dublin University Review* published his first lyrics in 1885. In London, trying to earn his living by his pen, he was desperately poor. But gradually, through perseverance, he began getting acceptances from English magazines. In 1889 his first book of poems, *The Wanderings of Oisin and Other Poems,* was published. In 1892 appeared his play *The Countless Kathleen.* In 1893 two works appeared: *The Celtic Twilight* and the three-volume edition of the poems of William Blake, in collaboration with Edwin Ellis. Soon, in 1895, he had published an early *Collected Poems.* It may be said that when *The Wind Among the Reeds* (1899) won the Royal Academy prize as the best book of poetry of the year, Yeats had arrived.

Yeats was fortunate in the women he knew, because they were almost invariably sympathetic. They were stimulating, and in writing them intimate letters he was able to formulate his ideas. An early literary friendship was that with Katherine Tynan. At that early date Yeats was still an unpublished poet, whereas her work had been published. The great passion of his life was for Maud Gonne, the tall Irish beauty and agitator for Irish independence, whom he first met at his father's house in 1889. His passion for her was hopeless, however, for they were as oil and water, she a woman of action and he, though at times active, a sedentary and contemplative man. When, in 1903, Maud married Major John MacBride, whom Yeats regarded as a "drunken, vainglorious lout" (see "Easter, 1916") it was a terrible blow to him emotionally. In 1894 or 1895, intervening during this barren passion, was his warm and sensuous love affair with Mrs. Olivia Shakespear, which developed into a lasting friendship. That friendship was significant in at least two ways. Mrs. Shakespear had a daughter, Dorothy, married to Ezra Pound and so brought Yeats into contact with Pound. She was the center of his life in London for more than forty years. Another invaluable friend was Lady Gregory, at whose home, Coole Park, in Galway in the west of Ireland, he spent his summers from 1897 for many years. Coole Park, with its woods, lake, and swans, came to be for him the dearest spot on earth. Lady Gregory released him from literary drudgery, and their relationship was that of mother to son. She was in part instrumental in realizing his dream for an intelligent national theater, the Abbey in Dublin.

Yeats waited till late in life to marry. He was fifty-two when in 1917 he married Georgie Hyde-Lees, whom he had already known for some time, a woman of great warmth and charm. The pattern of literary friendship with women continued to the end; his last friendship was with Dorothy Wellesley, to whom he paid many visits at her Sussex home on his way between Ireland and the Continent.

All his life he was open to new influences. When he was young and his father had moved to London, he met William Morris, William E. Henley, George Bernard Shaw, and Oscar Wilde. At the Rhymers' Club he met a number of poets, including Lionel Johnson and Ernest Dowson. He became closely associated with John O'Leary, the Irish Fenian leader, and also knew George Moore, the Irish writer and realist. He first learned about Indian tradition from a Brahmin, Mohini Chatterjee, in Dublin, when he was twenty-one. He knew Rabindranath Tagore, the poet of Bengal, and he did a translation of the Upanishads with Shri Purohit Swami. Then, too, he had a stimulating literary friendship with Ezra Pound, who introduced him to the Nō drama of Japan.

In later life he was no longer the poor publishers' drudge, copying in the British Museum; he was firmly established after his marriage. A daughter, Anne, was born to him in 1919; a son, Michael, in 1921. In 1922 he became a member of the Irish Senate and did not take his duties lightly, speaking out on divorce and other subjects. The recognition of the Nobel Prize in 1923 made him better known throughout the world. He wrote with more power and authority than ever before, as his two great volumes of poems, *The Tower* (1928) and *The Winding Stair* (1933), testify. He died at Roquebrune, France, in January, 1939, on the eve of World War II. His body was returned to Ireland on an Irish corvette in 1948 and was buried in Drumcliffe churchyard near Sligo "under bare Ben Bulben's head."

At the time Yeats was awarded the Nobel Prize few people would have doubted that he deserved the honor. He was recognized as a great lyric poet and was regarded with extraordinary respect by all who valued poetry both in Great Britain and in the United States. He consolidated his position further by writing, between 1892 and 1921, at least sixteen plays, which were performed at the Abbey Theatre, giving him a considerable reputation as a playwright to buttress his reputation as a lyric poet.

Very early in life Yeats made up his mind to be a great poet, and he never afterward swerved from his aim. His strength was derived in large part from the steadiness of his dedication. He was, however, slow in coming into his own. He never worked fast, and, in fact, he tells us in his *Autobiography* that "five or six lines in two or three laborious hours were a day's work." His method of composition was to say a line aloud over and over to get the sound of it. He lost himself in the imagination of the situation about which he was writing. As he put it, "I have a way of acting what I write and speaking it aloud without knowing what I am doing." One evening as he was working in his study, he heard voices full of derision; a woman and her family were a yard or two away at the opposite window watching. But nothing deterred him, certainly not the mockery of the ignorant.

Yeats's career as a poet extended from 1883 to 1939, a span of more than fifty years. His poetry is like finely woven tapestry, all of a piece, one continuous development from beginning to end. It should not be cut up into sections, but for convenience of evaluation I propose to study it in three phases: the early phase up to the reception of the Nobel Prize; the middle phase, or great period, including *The Tower* (1928) and *The Winding Stair* (1933); and the final phase.

Yeats's earliest work extends from poems published in the *Dublin University Review* in 1883 to *The Wind Among the Reeds* in 1899. The early work is usually condescended to by critics and dismissed with some comment about limpidity and vagueness. But his early work, though it has the qualities disparaged by the critics and though some of it is weak, deserves more serious study than it receives. Yeats was extremely romantic, both by temperament and because of surrounding influences, and his early poems are steeped in romantic feeling: Manfred on his glacier, Prince Athanase studying late in his lonely tower, or Alastor in his boat gliding down the stream. When Katherine Tynan

48

met him in 1885, he seemed to her "all dreams and gentleness." She remembered him standing in the rain, his umbrella tilted at a rakish and absent-minded angle, absorbed in reading Shelley's "The Sensitive Plant." Shelley's *Prometheus Bound* was his sacred book. Blake soon became and remained one of his gods. It was necessary that he pass through the romantic phase on the way to later achievement.

The *Wanderings of Oisin and Other Poems* (1889), his first book of poems, established Yeats as a lyrical poet when he was twenty-four. There he collected nearly all the verse he had written up to that time but also added an ambitious narrative poem, *The Wanderings of Oisin*, in three books. It was the longest poem he had so far written or, for that matter, was ever to write. Katherine Tynan, herself an established poet, had suggested that he write on a theme from Celtic mythology. Yeats, pleased by the idea, used Celtic legends; the hero (whose name is pronounced "Usheen") is the same as "Ossian" of the eighteenth century. The poem occupies much the same position in Yeats's canon as "Endymion" does in Keats's or "Alastor" does in Shelley's; they are similar in that they are youthful trials of strength. But Yeats's poem is more disciplined than Keats's, or at least is more structured. The pagan bard Oisin, who has spent three centuries in fairyland with the goddess Niamh ("Beauty" or "Brightness") returns to imperfectly Christianized Ireland and relates the story of the three islands where he has stayed. The first century was spent on the island of youth, dancing, and love; the second, on the island of maturity and accomplishment (Richard Ellmann, the Yeats scholar, calls it "Victory"); the third, on the island of old age and contemplation, or perhaps dreaming and forgetfulness. It is true that, as Yeats tells the story, it lacks the toughness of the original, but it has in it the essential rhythm of life. Looking back on it much later, he castigated his own epic effort as guilty of vagueness and lack of direction.

Some of his early poems are completely successful and belong in any anthology of his best work. One is "The Stolen Child" from his volume of poems *Crossways* (1889), published the same year as *The Wanderings of Oisin*. Another, "The Ballad of Father Gilligan," has the narrative movement and speed proper to a well-made ballad. In his "Down by the Salley Gardens" he has done as Burns did, taken a few lines of folk song and built upon them some lines of his own. At the very

49

beginning of his attempts at verse he blundered badly, not even understanding scansion. But to offset that lack he had a passion for rhythm
and developed an ear for subtle music of the verse line unexcelled in
English. His felicitous "The Lake Isle of Innisfree," with the metrical
wizardry of its bisection into rising and falling rhythm, is an example
of his new mastery. He called it "my first lyric with anything in its
rhythm of my own music." It was inevitable, Yeats's upbringing being
what it was, that his early poetry would have a visionary and dreamy
character, its incantatory rhythm the haunting romantic music whose
source is Coleridge's "Kubla Khan" or "Christabel," or Keats's "La
Belle Dame Sans Merci."

In the early poetry of Yeats gray or pearl gray and pale are the
favorite adjectives. Everything is misty, nothing clearly defined.
Islands abound, for they are surrounded by water, the mother element,
and they symbolize the condition of being cut off from the world and
of being in nearly absolute isolation from it. Alex Zwerdling has said
that the early poetry of Yeats is based on the dichotomy between
worldly reality and spiritual reality. Escape from the world to an
island or fairyland is a constant theme. In 1888 he wrote Katherine
Tynan, "I have noticed some things about my poetry I did not know
before, in this process of correction; for instance, that it is almost all a
flight into fairyland from the real world, and a summons to this flight."
"Innisfree," however, is not simply romantic escapism, for the motive of
the journey is Thoreauvian and ascetic.

One source of his dignity and passion as a young poet was his noble
and high ideal for Ireland. He was not a political activist, but he knew
John O'Leary, the Fenian leader, who had suffered exile for the Irish
cause, and respected his "moral genius." That O'Leary had high
ethical standards is reflected in his saying, quoted by Yeats, "There are
things that a man must not do to save a nation." Yeats's high dream
was for an Ireland culturally united, so that the two halves, Protestant
and Catholic, would come together. The foundation of this culture,
which was to fire the imagination of educated and ignorant alike, was
the old Irish heroic tradition. His ideal had nothing to do with nationalism, with flag waving, tub thumping, or drum beating—the ruthless,
unprincipled nationalism (essentially juvenile and immature) which,
unless something more humane replaces it, can be the end of humanity.

To realistic minds, quick to point out that he ignored economic, social, and political realities, his spiritual ideal will seem an impractical dream, but nonetheless Yeats had the right idea: true nationalism is the spiritual nationalism he advocated. To quote his own words:

Have not all races had their first unity from a mythology that marries them to rock and hill? We had in Ireland imaginative stories, which the uneducated classes knew and even sang, and might we not make those stories current among the educated classes . . .; and at last, it might be, so deepen the political passion of the nation that all, artist and poet, craftsman and day-labourer would accept a common design?

He passionately wanted "an Irish literature which, though made by many minds, would seem the work of a single mind."

In 1889, Yeats met Maud Gonne, who was to become the great, though frustrated, passion of his life. She said that posterity ought to be grateful to her for rejecting him, since the pain of it caused him to write some of his best poetry. It is true that some of his best poetry was inspired by her. Very early in the course of his love he sat down to write *The Countess Cathleen* (1892), the drama of a noblewoman who sells her soul to save her peasants from starvation. The role of the countess was, of course, created for Maud, an actress, to shine in.

In 1893 he published a new volume of poems called *The Rose*, in which the central symbol is not the island but the Rose of the title. The opening poem, "To the Rose upon the Rood of Time," is extremely romantic in feeling; the opening line is the refrain: "Red Rose, proud Rose, sad Rose of all my days!" Today someone reading what Babette Deutsch calls those "dim old lyrics"—the Rose of the World, the Rose of Peace, the Rose of Battle—is apt to feel that the roses have faded with time. But the Rose of the World carries a wealth of symbolic meaning. No doubt the rose is all involved with his feeling for Maud, but ultimately, at its deepest root, the rose is a religious symbol, signifying imperishable beauty and love. It is irrelevant to note here that in 1887 Yeats had joined the Rosicrucian Order of the Golden Dawn, whose ritual and symbolism centered upon the rose and the cross. To the Rosicrucian, the rose was the goal of man, for, representing as it did eternal beauty and love, it expressed the divine order. *The Rose* also represents a real advance for Yeats, for he uses symbols in the

51

manner of Blake or of Dante; that is to say, he has a system of meanings. His work is not all at random, but an ordered imagination is in control.

In 1895, Fisher Unwin published a one-volume edition of Yeats's work containing *The Wanderings of Oisin, The Countess Cathleen, The Land of Heart's Desire* (play, 1894), and a number of lyrics. Little intervened between 1895 and 1900 except a brief flirtation, sponsored by Arthur Symons, with French symbolism. Had Yeats died in 1900, he would have been known as a *fin de siècle* romantic, better perhaps than Lionel Johnson or Ernest Dowson or others of the "tragic generation," but still a minor poet. Yet there were signs, for those reading closely between the lines, of the promise of the great poet Yeats was to become.

In 1900 or thereabouts Yeats grew tired of romantic vagueness and symbolistic mistiness. As he himself put it, "Dissatisfied . . . with all that overcharged colour inherited from the romantic movement, I deliberately reshaped my style." But if, as he also said, "the self-conquest of the writer who is not a man of action is style," that self-conquest and self-discipline were hard won. The new, less dim and misty, more forceful style appeared at first only occasionally in his work, and it was many years before the conquest was complete. But it is possible to detect the difference quite early.

His collection *In the Seven Woods* (1904) contains poems of greater toughness, "Adam's Curse" (particularly the marrow-bones stanza) and "The Old Men Admiring Themselves in the Water." In 1905 he wrote significantly to John Quinn, "I believe more strongly every day that the element of strength in poetic language is common idiom, just as the element of strength in poetic construction is common passion." He wanted to gain genuineness and honesty in writing by fixing an emotion exactly as it was experienced. He was deeply moved by some verses written by a dying political exile who described the shore of Ireland as it appeared to him when he returned. The words were moving, Yeats says, "because they contained the actual thoughts of a man at a passionate moment of life." His new ideal was to write thoughts in as nearly as possible the language in which he thought them. He tried from then on to write out of his emotions as they came to him in life, not changing them to make them more beautiful. "If I can be sincere and make my language natural . . . ," he said to himself,

52

"I shall, if good luck or bad luck make my life interesting, be a great poet."

The main motive for Yeats's altered style was his desire for change. But the contributing factors are subtle and complex. The greater toughness in his poetry often came about through bitter experience, disappointment in love, or disappointment with the way things went in Ireland. He wrote poetry out of his pain; the comment that "mad Ireland hurt you into poetry" from Auden's elegy is one of the most penetrating ever made about Yeats.

A possible influence was that of Synge, Yeats's friend and associate at the Abbey Theatre. Synge thought that modern literature had grown anemic and that "before verse can be human again it must learn to be brutal." Sir Herbert Grierson's edition of Donne (1912) gave Yeats insight into metaphysical poetry. Possibly Yeats was emulating Donne in the blunt openings of his poems: "A sudden blow" (the Leda sonnet), and, "This is no country for old men" ("Sailing to Byzantium"). Then, too, of unquestionable impact was the criticism of Ezra Pound, who worked close to Yeats as his secretary from 1913 to 1916. Yeats asked him to comb through his poetry, pointing out all the abstract words he could find, and was startled by the large number (war against abstraction was one of Yeats's objectives). Pound convinced him, as Alex Zwerdling reports, "that a vague 'spiritual' language was the curse of the poetry of the Nineties, and that all poetry must be more strongly rooted in the actual and physical than Yeats's had been heretofore." Finally, among the contributing factors, was Yeats's work for the theater. The exacting discipline of writing and rehearsing plays, the problems of management when he was a director of the Abbey, helped in the hardening process, as did his championship of Synge when the mob became angered by *The Playboy of the Western World*.

The new firmness in his poetry appeared in successive volumes— *In the Seven Woods* (1904), *The Green Helmet* (1910), *Responsibilities* (1914), *The Wild Swans at Coole* (1919), and *Michael Robartes and the Dancer* (1921)—up to and beyond the receipt of the Nobel Prize and remained characteristic of his poetry to the end. One of the first poems in which this new firmness is found is "Adam's Curse" in the 1904 volume, already mentioned. This poem has the advantage of being quietly dramatic, a conversation between intimate friends in a London flat. The theme is the hard work that goes into all achievement, particularly in the arts. Yeats, speaking directly out of his own experience in writing poetry, says:

A line will take us hours maybe;
Yet if it does not seem a moment's thought,
Our stitching and unstitching has been naught.

Similarly, the growth of the poem out of actual experience is found in "The Fascination of What's Difficult," which is about the conflicts, the sweat, and the trouble involved in "Theatre business, management of men."

The final conquest over the old and the victory of the new came with *Responsibilities* (1914). The verse now has a leanness, a clean, windswept quality. It took anger to make Yeats throw away decorum and speak his mind as he did in "September, 1913." Sir Hugh Lane had a priceless collection, chiefly of French impressionist paintings, which he offered free to the city of Dublin, provided the city fathers would build a suitable gallery to house them. Perhaps moved by money considerations, the city fathers refused the offer. Angrily Yeats accused them of "fumbling in a greasy till." *Responsibilities* is full of strong poems, among them "The Cold Heaven," "That the Night Come," "The Magi," and "A Coat." "The Magi" closes with a line showing his sense of a force in history older than Christianity, primitive and savage: "The uncontrollable mystery on the bestial floor."

At times he could be startlingly frank. In a postscript to the book, the note of bitterness was probably occasioned by disappointment with the Dubliners, for whom he had written poetic and heroic plays in accordance with his ambition for a national literature which the Dublin public had little appreciated:

all my priceless things
Are but a post the passing dogs defile.

It is inconceivable that he could have written this in his early period. His famous remark about there being "more enterprise in walking naked" (in "A Coat") means that, instead of wrapping oneself in bardic robes, there is more enterprise in finding subject matter in experience immediately at hand and in stripping away pretensions, in

54

exposing what one truly feels, in the often painful honesty of getting at and expressing the true self. The new athleticism of his style did not, however, mean a loss of imagination or of the power to be symbolic and visionary.

This early phase of Yeats's poetry, up to the reception of the Nobel Prize in 1923, is one of consolidation and growing maturity. By this time Yeats is an assured craftsman, poetically mature, writing without stiffness and yet with authority. Characteristic of his style is the energy and the vigorous forward drive of his verse; the verse paragraph is meaty and compresses a complex thought; his work grows sinewy and at the same time subtle.

"Easter, 1916" is one of the great political poems of modern times, raising an abortive rebellion to mythic status. The point of the poem is that the most commonplace characters, the most ordinary men whom he met in the streets or at the club, are translated into heroes by laying down their lives. This thought is expressed in the refrain which ends three of the stanzas:

> All changed, changed utterly;
> A terrible beauty is born.

Here Yeats concedes that Major MacBride, the man who had married Maud Gonne and who was one of the executed leaders, was "changed utterly" along with the rest. But were the poem merely the celebration of heroes who have died for their country, it could hardly be the great poem that it is. It is the finely balanced thought of the third stanza, the only one not carrying the refrain, that redeems the poem from the ordinary. Here the imagery carries the thought. One image, that of the stone in the middle of the "living stream," carries a weight of significance centered around concepts such as the rocklike, the obdurate, the unyielding. To it is opposed a wealth of images all signifying an opposite context: the flowing, fleeting, flying character of life. The poem then becomes charged with the question of whether the obsession of the heroes for Irish freedom (which hardened them into stone) was a senseless obduracy or the price to be paid for the end to be achieved. Thus Yeats mingled lyric celebration with philosophy. It was his special gift.

Few poets have been more successful than Yeats in making poetic capital out of material that lay nearest to hand. In his early period he was constantly writing about his friends, celebrating their qualities and somehow dramatizing them, raising them a little above human stature. He also, even though relying on the esoteric and arcane, was apt to choose his symbols from things close to him, things which were a part of his world. In a splendid lyric, "The Wild Swans at Coole," he wrote about a flock of wild swans which came every autumn to a lake in Coole Park on Lady Gregory's estate. "In Memory of Major Robert Gregory," a masterly elegy, was about Lady Gregory's son, whom Yeats characterized as a fine rider to hounds, a man well able to advise about the furnishing of a house, an artist, a scholar, an example of the Renaissance ideal of the gentleman or courtier: "our Sidney and our perfect man." Later he was to write of "My House," "My Table," "The Road at My Door," and so on ("Meditations in Time of Civil War"). He used the winding stair of his tower, Thoor Ballylee, as symbol of the soul's ascension, turning upon itself but always at a higher level, and Sato's sword, which lay upon his desk, its scabbard wrapped in silk from one of Lady Gregory's court dresses, as his emblem of the life of action ("A Dialogue of Self and Soul").

Marriage in 1917 gave him a firmer hold on life. He understood—and this kind of understanding is always good for a poet—the common human feelings, such as a father's concern for his children. Just after the birth of his daughter, Anne, in February, 1919, he began writing "A Prayer for My Daughter," one of the great poems in the language. It begins on a note of foreboding, the baby innocently sleeping in its handmade cradle, the father anxiously pacing up and down while a storm is brewing on the Atlantic. The wind is violent, a "roof-levelling wind," and is symbolic of the violence that Yeats fears may engulf his daughter when she grows up. Among his prayers for her are that she will not be extravagantly beautiful, so as "to make a stranger's eye distraught," and that she will avoid the example of Maud Gonne, with her passionate political hatred, to become in the end "an old bellows full of angry wind." Rather, he prays that she have a loving, kind, and friendly nature and that she become "a flourishing hidden tree . . . rooted in one dear perpetual place." The tree is one of his favorite symbols; much more is implied here than simple security. The tree has a religious meaning, and, indeed, is tied to the idea of "radical innocence." In the last stanza, he prays for his daughter that she may find a good husband who will bring her to a house where ceremony, courtesy, and art are valued; the two symbols of the tree and the horn of plenty are entwined in the final lines. The poem satisfies because its creator had total control and is one of several expressing Yeats's deep love for a traditional way of life. This way of life was precious, precious and threatened by the burning of houses in the Irish civil war.

Yeats shares with the Hindus a lack of teleological feeling; human history does not move toward some grand climactic moment or judgment Day. Instead, the epochs of history, as also the lives of individuals, are cyclical in movement, an endless series of rebirths. Yeats, probably without benefit of Giovanni Vico and certainly independently of Oswald Spengler, saw history as moving in cycles of two thousand years. His view of history comprised two such cycles, Hellenic civilization from the Homeric or mythical age, roughly from 2000 B.C. to A.D. 1; and Christian civilization, from A.D. 1 to 2000.

Two poems, "The Second Coming" and "Leda and the Swan," are best understood in the light of his cyclical theory of history. "The Second Coming" is prophetic of the end of the Christian phase of civilization. Perhaps no other poem by Yeats or by any other poet of his time packs so much power in two stanzas totaling only twenty-two lines. Written in January, 1919, and preceding "A Prayer for My Daughter," it contains the same sense of threat and grows out of the same material which at that time was fermenting in his mind. When he writes in "The Second Coming" that "the blood-dimmed tide is loosed," he is no doubt thinking of the civil war in Ireland, for that was in the foreground of his thought. But the words of the first stanza have a wider application; they apply to what in his *Autobiography* he calls "the growing murderousness of the world." It is our sense that the words describe our time—what we know and have experienced—and are threatening and prophetic of what worse may yet befall, which gives the poem its extraordinary hold upon us.

We all feel the end of an old era, the beginning of a new, in the changes brought by the revolution in technology, the nuclear age, and the space age, though the coming of the new era, with today's accelerated rate of change, antedated Yeats's terminal date of A.D. 2000 by several decades. More especially the line "Things fall apart; the center cannot hold" comes home to us. For what is it that makes a culture or a civilization cohere? Surely it is shared faith and shared values; it is the crumbling of traditional values and traditional religion which we witness today; and especially what Yeats valued most, "the ceremony of innocence," has indeed been drowned. The imagery of the second stanza is ominous; we can only speculate as the "rough beast . . . slouches towards Bethlehem to be born." None of us knows what the new age will be like, but we all feel that it will be different.

"Leda and the Swan" refers to an event which ushered in the two thousand years of Hellenic history. The sonnet begins abruptly: "A sudden blow." The annunciation to the Virgin Mary, according to the Christian version, was gentle, the Holy Ghost coming in the form of a dove, but the annunciation to Leda was violent, rape in the form of a swan. Yeats spares nothing of physical impact in the Leda sonnet. Leda is pinned helplessly as Zeus, or the divine potency in the form of a swan, attacks her and works his will upon her. Her nape is firmly held in the bird's hard beak, his "dark webs" caress her thighs, she is "a staggering girl" seized with terror. There is, however, some relaxation in the second quatrain, possible acquiescence in a *fait accompli*, subtly suggested in "loosening," "feathered glory," and the intimacy, even though forced, of a "strange heart beating where it lies."

When Yeats moves in the sestet from the act to the consequences of the act, the transition is beautifully managed. He does not permit the poem to lose power in abstraction but continues with "a shudder in the loins" (the moment of conception), and what it entails: "the broken wall, the burning roof and tower," in short, the whole tragedy of Troy. As Helen Vendler has pointed out, the question asked at the end of the sestet, "Did she put on his knowledge with his power?" is not rhetorical but real. It is a genuine question, and Yeats does not know the answer, nor do we. But it may be suspected that the answer is no, for considering Leda's limitations as a mortal, it seems unlikely that she could put on divine insight into the future or into the final mystery of life. The poem masks other meanings than the obvious one of the initiatory rite of pagan history. A shattering experience discloses being in its terror and power; such an experience, which disturbs a person down to the roots, is not always harmful if it renews vital contact.

An interesting theory developed by Yeats is his doctrine of the mask. This doctrine illustrates his tendency to deal in opposites. The principle is that of progression by contraries; the self develops its anti-self or the individual struggles to become that which is most unlike himself. An example is the playwright Synge who, though dying, wrote with gaiety of people with the most robust vitality. Yeats himself put his own doctrine into practice by becoming the opposite of what he naturally was, one shy in the presence of strangers, gentle, and dreamy. No longer was he the sensitive and extremely idealistic young man from the Dublin art school, who wore a long, flowing black cape and floppy tie. Instead he had put on the mask of the man of action. He had become a public figure in Dublin, acknowledged leader of the Irish literary movement, vocal in public controversy, cofounder of the Abbey Theatre, defender of Synge in the fight over *Playboy*, and, in due course, senator of the Irish Free State. The discipline which he imposed upon his writing is another form of the same doctrine; the work of his middle period, with its facing of reality, is the opposite in many ways of the early romantic phase of pale pastel. The guiding thought is summarized in "Ego Dominus Tuus":

> By the help of an image
> I call to my own opposite, summon all
> That I have handled least, least looked upon.

His work at this point richly deserved the honor he received in 1923. He had consistently over the years turned out poetry of the first quality. Line after line has the characteristic of seeming inevitability; test the line, and exactly the right words have been chosen. He had demonstrated persistence and will power in the massive effort needed to remake his poetry in a new style. He showed vital growth; he was not afraid, as new experience came to him, to incorporate it into his poetry. "A writer," he once wrote, "must die every day he lives, be reborn . . . an incorruptible self, that self opposite of all that he has named 'himself.' " That was the secret of the joyous and creative life. He was no private, introverted poet. While his verse, born of experience or of passion, is unique, it is nonetheless universal. He has learned the art of concentration, of conveying weight of meaning in short space, as in "The Second Coming." Perhaps the quality for which his poetry as it matures is most to be valued is depth. Depth is

59

gained by opposed images, as in "Easter, 1916," through the clashing of opposites, and through the poem of dialogue, of which "Ego Dominus Tuus" and the later "A Dialogue of Self and Soul" are examples.

It is a remarkable fact that Yeats's greatest poetry was not written until after he was fifty and that most of it was written after he was honored with the Nobel Prize. Middle-phase Yeats was the period in which he published the two volumes containing his major poems, *The Tower* (1928) and *The Winding Stair* (1933). After that, though there is no decline in craftsmanship or mastery, there is never again the supreme effort of "Among School Children," "Sailing to Byzantium," and "Byzantium."

One problem about Yeats must be faced, and that is his lifelong concern with magic. His whole life was permeated by interest in the occult, probably a compensation for his early loss of Christian belief. His willingness to accept the supernatural causes much that he wrote to be suspect to people brought up in the modern scientific climate. Auden's question is pertinent here: "The reaction of most of us to all that is occult is, I fancy, the same: How on earth, we wonder, could a man of Yeats's gifts take such nonsense seriously?" As a matter of fact, he preserved an open mind, and his occult studies helped him to a wealth of imagery. As his biographer Joseph Hone has said, "Yeats felt mystery a primary necessity of his soul." The critic Richard Blackmur has stated that magic was Yeats's weapon for grasping reality.

It will not be possible here to do more than touch lightly upon Yeats's system. He worked upon it with some excitement from the time of his marriage until he assembled it in one of the strangest books of modern times, *A Vision* (1925). It is very complicated, involving gyres, cycles of history, and phases of the moon. Critics who are cold toward his concern with magic are equally cold toward *A Vision*. Personalities and civilizations are arranged in twenty-eight phases, corresponding to the phases of the moon in the lunar month. It should be realized that this was Yeats's way of imposing an imaginative order or system upon experience and at the same time a scheme of values. Human personality cannot achieve the absolute, and so no human life exists at phase 1 (total objectivity or the dark of the moon) or at phase 15 (total subjectivity or the full moon), when the soul of man rounds itself out through the creation of art or attains Yeats's ideal of Unity of Being. Between these two extremes is a whole spectrum of possibilities. The fundamental metaphor behind the entire work is that of the gyring cones, which are opposites, boring into one another, one the subjective, the other the objective. The movement of the subjective cone is toward perfect self-realization; that of the objective, toward self-negation. We seem to reach close to Yeats's heart in that passage in Book III, "Dove or Swan": "I think that in early Byzantium, and maybe never before or since in recorded history, religious, aesthetic and practical life were one." Here he is saying that Byzantium with its art of mosaics attained unity of culture (which he had so much desired for Ireland) when it approached the full orb of phase 15.

A *Vision* should not be regarded with condescension, but rather it should be accorded the same kind of imaginative validity, the same relevance to experience that is accorded to myth. Nor should it be assumed that Yeats himself believed in his system literally. He himself wrote that he regarded his circuits of sun and moon as stylistic arrangements of experience comparable to the cubes in the drawings of Wyndham Lewis or to the ovoids in the sculpture of Constantin Brancusi. Of the value of A *Vision* to Yeats there can be little doubt. This is something one can never know, but it seems likely that setting it down gave him a sense of confidence and strength. Not only did it make his greatest poetry and late plays possible but, as Northrop Frye points out, it furnished him with energy, almost of jet-propulsive force, out of which to write.

Yeats's great period is the time in his life when he wrote poems like "Among School Children" and "Sailing to Byzantium" (both 1926), which critical consensus regards as his greatest. "Among School Children" opens rather casually with the setting in a schoolroom. But before the poem is done, it has become a weighty meditation upon the whole meaning of human existence. Yeats by this time had developed a masterly architectonic power in building a poem; what is admirable here is the movement of thought from one stanza to the next, the way the poem mounts like one of his swans. The schoolroom naturally leads to thoughts of the contrast between youth and age; it

61

also suggests ironic reflections that perhaps "no possible life can fulfill" the children's "own dreams or even their teacher's hope." Not the least delightful parts of the poem are several touches of wry humor. In stanza V the poet wonders whether a young mother with a baby son on her lap, if she could see what her son would be like at age sixty, would think it worth all the pains of labor and the worry of bringing him up. In stanza VI he masterfully characterizes the teaching of three leading philosophers of Greece: Aristotle, Plato, and Pythagoras; but he brings the reader up short in the earthy last line: "old clothes upon old sticks to scare a bird." In stanza VII he takes up the old theme of disappointment, how the images of mothers, nuns, and lovers "break hearts," because ideals always mock man's ability to realize them. It is now time to reconcile opposites and to write the resolution of the poem, if any resolution is possible to the apparently insoluble problem. In the eighth and final stanza he interweaves all the major themes: the religious or saintly ideal of nuns, the ideal of lovers, and the search for wisdom of philosophers.

One of the marvels of the poem is the way themes reappear. Labor, the poet declares, is "blossoming or dancing" (here he skillfully anticipates the two great symbols which close the poem) when it is done for the joy of it, when body, intellect, and spirit coincide. The poem ends with two questions:

> O chestnut tree, great rooted blossomer,
> Are you the leaf, the blossom, or the bole?
> O body swayed to music, O brightening glance,
> How can we know the dancer from the dance?

The answer is that we cannot know. We cannot separate the dancer from the dance, so complete is the fusion between the music and choreography of the dance and the instrument of interpretation, the disciplined body of the dancer. The solution to the problem posed by the poem is that fulfillment is possible only when unity of being is attained. The poem rises from the particular, limited time and place of the schoolroom and mounts till it comes to rest in a moment of timeless ecstasy.

"Sailing to Byzantium" is similarly a quest for an existence transcending the limits of space-time. The two poems are close together in time of composition; "Among School Children" is dated June, 1926, and a typescript draft of "Sailing to Byzantium" is dated September 26 of that year. Both poems have the same central theme: the achievement of unity of being.

The immediate impetus of the poem was the finishing of A Vision at Syracuse in January, 1925, when he visited Sicily in company with Ezra Pound and Mrs. Pound to see the great mosaics at Palermo. But it was more than a matter of immediate stimulus; it has been well said that his whole life speaks through the poem. His lifelong dedication to art and his interest in Byzantine art in particular finds articulate voice. The poem owes much of its success to the choice of Byzantium as its central symbol, for a symbol of more extraordinary depth and richness would be hard to find. He surrounded ancient Byzantium and the great cathedral of Hagia Sophia with a halo; to him it was the artist's heaven. No doubt he idealized it, as the passage from "Dove or Swan" in A Vision quoted earlier shows. For him it realized that unity of culture which had always been his dream for Ireland, or for any true civilization in the world. His own statement is simple and sufficient: "Byzantium was the center of European civilization and the source of its spiritual philosophy, so I symbolize the search for the spiritual life by a journey to that city."

What gives the poem its strength? As is true of any good poem, it is not one element but several working together. Yeats's use of the simple, compact structure of ottava rima, which he had used in "Among School Children" and was to use later in "The Circus Animals' Desertion," is masterly. He is modern in his use of slant or half rhymes, and at moments of intensity rich assonance accords with the sacred character of the theme:

> O sages standing in God's holy fire
> As in the gold mosaic of a wall.

Another strength of the poem is its movement forward; it does not stagnate. True, in stanza I the speaker of the poem, or "I-persona," now feeling his age, is caught, so to speak, in the country of the young, where he feels out of place. But this immediately initiates in stanza II the strong statement of the motivation for the voyage. Stanza III is a fervent prayer for initiation, for the purification necessary before the all-too-human voyager can be admitted to the "artifice of eternity." In stanza IV the destination has been reached; the voyager has attained the active heaven of art where "once out of nature" he can "sing" (practice his craft) on an unlimited range of subjects, "past, . . . passing, or to come." Perhaps he can enjoy the best of both worlds, for though removed out of time, he is still in touch with earthly passions.

Other sources of the poem's strength are the toughness of its realism; the authority, dignity, and compression of its language; and the powerful tension set up within it. The old man is "a tattered coat upon a stick," and the condition of the human heart in old age is accurately depicted in these words: "sick with desire/and fastened to a dying animal." As for compression, Yeats has learned to subsume vast classes of objects under a single word or clause: "Fish, flesh, or fowl," "Whatever is begotten, born, and dies," "what is past, or passing, or to come." Throughout the poem, the precisely right word is chosen. Take for example the phrase, "Caught in that sensual music." "Sensual music" is perfect for the sexual enjoyment celebrated in the first stanza, but the verb "caught" fits exactly because of the earlier reference to "mackerel-crowded seas" and the implication of fish caught in a net. All living creatures, man included, are caught within the cycle of birth and death. No escape is possible for the seething fish within the net.

The tension is strong because the forces pulling either way are strong. On the one hand, there is the overmastering pull of the sensual life; on the other hand, the strong attraction of the ordered world of art. Not that, properly speaking, art is an escape from the sensual life; it is rather founded upon the sensual life, its completion and transference into another sphere. The critic John Senior has described Yeats as a "reluctant voyager," and all readers who have experienced his "rage against old age" in the later poems know that he did not relinquish the sensual life gladly. The first stanza of "Sailing to Byzantium" celebrated the abundance and fecundity of that life in what must surely be one of the most procreative lines in English literature, "The salmon falls, the mackerel-crowded seas." We know, too, from other sources, especially from "A Dialogue of Self and Soul," the intensity of his relish for life, his willingness to be reimmersed in it, even at the cost of undergoing all the suffering again. Yet one does not doubt the sincerity of his prayer to the holy sages to "be the singing masters of my soul." His devotion to art, above all to poetry, forbids one to doubt that he felt art to be sacred and sacrosanct, the shrine which held value protected from the ravages of time. One wonders whether it was a decision of an absolute either-or kind; unity of being would seem to require the holding of the two halves in balance.

"Byzantium," several years later than "Sailing to Byzantium," was written after an illness that had brought him close to death, in order, as he said, "to warm myself back into life." Here the poet is no longer sailing to Byzantium, but he is there. Byzantium is now the symbol of the after life. The dome—"moonlit" suggest the full creativity of phase 15—dominates stanza I. As in the earlier poem, opposition is generated between two poles: the dome, symbol of the immortality of art, and the human passions, "the fury and the mire of human veins."

Yeats's belief which undergirds the poem is that the soul seeks passionate experience during its lifetime. After death, it must assimilate and master that experience through reliving it, until it is purged and ready for "The Marriage," or reunion with absolute spirit; it then re-enters life afresh. The similarity to the Hindu doctrine of reincarnation, as well as to Plato's parable at the end of The Republic, is striking. The unwinding of "Hades' bobbin" in stanza II means the soul's reliving of its experiences in life so that it may master them. A curious experience, it would be like watching a motion picture of one's whole life in reverse, from death back to infancy. Yeats in his Autobiography calls this process of dreaming back, or living back, the soul's return to innocence.

The great fourth stanza celebrates the condition of fire in which is all peace and all rest, the condition of the holy sages in stanza III of "Sailing to Byzantium." Nothing can exceed the energy of this passage, the profound meaning of the dance symbolism, or the paradoxical power of "an agony of flame which cannot singe a sleeve." In the fifth and final stanza the warm-blooded dolphins are busy ferrying souls to the mosaic pavements, where they, too, will dance the ritual dance. The seething, sensual seas over which the souls pass are "gongtormented," that is, reverberate with the gong of Saint Sophia which summoned to worship in stanza I.

Yeats grew younger as he grew older, or so it seems in the poetry of

65

his last phase. No decline can be detected in the vigorous, bounding energy of his verse; witness section III of "The Tower" and the whole of "Under Ben Bulben," not the last, but one of the last poems he ever wrote (no doubt on account of its valedictory nature, it is placed at the end of his *Collected Poems*). His imagination is as hot, passionate, and "fantastical" as when he was young ("The Tower"). He explores new subject matter in the Crazy Jane poems, with their earthy frankness. The number of well-wrought and completely finished poems does not decrease. "A Dialogue of Self and Soul" gains much of its power from the opposition in the respective pulls of self and soul, and the decisive share of the argument is given to the self. Critics see this as a contradiction to the victory of the spiritual life in the Byzantium poems, but Yeats's thought perpetually vacillates between two poles.

A few of the many successful poems of his final phase may be cited: "Lapis Lazuli," that delightful poem about gaiety in spite of tragedy and old age; "The Spur," short and sharp, which Eliot praised for its honesty; "The Long-Legged Fly," on the silence and stillness out of which creative thought or decision is born; and "The Circus Animals' Desertion," where he reviews the heroic themes from Celtic myth which he once wrote about. The themes, or "circus animals" of the show he presented now desert him and he is left with nothing but his human heart.

Yeats directed as much time and energy to the writing of plays as he did to the writing of poems—probably more, for the total of his plays is large: twenty-five in all, or twenty-seven if his two translations from Sophocles, *King Oedipus* and *Oedipus at Colonus*, are included. He very early became ambitious to do great work in the theater, for his father exalted dramatic poetry above all other kinds. A similar development is observable in his plays and in his poems: from a misty romanticism to an austere exploration of reality. The change to bluntness of language is also found.

From the outset, and consistently throughout his career, Yeats was the determined enemy of realism in the theater. His response to Ibsen's *A Doll's House*, which he saw in his youth, was simply, "I hated the play." For one thing, the closeness of the dialogue to modern speech prevented any music of style. When in later life he saw Shaw's *Apple*

Cart, he disliked it, for it seemed to him that it was written off the top of Shaw's mind by the Shaw who made wisecracks or who participated in public debate. The inwardness of Shaw did not appear. In the last of his plays, *The Death of Cuchulain,* Yeats has the old man who speaks the prologue say that he spits upon the dancers of Degas. Why so violent a reaction to the work of a respected painter? The reason for the reaction is that the dancers of Degas are painted realistically. Yeats's great theme in the theater was the one he had announced in *The Secret Rose* (1897), namely, the war of "spiritual with natural order," and though he thereby doomed his plays to unpopularity, he stayed with this theme throughout with unflinching integrity.

The plays of Yeats divide naturally into two groups, those written before 1914 and those written after that date. The division is due to the fact that the later plays are written in a different tradition from the early ones, for they conform to the Nō tradition of Japan.

The first of Yeats's plays, *The Countess Cathleen* (1892), is the drama of a noblewoman who sells her soul to save her peasants from starvation. She sells her soul to the devil and remains unchanged. After the benefit of more experience in the theater Yeats said that, were he to do the play again, the moment the countess had signed the bond he would have her break out into loud laughter. His next play, *The Land of Heart's Desire* (1894), a one-act play produced in London as a curtain raiser for Shaw's *Arms and the Man,* is about a newly married girl, Mary Bruin, and the conflict for her soul between a fairy child and a priest, Father Hart. The conflict is real enough that the play crosses the footlights. Yeats himself later criticized it as "a vague, sentimental trifle" and condemned *The Countess Cathleen* as "tapestry." His next play, *The Shadowy Waters* (1900), was written during his French symbolist phase; as he tells us, it was intended to be "more a ritual than a play" and was designed for a few people who love symbols. The lovers, Forgael and Dectora, are shadowy rather than individualized; they are universal, archetypal figures, representing lovers of all times and places. At this particular stage in his development Yeats much admired *Axël* and the early plays of Maeterlinck.

In the years between 1900 and 1914, Yeats, without in any way compromising his antinaturalist stand, became a more seasoned man of the theater. The fact that the Abbey Theatre opened in 1904 and that in 1906 he became a director with Lady Gregory and Synge had much to do with the change. Before that, however, his prose play *Cathleen ni Houlihan* (1902) was enthusiastically received, no doubt because it had a patriotic Irish theme. Here the situation is reminiscent of *The Land of Heart's Desire*, but this time the wedding is yet to take place, and the spirit of Ireland comes to lure the groom away to serve in the cause of Irish independence. Yeats moved from the languid dreaminess of *The Shadowy Waters*; he wanted to make his language tougher, more masculine. This he effectively did in three racy lines that he added in 1907 in revising the last-named play, where he has the sailor say:

> I am so lecherous with abstinence
> I'd give the profit of nine voyages
> For that red Moll that had but the one eye.

Of the many plays that Yeats wrote during this period—*The Hour Glass* (1903), *The King's Threshold* (1904), *The Pot of Broth*, a farce (1904), *On Baile's Strand* (1904), *Deirdre* (1906), *The Unicorn from the Stars* (1908), *The Green Helmet*, a farce (1910), *The Hour Glass* (1914)—critics usually regard *On Baile's Strand* and *Deirdre* as the best. Both are without question acting plays, both are tragedies, and both deal with heroic Irish themes. The language, simple and bare, is fortunately un-Shakespearean.

On Baile's Strand is the first of five plays which Yeats wrote on the theme of the great hero of Irish mythology, Cuchulain. The other plays are *The Green Helmet*, *At the Hawk's Well* (1916), *The Only Jealousy of Emer* (1919), and *The Death of Cuchulain* (1938). In the play *On Baile's Strand*, Yeats wisely limits himself to one terrible episode in the life of the hero. The action moves at two levels: the main action, concerned with Cuchulain, the hero, and Conchubar, the High King; and the subplot, concerned with the blind man and the fool. The characterization is clear: Cuchulain is wild and Conchubar grave and weighed down with cares of state. The character contrast is doubled by the low comedy of the two characters in the subplot, for the fool is wild and the blind man cunning. The main plot is the Irish version of a story found so often in ancient myth in which either a son kills his father or (as here) the father kills his son. The unlikely circumstance

68

is given credibility because the son is the result of a love affair which Cuchulain had years before with the passionate warrior-woman Aoife, now his bitter enemy; in fact, she had raised the son with the specific purpose in mind that he would grow up to kill his father. A young challenger appears, and Cuchulain, not recognizing his son after so many years, fights the challenger and kills him. The two plots are cleverly interwoven, for it is through the old man and the fool that the hero discovers who the challenger is. Crazed with grief when he finds out what he has done, he jumps into the sea and battles the waves. At the end of the play the cunning blind man and the fool who provides his sight use the opportunity of the deserted houses (everybody has gone down to the shore to watch Cuchulain) to steal food from the ovens.

The play has a tight plot which moves steadily toward the catastrophe. When one realizes that it was begun in 1901 and written, so to speak, under the shadow of *The Shadowy Waters*, Yeats's sudden advance in mastery becomes all the more striking.

Deirdre (1906) is concerned with the final hours of one of the most famous heroines of Irish mythology. The play is short and concentrated in a manner similar to *On Baile's Strand*. It opens in the rough-hewn guesthouse of Conchubar, the High King of Ireland; on a table are a chessboard and chessmen, a flagon of wine, and a loaf of bread. The story, told by the musician, is that, twelve years before, King Conchubar found a beautiful child, Deirdre, being nursed by an old witch, and decided to raise her himself. When she grew older, she was so beautiful that he desired her for his wife. But his intention was thwarted when Naisi, a young follower of his, ran off with her. As the play begins, we are given to understand by Fergus, an old friend of Conchubar's, that the lovers have returned after six years of wandering and that they will be taken back into favor and forgiven; Fergus, in fact, has been instrumental in this forgiveness. When the lovers Deirdre and Naisi enter, however, many signs show that this is wishful thinking; the chess game that follows is ominous because it calls up memories of the story of another hero and his "sea-mew" wife who had played chess years ago on the very same board while waiting for death. Conchubar has sent no welcoming messenger, the flagon contains cobwebs, and the bread is moldy. Near the climax of the play

Conchubar sends Naisi into the curtained section of the room to be killed. The musicians make a final lament, as Fergus enters with support for the lovers, only to be told by Conchubar that he is too late. Conchubar then flings the curtain back, and it is indeed too late, for Deirdre has killed herself beside Naisi. *On Baile's Strand* and *Deirdre* have sufficient tragic power that together they form the greatest dramatic effort of Yeats's early plays.

In the winter of 1914, Yeats was introduced by Ezra Pound to the Nō theater of Japan, which he welcomed because he saw in it the ideal medium through which to present his ideas and symbolism on the stage. In Nō theater the language is simple and direct; among its conventions are a bare stage, a few choric attendants, the use of masks, dance, and a dominating image or symbol—Leonard Nathan calls it the "binding metaphor." The characters are few in number, the plot simple; the last drop of meaning is squeezed out of the situation. The result is a revelation of reality or unity of being. This was exactly what Yeats wanted. In many of his Nō plays, he adopted all the Nō conventions mentioned above. It is not, however, accurate to say that he merely imitated the Nō model; what is true, rather, is that he adapted Nō to his own purposes, that is, to tragic or heroic Irish themes, and that, as Nathan puts it, the Nō theater acted as the "catalyst" for his own ideas.

At the Hawk's Well (1916) has the distinction of being the first Nō play in English. It was produced in Lady Cunard's drawing room in London with Mischio Itow in the role of the hawk. The play is highly stylized in the Nō manner. The characters either wear masks or have their faces made up to resemble masks. The plot is simple. Once at long intervals the magic well guarded by the hawklike woman bubbles up with a spring of immortality. The young Cuchulain, with his heroic fame still ahead of him, comes to the well, but is so determined to conquer the hawk that he pursues her. Meanwhile the well bubbles up, and he loses his chance of drinking at the immortal spring. Clearly the play moves simultaneously at a symbolic and a physical level.

The next play, *The Dreaming of the Bones* (1917), probably adheres more closely to the Nō drama than any other play in English, employing the *Nishikigi* motif of ghostly lovers. A young man who has taken part in the Easter Rebellion, who has been in the Post Office in

Dublin, and who, if caught, will be put against a wall and shot, is escaping to the Aran Islands. He meets with the two lovers Diarmuid and Devorgilla, not realizing at first that they are ghosts. When he discovers that they are the lovers "who brought the Norman in," and who therefore brought about Ireland's domination under foreign rule, he refuses to forgive them, and so the souls of the lovers go unappeased. The play, as Helen Vendler has pointed out, is on one of the obsessive themes in Yeats's work, namely, of the soul's "dreaming back" the events of its past life and its eventual self-forgiveness (not attained here) and recovery of radical innocence

The Only Jealousy of Emer (1919), one of Yeats's more powerful plays, is a sequel to *At the Hawk's Well*. Cuchulain, "that amorous, violent man," has fought the waves, been overwhelmed by the tide, and lies in a state of stupor, captive in the other world to the sea goddess Fand (identified as the Hawk-Woman of the earlier play). The present play develops into a three-way struggle for the possession of Cuchulain among Fand, who belongs to the world of the immortals, Emer, his wife, and Eithne Inguba, his young mistress. The plot has a twist to it, for it appears that only Emer can summon him back on condition that she renounce forever her claim on his love. Hard as the condition is, Emer submits to it, and for thanks has to see the young mistress in the arms of Cuchulain. Beneath the plot surface lie deeper implications of a passionate man's relationship to muse, to wife (the one who probably loves him best), and to mistress, the one who has glamor and youthful appeal. One of the most poetic of Yeats's plays, the language is throughout dignified and, in the songs, lyrical.

The afterlife was a subject that from his earliest days persistently fascinated Yeats. It is not surprising, then, that he wrote two plays on the subject of Christ's life after his crucifixion, *Calvary* (1920) and *The Resurrection* (1925). In the first-named play, Christ re-enacts in his imagination the suffering of his walk to Calvary. The play is arranged as a series of encounters, the first being with Lazarus, who is ungrateful for having been raised from the tomb; he would have preferred to remain dead. The next encounter is with Judas, who had already recognized that Jesus was the Son of God and had not needed the evidence of miracles. He betrayed Christ because he could not bear to think that Christ had but to whistle and he had to obey. Judas

71

belongs to the old order of subjectivity; for him the essence of being is freedom of choice. He cannot bear the new reign of objectivity, detests the thought that Christ must in all things obey his Father's will. At this point, the play is nearly over; indeed, so compressed is it that it seems ended almost before it has begun. The dialogue is frigid, and the play, though interesting for its theme, is not among Yeats's more successful productions.

The next play, *The Player Queen* (1922), is one on which Yeats worked for years. As was the case with his father's painting, it would seem that the more a play is worried the less it coalesces into unity but instead betrays conflicting intentions. It is not really stageworthy and, even with the most intelligent direction, mystifies audiences. Not that all is clouded. The theme, as in *Calvary*, is one of a new dispensation superseding the old. Septimus is clearly a poet who lacks popular appeal. The presiding symbol is the unicorn. Popular superstition regards the Queen as a witch, because she shut herself up in the castle from the day her father died and has not shown herself to the people. She preserves her "quaint virginity," which the unicorn also symbolizes, just as the poet Septimus keeps his poetry unspotted from the least taint of commercial realism. Timidly, at the first whisper of revolution, the Queen retires to a convent; the Player Queen, the bold Decima, has an appetite for rule, marries the prime minister, and inaugurates the new regime. While it is partly tragic in intention, the play has farcical elements; the troupe of players, of whom Septimus and Decima are members, are about to perform a play about Noah and the animals going up the gangplank into the ark. But revolutionary events supervene, and the play is never performed, though we see players, dressed as animals, prancing about the stage. The play, as a whole, leaves a mixed impression; it has the theme of *Calvary* impudently treated.

By this time Yeats had completed an impressive number of plays, and his achievement in the theater favorably swayed the opinion of the judges who awarded him the Nobel Prize in 1923. With plays like *Deirdre* and *On Baile's Strand* he had given Ireland a heroic theater, and he had been tireless with experimentation, particularly in adapting the Nō theater to heroic Irish themes. It is significant, however, that when Yeats went to Stockholm the play chosen for performance

72

at the Royal Theatre in his honor was not one of the more esoteric ones but the one with popular appeal, *Cathleen ni Houlihan.* Yeats's career in the theater was by no means over, and some of his greatest plays were still to come. *Resurrection* (1925), at first intended for the drawing room rather than the theater and not publicly performed until 1934, in Dublin, is a companion piece to *Calvary.* It has the theme of so much of Yeats's work, including "The Second Coming": of the bloodshed and threat attendant upon the dying of an old order— in this case the Greek "subjective" civilization—and the coming of the new, the Hebraic, Christian, objective dispensation. Throughout this play, like figured bass, is the throb of primitive Dionysiac rites, the drumbeat and orgy of a wild ritual performed by the mob. The basic plot situation is that a Hebrew and a Greek are together guarding the eleven disciples on the third day after Calvary. The dialectic is found in the totally dissident attitudes of Hebrew and Greek toward Christ. To the Hebrew, Christ is simply a man who in a weak moment was fooled into believing himself the Messiah. To the Greek, who is clinging to the last vestiges of the rationality of Hellenic culture, the orgies of the mob are revolting, and it is simply not credible that Christ, after entombment, should be anything more than shade or specter. When, toward the climax of the play, the Greek touches Christ and finds a living body, he is so shocked that he screams. Christ represents a superhuman objectivity in that he has no concern for self but infinite compassion for others. Neither Hebrew nor Greek had penetrated the mystery of the God-man, though the Hebrew came much nearer than the Greek. This play, like the others in the Nō cycle, begins and ends with choric song, and the poetry which celebrates the dying of the old and the coming of the new order is incomparable, among the greatest Yeats ever wrote:

> Everything that man esteems
> Endures a moment or a day:
> Love's pleasure drives his love away,
> The painter's brush consumes his dreams;
> The herald's cry, the soldier's tread
> Exhaust his glory and his might:
> Whatever flames upon the night
> Man's own resinous heart has fed.

The Words upon the Window Pane (1934), one of the most attractive of Yeats's plays, was written in his seventieth year. It by no means has all the elements of Nō drama, yet in essential theme and spirit it is a Nō play, for at its heart it is concerned with the *Nishikigi* motif of ghostly lovers, which he had used previously in *The Dreaming of the Bones.* For once Yeats has admitted the modern and the realistic, for the setting of the play is modern Dublin. For once, too, the characters are not wearing masks and do not have heavy makeup on their faces to resemble masks but can be their natural selves. One of Yeats's lifelong interests finds expression in this play, for what is represented is a séance in session. The play is a tour de force which comes off, for we never see the lovers, Swift, Vanessa, and Stella, and yet we hear their voices and feel their presence; their passion comes very much alive. The two women who love Swift cannot both speak at once, but through the conductorship of the medium only one voice is heard at a time. The right ironic note of skepticism is provided by John Corbet, a student who is doing a study of Swift for his Cambridge doctorate. Dramatically, this is probably the most successful of all Yeats's plays.

The last five plays that Yeats wrote are, in order, *The King of the Great Clock Tower, A Full Moon in March, The Herne's Egg, The Death of Cuchulain,* and *Purgatory.* It will be convenient to take *The King of the Great Clock Tower* and *A Full Moon in March* together, for the latter is a revision of the former play.

The King of the Great Clock Tower employs all the Nō conventions —bare stage, choric attendants, masks, dance, and dominant symbol— to reveal fullness of being. A stroller who is a poet comes to the castle and confidently foretells that on the stroke of midnight he will be kissed by the Queen. The King orders him instantly beheaded for his impudence. At this the Queen enters into her dance. The King places the decapitated head on the throne and challenges it to sing. To his horror it sings, and on the stroke of midnight at the climax of the Queen's dance she kisses it on the lips. Thus the prophecy of the stroller is fulfilled.

A Full Moon in March is the same play completely revised and written with greater economy. The King is eliminated as unessential to the theme. The stroller poet again appears, only this time far less ele-

74

gant and more difficult to accept, for he is a dirty swineherd. Nevertheless, he represents passion, vitality, and fearlessness. The Queen orders his decapitation for his presumptuousness. She holds the severed head above her and her hands are red with blood (symbolically represented by red gloves). The Queen then lays the head upon the throne and enters into her dance. The severed head sings, or, more precisely, an attendant sings for the severed head). The Queen dances to drum taps, her dance grows more and more ecstatic, she presses her lips to the lips of the head, and she then sinks slowly down with the head upon her breast. The play closes with a choral interchange between the first and second attendant. The first attendant asks why "holy, haughty feet" must descend from ivory towers or "emblematic nitches." The second attendant replies, "For desecration and the lover's night."

A Full Moon in March invites comparison with Wilde's Salomé, but Yeats's is not a decadent play, while Wilde's is. Yeats is not retiring into ivory towers where secret lust is cultivated; he is confronting reality in its full scope. The "desecration and the lover's night" are necessary to the completion of being. This theme of the copresence of the physical and the spiritual is one which permeates the work of Yeats; it is present in the dance image at the close of "Among School Children." No matter how foul might be the rag shop "where all the ladders start," Yeats was not one to turn his back on reality. The "Full Moon" of the title has significance; it means phase 15, or being at the full.

The Herne's Egg (1938) is a departure from anything Yeats had done before, and can perhaps best be described as heroic farce. It is the Leda theme treated not with tragic seriousness but rather with primitive humor such as Homer's "inextinguishable laughter shook the immortal gods." Yeats himself called the play "the strangest and wildest thing I have ever written." Though it includes the rape of Attracta by many soldiers and has its moments of broad comedy, it is too confused, too uncertain in tone between seriousness and farce, to come off successfully.

In The Death of Cuchulain (1938), Yeats returned to the Irish hero cycle, and this tragedy is the fitting climax to the earlier plays he had written upon this theme. The subjective hero, Cuchulain, is at the end of an age now falling into objectivity. The play is unfinished; it was still under revision when Yeats died.

It has a bad-tempered prologue spoken by an old man, and its attitude of contempt for the public, "people who are educating themselves out of the Book Societies and the like, sciolists all, opinionated bitches," is unbecoming to a dramatist. The unpleasant, bitter tone is condensed into the reiterated "I spit! I spit! I spit" with which it closes.

The play itself lacks exposition and plunges at once into the action, which is swift and compressed. Always inventive, Yeats treats the saga freely and departs from it for his own purposes. In the saga Cuchulain is still young at the time of his death; Yeats makes him old. In the saga Cuchulain's savage anger in battle is the prelude to his death; here his death is to be inferred, for the stage darkens, and when the lights go up, Cuchulain enters wounded. Female figures or influences dominate the play—all the women in Cuchulain's past life: his wife, Emer; his mistress, Eithne Inguba; Aoife, with whom he slept in still earlier times; his old enemy, Maeve, who does not actually appear on the stage, but who bewitches Eithne Inguba so that she sends him to his death; and the Morrigu, goddess of war, who corresponds to the Hawk-Woman in *At the Hawk's Well*. The old heroism is not absent, for, even though he is aware of Eithne Inguba's bewitched treachery, Cuchulain still wants to meet the foe:

> I am for the fight,
> I and my handful are set upon the fight;
> We have faced great odds before.

Nevertheless, Cuchulain is old and tired. Eithne says to him:

> You're not the man I loved,
> That violent man forgave no treachery.
> It is because you are about to die.

Wounded to death, with weak and fumbling hands he attempts to strap himself to a pillar so that he may die standing—surely a heroic gesture, like the dying Roland blowing his horn. The beheading of Cuchulain is performed by the blind old man from *On Baile's Strand*. Yeats avoids realism and substitutes abstraction. The stage darkens, and when the curtain rises, the Morrigu holds up a black parallelogram, representing the hero's head. Six other parallelograms near the backdrop represent the heads of the six Irish chieftains who gave Cuchulain his death wounds but whom he killed. The Morrigu lays the hero's head upon the ground, and Emer enters to perform the final dance. Her anger seems directed against the six heads in the background, but her dance, inasmuch as she is well into middle age, can hardly be as passionate as the Queen's in *A Full Moon in March.* Cuchulain feels himself antiquated, even anachronistic, as the heroic age yields to the modern world, represented by the lively music of an Irish fair.

Purgatory (1938), a one-act play contemporaneous with *The Death of Cuchulain,* may fittingly close the review of Yeats's plays. His last public appearance was at the Abbey in August of that year, to see it performed. The bitterest, the bleakest, the most unpleasant of his plays, it has somehow attracted more critical interest than any other. It has resemblances, perhaps not altogether fortuitous, to Samuel Beckett's *Waiting for Godot,* especially in the bareness of the setting; though the intellectual climate of the two plays is different, both have the same feeling of a dead end. *Purgatory* is written on the Greek theme of the House of Atreus, a house in which the curse of the elder is passed on to a younger generation. Yeats has retained some, though not all, of the Nō conventions—bare stage, few characters, extreme concentration, and what Nathan calls "binding metaphor," the blasted tree which cannot even bud forth any new leaves. Experimental to the end, the poet has at last broken with iambic pentameter as norm, substituting, as Eliot has pointed out in his fine essay on Yeats, the freer fourbeats to a line, the number of light syllables not being strictly counted. The advantage is a greater approximation to actually spoken speech.

One reason for the prison feeling created by this play is that the world here is wholly given over to the objective phase and is lit by imagination, symbolism, the supernatural, or religion almost not at all. It could be a technological, computer world, so hard are its outlines. The only imaginative glimpse, aside from the old man's nostalgia for the great ancestral houses of Ireland, is that of a window lit up for little more than a few seconds, when the girl who ruined her life by a foolish choice of husband is made visible. The old man's killing of his son to stop the inherited curse is a gratuitous murder, leading to nothing except the extinction of a line. It is impossible either to see or read this play and feel any sense of noble catharsis; there is no precipitation of that tragic joy which Yeats in a marvelous late poem, "Lapis Lazuli," called gaiety.

Eliot's criticism of *Purgatory* in his essay on the poetry of Yeats— "I wish he had not given it this title, because I cannot accept a purgatory in which there is no hint, or at least no emphasis upon purgation" —will be accepted only by those who insist upon a Catholic interpretation of Purgatory. But if we do not insist upon a restrictive theological interpretation, requiring only that it mean suffering which may or may not purify, then the play is well named, for suffering is not only very real but also central to the play's action or passion; the suffering of the Old Man's mother is continually re-enacted and that of the Old Man himself (compelled to watch his mother suffer) is unalleviated. Not only so, but the theme of purgation runs through Yeats's plays, for example, *The Dreaming of the Bones* and *The Words upon the Window Pane.*

When one looks at Yeats's achievement in drama as a whole, it is hard to arrive at a balanced judgment. On the one hand, it is clear that he was no born master of the theater, a Sophocles, a Shakespeare, or a Molière. He had no particular natural genius for the stage but rather a persistent ambition to be successful in that medium, and he was willing to work to get what he wanted. His great lack as a dramatist was a good ear for human talk; he did not have that extraordinary gift possessed by Synge for the colloquial Irish idiom. Once in a while a turn of phrase will have the ring of Irish speech—for instance, "It's too snug he was in his bed," from *The Player Queen*—but when it came to a dialect play, *The Unicorn from the Stars,* Lady Gregory had to help him out. This is not to say, however, that his plays lack the ability to move. They are moving and come alive across the footlights, as such enthusiasts as Kenneth Rexroth testify.

On the other hand, it is equally clear that Yeats had high standards and that he wrote to the standards he set for himself. Judged by standards of realism, Yeats's plays are failures, but his plays ought not to be judged by realistic standards; he was not aiming at realism, but at

78

reality. Indeed, one major reason for admiring Yeats is the integrity with which he kept to that ideal, stated in *The Secret Rose* (1897) of preserving as his theme nothing less than the war of "spiritual with natural order," which he saw as the heart of human reality. It is tempting for the critic to complain that Yeats, especially when in his late plays he retreated into the fortress of the Nō, was writing for a coterie theater, for a restricted, aristocratic drawing-room audience, or for the brave little-theater groups which did not depend for life upon box-office receipts.

Actually, it is to be regretted that Yeats did not have a living theater that was not special or elite but which responded to his high themes. It is also to be regretted that he did not more often lower his sights to include the contemporary and the human, for no dramatist can live without some measure of popular appeal. We are all experts in human nature, inasmuch as we are all human, and the high moments of plays can have reverberations in an unselected audience. Yeats never entirely outgrew the symbolistic influence of *Axël's Castle*, with its notion that poetry is for those who live in an ivory tower: "As for living, our servants will do that for us." Even in Dublin his plays were never favorites, and most of them have disappeared from the repertory of the Abbey Theatre.

It will not do, of course, to make the trite critical complaint that Yeats was a lyrical poet who somehow blundered into the theater. In every Yeats play, as Eric Bentley has pointed out, there is a central dramatic situation, for the simple reason that almost everything else has been cut away. His plays will always be treasured by those who care deeply for language and symbol. Yeats being Yeats, the spiritual and the supernatural cannot be separated, and the central problem of his plays is how to make the supernatural acceptable in the theater. He successfully solved this problem in all his best work, particularly in plays like *The Dreaming of the Bones, The Words upon the Window Pane*, and *Purgatory*. To give Yeats his due, his contribution to the tragic theater of the world is unique and enduring. He did not make the mistake of avoiding the violent and the primitive; his plays, too brief, most of them, for an evening in the theater, are drama pared to the quick or cut to the bone.

Yeats was continually growing. From his earliest volume of poems, *Crossways* (1889), to his posthumously published *Last Poems* (1940), there is continuous development, and there is more energy in his final volume than in his first.

One of the best ways to explore Yeats is to discover persistence of certain themes in his poetry. Yeats enjoyed a pagan freedom, never afraid to let "holy feet" descend "to desecration and the lover's night." This passional descent was even seminal and necessary. Yeats used the dance as sacred symbol of unity of being; in the excited question which ends "Among School Children" the body is not left behind. It is true that in the later "Byzantium," "blood-begotten spirits" leave "all complexities of fury," but in Yeats's system the progress of consciousness is cyclical; he is describing a phase, en route to rebirth, rather than continuous ecstasy of heaven. While Yeats despised the commercialism and other aspects of our time, no one would dream of applying the word "reverend" to him. Yeats's poetry has severed all connection with Christian moorings, though imaginatively it has not lost all connection with Christian myth. Yeats's poetry is passionate and pagan.

As Richard Ellmann points out, Yeats "waited almost until his marriage to write directly of sexual intercourse." Then it became "a more and more constant subject in his work as he realized its symbolic possibilities." He wanted a symbol that was at the same time physical and transcending the physical. "Solomon to Sheba" shows the beginning of his exploration of the union of sexual and spiritual ecstasy, later to become one of his principal themes. In "Leda and the Swan" he writes powerfully of rape, leaving it an open question whether the god-inflicted rape was ever elevated into raptness or rapture. In "Chosen" he does not write of the moment of keenest, even excruciating sexual pleasure; rather he celebrates the moment of peace after orgasm is over. The woman is speaking, and she says:

> If questioned on
> My utmost pleasure with a man
> By some new-married bride, I take
> That stillness for a theme
> Where his heart my heart did seem
> And both adrift on the miraculous stream.

But he is realist enough to know that the miracle (when it happens) is all the more a miracle because of the inherent difficulties of marriage:

> Maybe the bridebed brings despair,
> For each an imagined image brings
> And finds a real image there.

It is clear that Yeats was not afraid of the physical. He acquired suppleness and resilience in his mature work; he could move at will from the earthy to the visionary. A sentence from his *Autobiography* is a profound critical commentary that could apply equally well to himself: "Donne could be as metaphysical as he pleased, and yet never seemed unhuman and hysterical as Shelley often does, because he could be as physical as he pleased." Another passage is equally significant: Yeats tells us that he sought for roots, a tradition of belief "older than any European Church, and founded upon the experience of the world before any modern bias." One of his characters, Ribh, finds Christian love insufficient, and Yeats gloried in Homer and his "unchristened heart." In his late poems Yeats had something that he valued, the possession of being undeceived; he felt that poets and writers are weakened if the world they present in their writings is nothing but an ideal world. Evil in Yeats is recognized as the complement of good, the persistence of violence in the world is reckoned with.

A constant theme of Yeats's poetry is the reconciliation of opposites. In the early play *The Shadowy Waters*, the rose is the point where opposites are reconciled. Fire is another symbol of consummate union, for "in the condition of fire is all music and all rest." The sages in "Sailing to Byzantium" are entreated to "come from the holy fire." The dancer at the end of "Among School Children" is clearly another such symbol. Dance and fire are combined, as we have seen, in "Byzantium." Unity of being, however difficult it may be to attain, is the supreme goal.

One uniquely distinguishing characteristic of Yeats as a poet is his paradoxical union of passion and coldness. Most likely it was a temperamental preference, but the "cold and passionate" theme is a striking example of the reconciliation of opposites. No doubt the coldness heightened the passion by contrast, and vice versa. It was a way of gaining intensity where he tells us in the *Autobiography* that he deliberately reshaped his style, he adds that he "became as emotional as possible, but with an emotion that I described to myself as cold." Elsewhere in the *Autobiography*, in a similar vein, he says, "I take pleasure alone in those verses where it seems to me I have found something hard and cold." "Ice burned and was but the more ice," he writes in the passionate lyric "The Cold Heaven." In "The Wild Swans at Coole" the swans paddle in the "cold/Companionable streams," where "Passion or conquest . . ./Attend upon them still." In "The Fisherman" he finds his ideal listener in the peasant wearing homespun cloth for whom he hopes to write one

> Poem maybe as cold
> And passionate as the dawn.

In reaction to Rilke's attitude to death, he commands that these words be cut on his gravestone:

> Cast a cold eye
> On life, on death.
> Horseman, pass by.

All of this should not be interpreted as a remoteness from human life or a want of emotion in Yeats but rather as a desire for a clear-eyed view of reality.

John Crowe Ransom has spoken of the "special gravity" of Yeats's verse. It does, indeed, have dignity, weight, and authority, but it also has bursts of earthy realism. Yeats has been reproached with loving the big country house, and a common criticism of him is that he ignores large areas of modern life; the industrial city is outside his scope, for example. But in a powerfully prophetic poem like "The Second Coming" he speaks to the modern consciousness. He speaks to us because of his resolute and courageous facing of life. He made the human his central concern, nor did he ever blink the fact that human passion can flare up in violence. He penetrated as deeply as any poet has to the core of human reality.

GEORGE BERNARD SHAW
by Edwin B. Pettet

I<small>F</small> S<small>HAW'S</small> <small>YOUTHFUL</small> <small>DREAMS</small> had materialized, the world would have celebrated another Michelangelo, a second Mozart, or, at the very least, the noblest operatic baritone of them all. Shaw never for a moment doubted that he was destined to become a great man, and yet it never crossed his mind to become a writer. As he later said, "You cannot want a thing and have it too." Music, to that genteelly impoverished Protestant Irish household in which Shaw rummaged through his boyhood, was the family totem and his mother's remarkable singing voice the center around which all else revolved. While she cultivated it under the hypnotic influence of her mentor, George John Vandaleur Lee (who somewhere along the line joined the Shaws in a Platonic *ménage à trois*), the youngster, left to his own devices, cultivated himself. By the time he was fifteen, he could whistle from beginning to end many works of Handel, Beethoven, Gounod, and Verdi; had "saturated" himself with Dickens, Bunyan, Shakespeare, and the Bible; and had taught himself art history by wandering the corridors of the Dublin Gallery—alone, he said, except for the guards.

But no artistic talent asserted itself then. He sketched a little and taught himself to thump the piano well enough to accompany arias, but that was the end of it. In his private world he was always playing a part, making up fabulous incidents in which he played the hero (or the villain when he discovered that villains were more interesting), supreme in war and irresistible in love. Dramatizing events was for him like breathing; his imaginary play acting gave him no clue to the future. His abilities as a businessman, on the other hand, were clearly evident by the time he was sixteen. In a Dublin estate office where an uncle had secured him an appointment, Shaw, in addition to teaching his fellow clerks operatic arias, or debating with them the existence of God (he became an atheist upon reading Shelley), handled the firm's accounts with such speed and accuracy that when the cashier resigned a few years later Shaw was promoted to replace him at eighty-four pounds a year—an unheard-of sum for a stripling in 1875. But it was not in Shaw's dreams to become an estate agent. Politely declining additional financial inducements to remain, he resigned his post and, except for a few months in London when he was employed by the Edison Telephone Company, never again sinned against his nature by "working" for a living.

Shaw once remarked when urged to write his autobiography that all his wares were in the shop window; the rest were merely breakfast, lunch, and dinner, sleeping and wakening. He might have added that even his eating and sleeping got into the shop window, for he never missed an opportunity to advance the cause of vegetarianism, and his two most memorable romances came to public view in the form of published correspondence with Ellen Terry and Mrs. Patrick Campbell. He wrote of his sexual encounters (such as they were) with clinical frankness, making no more of them than what they were: minor experiences wholly without urgency or romantic anxiety. According to his own account, he lived a "continent virgin" until he reached twenty-nine, at which age he finally took the plunge, reporting his findings with typical Shavian matter-of-factness: "I liked sexual intercourse in intellectual ecstasy," he testified, "because of its amazing power of producing a celestial flow of emotion and exaltation of existence which, however momentary, gave me a sample of what may one day be the normal state of being for mankind." When he married Charlotte Payne-Townsend, she was forty-four years old; their sexual lives were behind them. "As man and wife we found a new relation in which sex had no part. It ended the old gallantries, and philanderings for both of us." For forty-five years, until her death in 1943, their marriage was marked by affectionate companionship, unobserved by gossipmongers and free from even a whisper of scandal, and yet it was as public a private life as can be imagined. Because Shaw lived more publicly than is usual with writers, biographers in search of the interior man, the secret G.B.S., the face behind the mask, have found little reward. He was wholly a "work machine," as he defined himself, with few interests besides his public ones. Even his hobbies, if they can be called that, were public: swimming, walking, cycling, and motoring.

It was inevitable, of course, that even among his closest acquaintances Shaw should be thought something of a cold fish. In Frank Harris' opinion—characteristically extreme and irresponsible—Shaw was some sort of unsexed monster, unnaturally immune to the lures of the flesh. Saner, kindlier friends, among them G. K. Chesterton, accepted the Puritan in their midst with affectionate grace but could not resist suggesting that the playwright, like some of his stage characters, was wanting in a certain emotionalism or "finer feeling," the remedy for which lay easily at hand in the shape of a seven-course Edwardian dinner complete with a bottle of Madeira and a fine cigar. In a society of clubmen, *bon vivants*, and exuberant stage personalities, Shaw was undoubtedly something of an anomaly with his vegetable plate and his barley water; and if Oscar Wilde's remark that Shaw hadn't an enemy in the world but that none of his friends liked him hardly squares with the facts, it nevertheless suggests that an eminent man constantly in the public eye who was never known to utter a swear word, touch alcohol or tobacco, or eat meat or fish and who considered his occasional glass of ginger beer the appropriate draught for a gala evening, might well have caused his more robust companions some slight disquiet.

Shaw's Puritan streak (to use Harris' phrase) was no matter of personal idiosyncrasy, a peculiarity of genius, or some deficiency in his emotional constitution correctable by occasional dosages of mutton chops and roast beef. Shaw's asceticism, his old-maidishness, as some would have it, was nothing else than the personal expression of a philosophy that in all its corollaries was antithetical to the romantic-heroic view of life. Whether Shaw practiced what he preached, or preached what he practiced, will never be known. Nor does it matter. What is certain is that between the practice and the preachment there

85

was no gulf. Shaw was his own philosophy on the hoof; and if, despite charm and an unflagging wit, his unrelenting single-mindedness in the service of Creative Evolution seemed to take some of the fun out of life, it was because to his mind the business of life was a deadly serious matter if man was not to be ultimately superseded as he had superseded the ape.

By the time he was twenty, Shaw's earlier dreams of the art gallery and the opera stage had evaporated. In 1876 he joined his mother and sister in London, where, as he tells us in *Sixteen Self Sketches*, he did not throw himself into the struggle for life but threw his mother into it, living off her income as a music teacher and the pound a week sent from the abandoned father in Dublin. There he took his first step as a literary man with the wrong foot forward. He turned to novel writing, producing during the five years from 1879 to 1883 five volumes of awesome length for which, to his amazement, no publisher was to be found on either side of the Atlantic. For the first nine years in London, until 1885, his literary efforts brought him a total of six pounds, five of which he received for an article on patent medicine commissioned by a solicitor friend. When he was not penning his self-imposed five pages a day or wandering the London streets shabbily dressed, avoiding his mother's well-meaning friends who were determined (for her sake) to find him some employment, he was to be found holed up in the reading room of the British Museum or attending meetings at one or another of London's many debating societies. At twenty-nine, Shaw was neither painter nor opera star—nor, evidently, writer.

"Things do not happen to me," Shaw wrote. "I happen to things." Unquestionably true, once he was in full flight. But until he went aloft, things *did* happen to him, and it is fortunate for the future of English socialism, criticism, and drama that they happened as they did. In 1884 he heard Henry George lecture in Memorial Hall. He read the great man's *Progress and Poverty* and promptly became a single-tax socialist, the first important happening. Told by Henry Mayers Hyndman, leader of the Social Democratic Federation, England's doctrinaire communist society, that he would know nothing of socialism until he had read Karl Marx, Shaw forthwith repaired to the British Museum, read *Das Kapital*, and promptly was converted to Marxism. That was the second happening. It was in the British Mu-

86

seum that William Archer, the famous drama critic, happened upon the diffident Shaw, a Wagner score open before him, simultaneously reading Marx in the French edition. It was a momentous encounter for Shaw. With Archer's influence Shaw became successively a book reviewer for the *Pall Mall Gazette*, art critic of *The World*, music critic for the *Star* and the *World*, and ultimately drama critic for the *Saturday Review*, in which exalted role he "happened" to the London theater, its actors, producers, and playwrights with such knowledgeable power that Archer advised him to take up playwriting, which, obligingly, he promptly did.

The popular image of Bernard Shaw, red-bearded and Mephistophelean, scandalously forcing himself into the forefront of national attention, was largely a product of Shavian art. The workaday Shaw was a shy and obliging fellow with a face "like an unskillfully poached egg" as some wag described it—shy to the point of panic in public gatherings until by repeated efforts, shaking and inarticulate at first, he made himself into one of England's most wanted orators, and obliging sometimes to the point of utter exhaustion when called upon to address meetings, chair debates, or sit on committees.

As a Fabian committeeman he was indefatigable, always amiable and patient, skillful at reconciling differences among members by the canny device of diverting their irritability toward himself. A Fabian workhorse, he was always prepared to take up the slack during a dull Fabian summer month with a lecture or two (there was as much "let George do it" among the Fabians as elsewhere). One of the summer season lectures, published later as *The Quintessence of Ibsenism*, was acknowledged by some as the most incisive analysis of Ibsenism to date—and by others as a thinly disguised exposition of Shavianism. For six years he acted as vestryman and councilman for the Borough of St. Pancras, serving with such exceptional common sense and administrative ability that he was shamelessly exploited by his colleagues, who left to England's greatest dramatist the lion's share of work on the borough's parliamentary, electric lighting, housing, drainage, and health committees, the last of which landed him, ironically, with the chore of holding inquests on tubercular cattle. Characteristically, from the St. Pancras experience came *The Common Sense of Municipal Trading*.

87

His kindness to others was as remarkable as his indefatigability. Shaw drew up a petition in support of the imprisoned Oscar Wilde, which nobody signed, and another in support of the Chicago anarchists, which only Oscar Wilde signed. When Frank Harris died leaving an impoverished widow and an unpublished biography of Shaw, he edited the volume at Mrs. Harris' importuning, correcting errors of fact but retaining all of Harris' outrageous misinterpretations and falsified anecdotes, and finished off his good work with a postscript to ensure the book's sale. Although he let it be known that he would refuse the knighthood under consideration for him, he was instrumental in forwarding that honor on behalf of Arthur Wing Pinero, whose plays he had attacked mercilessly when writing for the *Saturday Review*. According to Mrs. Patrick Campbell, one of the letters she had from Shaw read:

Dear Stella:

While the prices of my manuscripts are so altitudinous, I suggest that you establish a pension for yourself. Sell immediately my love-letters to you. But for God's sake, keep copies.
Yours ever,
Joey.[1]

Friends considered him the ideal weekend guest. He helped with the washing up, played with the children, was always amusing, and was more than eager to proffer advice on every conceivable subject. Hesketh Pearson records that one of his hostesses left this description:

You invite him down to your place because you think he will entertain your guests with his brilliant conversation and before you know where you are he has chosen a school for your son, made your will for you, regulated your diet, and assumed all the privileges of your family solicitor, your housekeeper, your clergyman, your doctor, your dressmaker, your hairdresser, and your estate agent. When he has finished with everybody else, he incites the children to rebellion. And when he can find nothing more to do, he goes away and forgets all about you.[2]

[1] Mrs. Patrick Campbell, *My Life and Some Letters*, 340.
[2] Hesketh Pearson, *G.B.S.: A Full-Length Portrait*, 122.

He wrote plays to accommodate managers (designed and produced them, too) and parts to accommodate actors. He wrote the "Manifesto" for the Fabian Society and a defense of William Morris against accusations of decadence which later appeared in print as *The Sanity of Art*.

Music criticism, at the time Shaw took up his duties on the *World*, had the distinction of being virtually unreadable except by the small band of academics who were responsible for writing it. It reveled in technical jargon and analytical description as dull as was delightful Shaw's "analysis" of Hamlet's "To be or not to be" soliloquy in the same pretentious "scientific" manner. Written to parody the style of contemporary music reviews it goes:

> Shakespear, dispensing with the customary exordium, announces his subject at once in the infinitive, in which mood it is presently repeated after a short connecting passage in which, brief as it is, we recognize the alternative and negative forms on which so much of the significance of repetition depends. Here we reach a colon; and a pointed pository phrase, in which the accent falls decisively on the relative pronoun, brings us to the first full stop.

Corno di Bassetto, as Shaw called himself, put a full stop to that sort of rodomontade once and for all, introducing in its stead unashamed partiality, passion, and his unmistakable brand of irreverent gaiety. For the first time in English history the man in the street could read a passage of music criticism and enjoy it. "Never in my life have I penned an impartial criticism; and I hope I never may," went his critical credo.

A few snatches from his own reviews will illustrate his point. Of Gounod's *Redemption* he said, "I have no more to say generally than that if you will only take the precaution to go in long enough after it commences and to go out long enough before it is over you will not find it wearisome." Or, "By simply assassinating less than a dozen men, I could leave London without a single orchestral wind instrument player of the first rank." And, "There is nothing that soothes me more after a long and maddening course of piano-forte recitals than to sit and have my teeth drilled by a finely skilled hand." To those who claimed that such levity was a cover for superficiality, he retorted,

"Seriousness is only a small man's affectation of bigness." For the rather large number of musically knowledgeable Londoners who were of the opinion that Shaw was a know-nothing blabbermouth, he had this warning: "Don't be in a hurry to contradict G.B.S. as he never commits himself on a musical subject until he knows at least six times as much about it as you do." Shaw won the distinction, the only time in English musical history, of being refused complimentary tickets to Covent Garden. He had had a few words to say about the traditions of staging opera in that venerable hall. But lest new enjoyment of the man in the street render him too cocky, there was a touch of the Shavian lip for him to ponder, too: "It is all work and no play in the brain department that makes John Bull such an uncommonly dull boy." The English brain was so dense, he announced, that it was only by a strenuous and most desperately serious effort that the Englishman could set his intellect in action. The average Londoner, he told his public, was as void of feeling for the fine arts as a man could be without collapsing bodily.

When in the first week of January, 1895, Shaw changed hats and took up his new duties as drama critic for the *Saturday Review*, the theatrical world girded for the attack. It was immediately mounted and continued for three and a half years until, through the success of his own plays, he managed to do by example what he had failed to do by exhortation. For a hundred years before Shaw's arrival on the scene the English stage had produced not one playwright of note. Playgoers in the 1890's were treated to hack translations of French farces, the unending works of Dumas, mangled Shakespeare and Shakespeare imitations by Tennyson, sentimental melodramas, and thrillers with titles now happily forgotten. Hoisting his critical credo, Shaw waded into this bog of second-rateness, praising extravagantly where he saw a glimmer of hope and berating without mercy managers, actors, and playwrights who persisted in considering the theater an amusement booth instead of a house of correction.

He centered on three targets: the leading actor-manager of the day, Henry Irving; Pinero's fashionable, sham-problem adultery plays; and the empty, "well-made" melodramas of the Augustin Scribe–Victorien Sardou school. On Irving's head fell Shaw's heaviest and most persistent blows, for his mutilation of Shakespeare, his refusal to acknowledge Ibsen and the New Drama and, not least of all, for his keeping in thralldom Ellen Terry, Irving's leading lady and Shaw's paper inamorata. Irving, however, was as stubborn as Shaw. To his dying day nothing but the second-rate and the chopped-up Shakespeare tempted him, not even Shaw's *Man of Destiny*, which, in a desperate effort to break him loose, the playwright offered him.

In a letter to Shaw's official biographer, Archibald Henderson, Sir Arthur Wing Pinero wrote:

> It is among the misfortunes that attended my long life that I have never been brought into close association with Mr. Shaw. But, like so many others, I have received at his hands numerous acts of kindness, consideration and good will. I count Mr. Shaw as one of the most generous of men.[3]

Perhaps Sir Arthur was really the generous one (he never knew of Shaw's efforts in behalf of the knighthood), or perhaps Pinero had forgotten these lines about him:

> In literature, he is a humble and somewhat belated follower of the novelists of the middle of the 19th century and who has never written a line from which it could be guessed that he is a contemporary of Ibsen or Tolstoi.

One of Shaw's best-known attacks upon the trashy melodramas that enriched the managers while Ibsen waited in the wings appeared under the title "Sardoodledum." Although he had once written that the "attention given to criticism is in direct proportion to its indigestibility," surely this review is a delight to any palate. It runs in part:

> Up to this day week I had preserved my innocence as a playgoer sufficiently never to have seen Fedora. Of course, I was not altogether new to it since I had seen Diplomacy Dora, and Theodora and La Toscadora and other machine dolls from the same firm. And yet the thing took me aback. To see that curtain go up again and again only to disclose a bewildering profusion of everything that has no business in a play, was an experience for which nothing would quite prepare me. The postal arrangements, the telegraphic arrange-

[3] Sir Arthur Wing Pinero to Archibald Henderson, London, July 1, 1931, quoted in Archibald Henderson, *George Bernard Shaw: Playboy and Prophet.*

ments, the police arrangements, the names, and addresses, the hours and seasons, the tables of consanguinity, the railway and shipping time-tables, the arrivals and departures, the whole welter of Bradshaw and Baedeker, Court Guide and Post Office Directory, whirling round one tiny little stage murder and finally vanishing in a gulp of impossible stage poison, made up an entertainment too Bedlamite for any man with settled wits to preconceive.

Shaw's fellow drama critics condemned him as a proselytizer and self-advertiser, no critic at all. William Archer, the man responsible for starting Shaw off, considered him an actual danger, a "power for evil." Wrote Archer: "All that he could do he did, to discredit, crush and stamp out the new movement"[4]—the leader of the new movement to that intelligent translator and supporter of Ibsen being none other than Arthur Wing Pinero.

It is scarcely surprising that Shaw's appearance as a dramatist was not hailed with critical enthusiasm or that managers did not fight among themselves to lay hands on his scripts. His first play, *Widowers' Houses*, which ran for two nights at J. T. Grein's newly formed Independent Theatre, had as its subject the evils of slum landlordism; his second play, *The Philanderer*, was judged too advanced in ideas for production in London's Gay Nineties; and the third, *Mrs. Warren's Profession*, on the subject of prostitution, was obviously unacceptable to the censor. But despite Archer's opinion, written after witnessing the first performance of *Widowers' Houses*, that it "does not appear that Mr. Shaw has any more specific talent for the drama than he has for painting or sculpture," Shaw plunged ahead. "Man is a creature of habit," he said. "You cannot write three plays and then stop."

By the turn of the century Shaw could write his own contracts—which, incidentally, he ultimately did and producers were glad to sign them—yet England's greatest dramatist since Shakespeare could not find takers for some of his early work even among those who perceived his genius. An example is *Candida*. Shaw read it to one of England's finest actors, Charles Wyndham, who remarked that it would be twenty-five years before such a play would be possible on the English stage. Another actor-manager, George Alexander, offered

4 William Archer, *Morning Leader*, August 22, 1903, p. 47.

to do it if Shaw would make the poet Marchbanks blind in order to secure sympathy. But to Richard Mansfield, the American actor who had successfully produced *Arms and the Man* and *The Devil's Disciple* in the United States, goes the first prize for denseness. He had already rejected *The Philanderer*; now with a chance at *Candida*, he wrote to Shaw:

> There is no change of scene in three acts, and no action beyond moving from a chair to a sofa, and vice versa. O, ye Gods and little fishes . . . Your play *Candida* is lacking in all the essential qualities . . . *Candida* is charming . . . it is delightful but—pardon me—it is not a play—at least I do not think it is a play . . . Here are three long acts of talk, talk, talk—no matter how clever that talk is—it is talk, talk, talk . . . If you think a bristling, stirring, bustling, pushing, striving American audience will sit out calmly two hours of deliberate talk you are mistaken and I'm not to be sacrificed to their just vengeance. . . .[5]

So much for one of the most moving plays in English literature.

Shaw's habit of writing about people he approved of as though they were committed Shavians makes it difficult to assess the extent of Ibsen's influence upon him. Certainly, in *The Quintessence of Ibsenism*, the two men appear to see eye to eye on how plays should be written and on subject matter appropriate to the stage. Like Ibsen, Shaw scorned the plots of sexual intrigue and police-blotter action and lauded the technique of "discussion," the "Let's sit down and talk it over" device of *A Doll's House*, at which Shaw in some of his plays may be said to have outdone the Norwegian. In Shaw's analysis of the Philistine, the Idealist, and the Realist in *The Quintessence*, however, Ibsen is visible only in the dim distance. The ideas are pure Shaw, emerging as definitions of disparate attitudes toward society that not only account for the conflicts in his plays but also are responsible, he believed, for conflicts offstage. The Philistine, according to Shaw, accepts a social institution or convention (marriage is the example in *The Quintessence*) because he is comfortable with it; the Idealist is at odds with it, but from fear, cowardice, or ignorance insists upon its rightness—idealizes it—even to the extent of forcing it upon those who

---

[5] William Winter, *Life and Art of Richard Mansfield*, II, 232.

find it incompatible. The realist, he of twenty-twenty vision (like Shaw), recognizes that what may be sauce for the goose is not necessarily sauce for the gander and is prepared to adjust or eliminate the institution if the need arises. It is the conflict between the Realist in man's nature on the one hand and the complacent Philistine and the militant Idealist (and his minion, the Romanticist) on the other that makes of a Shavian play a battlefield on which man's passionate drive toward change and growth is met by his equally passionate determination to protect and maintain.

The hero as total realist seldom enters the Shavian scene. Shaw is no morality playwright, despite his admiration for Bunyan and the occasional appearance of type-names like Hushabye, Shotover, Undershaft, and Broadbent among his casts of characters. There are no blacks and whites on the Shavian palate; there are only vital ideas and obstructive ones and, as a man may grasp the right end of the stick on one occasion and heft it from the wrong end on another, so with Shaw's characters: none has the exclusive use of the vital virtues or is forced to vector the obstructive vices. Shaw knew better than to make the case for Creative Evolution by stacking the cards or fighting sham battles; each of the combatants enters the arena armed with his fair share of Shavian wit—which makes for some mighty fine battle scenes. It also allows the auditor, if there is intelligence in him, to come to his own conclusions. Sometimes, notably in the case of *Saint Joan*, the tuning is so fine that it is the rare auditor indeed who has not found himself in the course of the play persuaded to endorse the claims of both Catholicism and Protestantism, the values of both nationalism and feudalism, the case for inquisitor and heretic alike, and at the final curtain ushered from the playhouse in a state of ecumenical bliss. Roman Catholics liked *Saint Joan* as much as Protestants did. In fact, the case Shaw had made for the Mother Church prompted someone to ask him whether he planned to become a Catholic. "There's no room for two Popes in the Roman Catholic Church," he retorted.

Frequently the Shavian agon, the arguments between characters, is supplemented by an act of conversion not to doctrine or program but from romantic illusion to the fact-facing realist's manner of seeing life as it is. In *Heartbreak House*, for example, Ellie Dunn discovers that the man she thinks she loves is married. She says, "Damn; how could I be taken in so," allows herself a few moments to mend her broken heart, and straightway begins to view everything about her with more penetrating eyes. Similarly, the lovelorn romantic Marchbanks in *Candida* suffers a shattering of illusions when he discovers that his inamorata cannot follow his poetry, peels onions, and has more mother in her than lover. Out into the night he goes a changed man. In both plays the conversion from romantic to realist was triggered by the misfortunes of love, but we are not to suppose that the new realists are realists only with respect to that indulgence. The effect is far greater than the cause. The comfortable Philistine, Candida, whose profession is domesticity, says after the departing Marchbanks: "He has learned to live without happiness"—but that remark simply describes her limitation. The secret in the poet's heart is even simpler than that: he has learned to live with his eyes open. In *Major Barbara* the conversion occurs in the context of a specific social problem— poverty and the Salvation Army's relation to it—which gave Shaw the opportunity to exemplify the difference between the romantic and realistic approaches to problem solving. When Barbara ceases to romanticize poverty, she turns like a good realist from effect to cause: she will no longer seek to alleviate it but to prevent it.

The most interesting Shavian conversions, because closer to the bone of his religious philosophy, are those that occur without external cause. What happens to Blanco in *The Shewing-up of Blanco Posnet* and to Dick Dugeon in *The Devil's Disciple* is not in consequence of events outside themselves but of the sudden "dawning of a moral passion," that unaccountable surge of rectitude which, in Shaw's view, accounts for the actions of men more often than they are prone to admit and might be described as a kind of creative evolutionary short-cut. Blanco Posnet's and Dick Dugeon's self-sacrificing acts have no apparent motivation. One returns on a horse he stole to save a baby with the croup; the other substitutes himself for a man hunted by the military. Both are spur-of-the-moment deeds leaving the doers baffled by their own nobility. Blanco explains it as best he can: ". . . there's a rotten game and there's a great game. I played the rotten game but the great game was played on me; and now I'm for the great game every time."

95

Shaw's Creative Evolution, the philosophy of the Life Force, developed as an answer to what he considered the defeatism of Darwin's theory of Circumstantial Selection. It was inconceivable to Shaw that life had advanced through its many stages to man without purpose or will but simply as the result of a series of senseless accidents. Echoing Samuel Butler's cry that Darwin had banished mind from the universe, he sailed into the "unnatural Selectionists" in the preface to *Back to Methuselah*, shredded their theory to his own satisfaction, and raised the standard of Butlerian Lamarckism as the new religion. Two assumptions underlay Shaw's thesis: the existence in life of a will to control its environment, produce new organs, and evolve new species: and the inheritance of characteristics acquired through the exercise of the will. "You are alive; and you want to be more alive," Shaw wrote in the *Back to Methuselah* preface:

> You want an extension of consciousness and of power. You want, consequently, additional organs or additional uses of your existing organs; that is additional habits. You get them because you want them badly enough to keep trying for them until they come. Nobody knows how: nobody knows why: all we know is that the thing actually takes place.

Then, as new usages form new habits, they lose the need for conscious effort to exercise them, pass into the genetic structure of the organism, and are thereby transmitted by inheritance.

Shaw's new Religion of the Twentieth Century, as he labeled his "metabiological" philosophy, did not take the world by storm. Scientists dismissed it as romantic folly; churchmen did not welcome the notion of God as a natural "urge"; and the agnostic scorned it as a cosmic fantasy invented by Shaw to reinforce his moral Puritanism with the authority of natural law. The production and subsequent publication of the massive five-play sequence *Back to Methuselah* did little to encourage converts. The first play, *In the Beginning*, Shaw's interpretation of the Adam and Eve, Cain and Abel legend, is charming travesty, but the following three parts seem labored by comparison and discursive to the point of tediousness. *As Far as Thought Can Reach*, the fifth part, set in the year 31,920, is a Shavian pre-view of the life man will enjoy once he has formed the habit of living seven hundred years or more. Few found it an invigorating prospect. The conquest of matter to the extent that life exists wholly without love, sex, art, conflict, or challenge, merely in a whirlpool of pure intelligence with nothing left but the infinite to contemplate, seemed a rather empty victory—if the play is accepted on its literal level. As a Shavian parable on responsibility, its lesson is clear: put aside childish things and act as though you expect to live long enough to reap the consequences of your action.

Seventeen years before *Back to Methuselah*, Shaw had written a brighter Life Force play that, despite its chase-farce plot, its levity and wit, makes more understandable the serious implications of the Shavian philosophy than does the later play. Written in response to A. B. Walkley's mischievous request that Shaw write a Don Juan play, *Man and Superman* is "all about sex" in the Shavian definition of the term. Shaw called it "the only play on the subject of sex ever written." It is undoubtedly the only play ever written in which the "subject" of sex is discussed in depth without—except for a rather chaste embrace in the last act—sex itself rearing its ugly head. But then, Shaw thought sex neither ugly nor beautiful but simply an impersonal act whereby the Life Force seeks to achieve the superman by setting the female in pursuit of the male, whose business it is to avoid capture, if, paradoxically, he himself is sufficiently in the grip of the Life Force to father the superior child. Ann Whitefield, who is the Life Force's Everywoman in the play, does capture John Tanner in the last act after pursuing him from England to Spain, and we are left to wonder whether in this instance the Life Force outwitted itself or achieved its goal.

However, in the third-act dream sequence—the ultimate in "Let's sit down and talk it over" scenes—Shaw enlarges the subject matter of the other acts into a full-scale exposition of the moral imperatives implicit in the vitalist view. With Tanner—Don Juan as his spokesman, Shaw sings: ". . . the philosophic man: he who seeks in contemplation to discover the inner will of the world, in invention to discover the means of fulfilling that will, and in action to do that will by the so-discovered means."

The Devil, on the other hand, advocates the unphilosophic man who seeks in every way he can to enjoy the earthly pleasures without reference to any will but his own. At times in the debate the Devil seems to have most of the good tunes; he certainly has all the romantic ones that sing of joy, happiness, love, and beauty to counterpoint the astringent Don Juan-Shavian theme of:

> I tell you that as long as I can conceive something better than myself I cannot be easy unless I am striving to bring it into existence or clearing the way for it. That is the law of my life. That is the working within me of Life's incessant aspiration to higher organization, wider, deeper, intenser self-consciousness, and clearer self-understanding.

The theme runs throughout Shaw's work like a leitmotiv. In a lecture delivered in Kensington Town Hall early in the century he said:

> When you are asked, "Where is God? Who is God?" stand up and say, "I am God, and here is God," not as yet completed, but still advancing towards completion, just in so much as I am working for the purpose of the universe, working for the good of the whole of society and the whole world, instead of looking after my personal ends.

The cardinal virtue on the Shavian scale is responsibility: man's responsibility through conscious effort to direct the will of life to fuller control of environment. The key word is "direct" (Shaw uses "navigate" and "steer" in *Heartbreak House*), for until life evolved the philosopher's brain it was a blind force blundering through mishap after mishap. Speaking for the Life Force, Don Juan says:

> I have done a thousand wonderful things unconsciously by merely willing to live and following the line of least resistance: Now I want to know myself and my destination, and choose my path; so I have made a special brain—a philosopher's brain—to grasp this knowledge for me as the husbandman's hand grasps the plow for me. And this [says the Life Force to the philosopher] . . . must thou strive to do for me until thou diest, when I will make another brain and another philosopher to carry on the work.

The notion that life fumbled its way to human consciousness—the concept of an incomplete God—earned for Shaw the flippant headline: "God Makes Mistakes: Bernard Shaw." It also provoked serious ques-

GEORGE BERNARD SHAW

tioning of the means whereby Shaw, or anyone else, could determine in which direction life wills to go. Perhaps life has evil goals, or wills its self-destruction. Perhaps indeed there is no will at all and no purpose. Perhaps man is to God as flies to wanton boys. Or perhaps life is a cosmic joke. Shaw conceded the possibilities. Vitalism was as unprovable as Darwinism or Genesis or the salvation of man by redemption; it was, like the rest, a matter of faith arrived at by observation and "divination." But if life evolved by accidental selection, then "only fools and scoundrels could bear to live," said Shaw. As for life's direction: "It is quite useless," he said, "to believe that men are born free if you deny that they are born good." How did he know there was a will striving for consciousness? He echoed Samuel Butler: "I *bet* that my Redeemer liveth." Life a cosmic joke? "Suppose the world were only one of God's jokes, would you work any the less to make it a good joke instead of a bad one?" He did not presume to ultimate answers. Through Lilith's closing words in *Back to Methuselah* Shaw could say: "And for what may be beyond, the eyesight of Lilith is too short. It is enough that there is a beyond." Or with Lavinia in her reply to the Captain's "What is God?" in *Androcles and the Lion*: "When we know that, Captain, we shall be gods ourselves."

Shaw's economic theory follows from his religious philosophy as a logical corollary: increased control of the environment through the step by-step replacement of capitalist production and distribution of wealth by socialism. Shaw rejected Marxism for the same reason he had earlier rejected Darwinism: its determinism, its reliance upon "historic inevitability" as the agent of social progress. The notion that capitalism in full swing on Monday could be changed into socialism in full swing on Wednesday by storming the Bastille on Tuesday he considered a delusion. Moreover, as John Tanner had written in his "*Revolutionist's Handbook*": "Revolutions have never lightened the burden of tyranny: they have only shifted it to other shoulders." What Shaw realized and Marx did not was that in highly developed industrial societies there is no revolutionary proletariat aglow with the historic mission to destroy capitalism. Many whom Marx considered proletariats Shaw believed would fight for the maintenance of capitalism no less vigorously than the capitalist himself, for, as he wrote in

99

The Intelligent Woman's Guide to Socialism and Capitalism, the line that separates

> those interested in the maintenance of Capitalism from those interested in its replacement by Socialism is a line drawn not between rich and poor, capitalist and proletariat, but right down through the middle of the proletariat to the bottom of the very poorest section.

Change would be effected in Shaw's view not by the barricaders and their ready-made programs for instant socialism but by the continuing efforts of trained economists working through the existing political system by parliamentary methods, by "permeating the Liberals" with carefully-thought-out items of social legislation that could be incorporated into the national economy without throwing the whole into chaos. In *The Illusions of Socialism,* written in 1896, Shaw declared flatly:

> Socialism will come by prosaic installments of public regulation and public administration enacted by ordinary parliaments, vestries, municipalities, parish councils, school boards and the like; and that not one of these installments will amount to a revolution.

The romance of slogans and flags, villains and martyrs had no appeal to Shaw the realist. "The lot of the Socialist," he warned,

> is to be one of dogged political drudgery, in conflict not with the wicked machinations of the capitalist, but with the stupidity, the narrowness, in a word the idiocy . . . of all classes, and especially of the class which suffers most by the existing system.

Shaw was, Lenin once said, "a good man fallen among Fabians."

Credit for many of the Fabian Society's specific reform measures, particularly those that served in the creation and reconstitution of the British Labour Party, goes to Sidney Webb (whom Shaw brought into the society) and to his wife, Beatrice. Nonetheless, Shaw's contribution in the formation of Fabian policy was considerable, notably in devising the Fabian "Manifesto" which set for the young society its principles and goals. The "Manifesto" announced that "the Fabians are associated for the purpose of spreading the following opinions held by them, and discussing their practical consequences."

Many Fabian tracts by Shaw followed this maiden effort during the twenty-seven years of his service to the society. Yet it was after his resignation from the Executive Committee in 1911, at the age of fifty-five, that he made his most important and startling—contribution to socialist theory: the principle of equal income for everyone. Although the "Manifesto" contains the seed of this belief, its flowering occurred in 1913 in a lecture given before the National Liberal Club and later published in New York under the title *The Case for Equality*. Equality of income, said Shaw, means that "if one person is to have half-a-crown, the other is to have two and sixpence. It means that precisely." No way exists, Shaw pointed out, for measuring human value or for measuring the differences in social importance between one man's contribution and another's; *ergo*, inequalities in income are arbitrary, irrational, and the cause of (at least) two undesirable social consequences: class government and class marriage. Shaw made much of this last objection to inequality of income, stressing that as mutual sexual attraction was life's device for the constant improving of the racial strain, any program of income distribution which did not ensure complete intermarriageability in the community was a drag upon the development of the human species. Shaw reiterated, "I say, therefore, that if all the other arguments did not exist,"

the fact that equality of income would have the effect of making the entire community intermarriageable from one end to the other, and would practically give a young man and a young woman his and her own choice right through the population—I say that that argument only, with the results which would be likely to accrue in the improvement of the race, would carry the day.

The Case for Equality won immediate and overwhelming unpopularity. The *Metropolitan*, which had published the lecture in New York, ran a competition offering five hundred dollars for the best reply to Shaw of not over two thousand words. Between two and three thousand entries were received—many of them sent directly to Shaw himself. The winner was Lincoln Steffens, with his "The Case for Inequality" with runner-up Lewis C. Mumford's reply, "Jones and I," also given publication along with Steffen's essay. Shaw was not to be rebuked. He called his essay "the most important departure in Socialism since Karl Marx," and went on to expand it into a full-length volume of 463 pages finished in March, 1927, and published the next year under the galloping title of *The Intelligent Woman's Guide to Socialism and Capitalism*. Archibald Henderson, Shaw's official biographer, believed the work would assure Shaw's fame as "writer and economist had he never published another line" and called it "the ablest and most comprehensive view of practical Socialism put forward since Marx's *Capital*." Unquestionably, it is a highly knowledgeable and sane view of politics, society, government, banking, marriage, education, and religion, and if it brought no more converts into the fold of equality than had *The Case for Equality*, it was not for want of logical cogency.

Shaw's common sense kept him from making of socialism an "Ideal," as the more righteous among his fellow socialists were prone to do. Socialist theory, he realized, faced the danger of becoming an institution as rigid and restrictive as any other institution if the Calvinist attitude of "principle at all cost" prevailed. He disassociated himself from "the fanatics who are prepared to sacrifice all considerations of human welfare and convenience sooner than flinch from the rigorous application of 'their principles.' " He warned that many socialists were guilty of using "a formula to save themselves the trouble of finding sensible answers for practical questions, and the humiliation of confessing that their panacea will not cure all ailments." Not surprising, therefore, is Shaw's "practical view" that socialism may

> not prove worth carrying out in its integrity—that long before it has reached every corner of the political and industrial organization, it will have so completely relieved the pressure to which it owes its force that it will recede before the next great movement in social development, leaving relics of untouched Individualist Liberalism in all directions among the relics of feudalism which Liberalism itself has left.

In other words, socialize and nationalize wherever it is essential to do so for the economic health of the nation, but once the *livelihood* of the people is made independent of private capital and enterprise, then "the more private property and individual activity we have the better." For Shaw the point was not "Are you a Socialist or not?" but "How much are you a Socialist?"

The question at once arises how to reconcile the relativism of Shaw's "practical" view with the formalism of his half-a-crown–two-and-sixpence equality of income? How could Shaw's brand of civil service socialism with its apparently desirable loose ends manage so rigid a program as equal wealth distribution? During the vigorous years of his socialist pronouncements, Shaw seems not to have anticipated the question, for not until 1944 and the appearance of *Everybody's Political What's What* did he resolve the problem by retreating from the rigidity of *The Case for Equality* to the more manageable principle of "minimum income." Shaw's persistent fear had been the "great corruption of socialism" into state capitalism (fascism) with socialist production and unsocialist distribution fixing the rich-poor dichotomy, which even at its worst under laissez-faire capitalism had retained a certain flexibility. Moreover, Shaw's program, whatever its merits, represented one of the few attempts by socialist thinkers to insert a rational income-distribution plank in the socialist platform as an alternative to the sentimentalism of Marx's "to each according to his needs." Still, Shaw realized that the formula of exact income distribution had in it something of the fanaticism he detested—and more than likely was impossible of achievement without a drastic lowering of the standard of living in any nation that attempted it. Consequently, in *Everybody's Political What's What,* he states that

> mathematical equality is not an end in itself . . . When democratic Socialism has achieved sufficiency of means, equality of opportunity, and national intermarriageability for everybody, with production kept in its natural order from necessities to luxuries, and the courts of justice unbiased by mercenary barristers, its work will be done; for these, and not a mathematical abstraction like equality of income are its real goals.

Instead of equality of income the new phrase is "Basic Income," to be ultimately equal for all but "enjoyed at first by only 10 per cent of the population: with the rest gradually working their way up to it." Once a basic income is enjoyed by all, it made little difference, said

Shaw, if cinema actors, prize fighters, and other national heroes received more than the basic. The purpose of socialism was to "keep civilisation safe and steady," not to denature it.

The major contribution of *What's What* is a political program designed to overcome the absurdities Shaw believed inherent in government "by the people," or "Mobocracy," that "mock democratic folly," as he described it, "of pretending that the intellectual and technical work of Government can be dictated, or its ministers directly chosen, by mobs of voters." Shaw proposed a vast hierarchical state based on occupational franchise with the higher functions of government removed from direct popular control. He advocated political and economic schooling for would-be office seekers with examinations more or less on the order of civil-service tests required before each step up the ladder. Government by amateurs was, to his mind, merely an invitation to demagoguery. In Shaw's state there would be

a basic representative Congress to keep in touch with its subjects. This Congress would have sufficient local knowledge to elect the local chiefs of industry throughout the country. These local chiefs can elect provincial chiefs who can elect national chiefs. The national chiefs—you can call them if you like a cabinet—in their turn have to elect the national thinkers, for a nation needs two cabinets: an administrative Cabinet and a thinking Cabinet.

He frankly disavowed the two-party system—for which he was labeled both Bolshevik and fascist—but proposed a scheme whereby those at the bottom of the hierarchical pyramid, the mass of people, would periodically pass judgment on the government as a whole. Shaw wanted room at the top for the superman, but at the bottom the power to decide just how super he was.

Following one of his lectures, Shaw overheard a member of the audience remark to a companion, "I wish I could talk the way he does." Shaw immediately collared the man and warned him not to be taken in by what he had just heard, for, said Shaw, he could argue just as eloquently on the opposite side the next night. Since the gentleman had said not that he had been persuaded by Shaw, but merely wished he could talk like him, Shaw's admonition was somewhat gratuitous. In later years Shaw was to acknowledge ruefully that between the brilliance of his eloquence and its efficacy yawned a noticeable gap. But Shaw never was a switch-hitting debater. The allegation that he did, in fact, lend his eloquence in support of opposing views reflects the difficulty some have had—well-wishers no less than detractors—in grasping the implications of the Shavian philosophy or in rolling with Shaw's literary punch. In seventy years of making public pronouncements some modification of judgment was to be expected: from social revolutionist to social evolutionist, for example, or from equal incomes to basic incomes. But apart from changes of this order, enough seeming contradictions and paradoxes remain to puzzle any reader not an expert in Shavian strategy: the anti-Marxist writing approvingly of the Soviet Union; the anti-imperialist supporting the British Crown in the Boer War; the anti-romantic championing Wagner; the natural scientist claiming that "science is always wrong and religion is always right"; the mystic avowing that all problems are finally scientific problems; the prophet of democratic socialism saying, "I do not believe in democracy." To the mind accustomed to thinking in moral abstractions or in consistent structures—or having once committed itself to the rightness of "A" unable to admit any virtue to "B"—Shaw's vitalist pragmatism—a willingness to support the good wherever he found it and to denounce whatever he considered bad even in the best of things—seemed to be a shocking want of principle and responsibility.

His trick of redefining words to suit his own purposes seemed like perverse paradoxing: for example, the pejorative usage of "Ideal" and "Idealist" in *The Quintessence of Ibsenism*, or his insistence that "moral" derives from "mores" and means "customary," not "good." "I write immoral plays," he would proclaim, meaning that they opposed the customary social behavior of a specified group. But Shaw was not playing word games. He was irritating his audience into a re-examination of concepts and attitudes that lay behind labels that had lost their meaning or become degraded. When Shaw announced that "men need religion as a matter of life and death," churchgoers and atheists alike were jolted into reappraising the meaning of the word religion. Similarly, by overpraising the second-rate French playwright Eugène Brieux, Shaw was forcing an awareness of a new class of playwriting that realistically dramatized harsh and disquieting social problems like syphilis upon audiences who were still thinking of the theater only as a palace of pleasure. Still, Shaw's practice of overemphasizing partial truths as a corrective device was not universally appreciated. It seemed much of the time like pigheadedness and contrariness, and for more than a few of his contemporaries the Dauphin's exasperated snap at the Maid in *Saint Joan*, "It always comes down to the same thing; she's right and everybody else is wrong," about summed up their reaction to G.B.S.

The reaction was understandable enough; not everyone enjoys being rolled into virtue on waves of Shavian rhetoric. His statement that "it is always necessary to overstate a case startlingly to make people sit up and listen to it, and to frighten them into acting on it. I myself do this habitually and deliberately," had echoes in it of the schoolroom and in practice it could cut two ways. Without his abundant humor and unparalleled wit, Shaw might have been a scold. But precisely because of them the exaggerative overstatement is simultaneously armed and disarmed. By appearing to mock amusingly, Shaw is able to make his case in strength—which is exactly what he intends. The exaggeration *is* the Shavian truth; it is also, ironically, its own disguise. It became the comic device by which Shaw played Lear's fool to the world.

Shaw's prose style has been both praised and disparaged under the label "journalistic"—praised for its readability by the man in the street and disparaged as appropriate stuff for the popular press. Actually, Shaw's was a new order of journalism: subjective, self-revealing, erudite without pretensions of scholarly diction, and wholly free from the vice of condescension. Nor was the style subject to change. The Shavian manner is as apparent in the pages of *The Intelligent Woman's Guide* as it was in the early reviews or in the Fabian essays and continues to enliven the text of *Everybody's Political What's What*, written when its author was eighty-eight. Between the early novels and the prose and dramatic works that followed them there is a discernible shift not of style but of focus: the reader is directly spoken to as though he were a participant in a dramatic dialogue. After the novels Shaw's prose reflects the direct man-to-man conversational quality that sparked his platform style. Indeed, parts of various prefaces to the plays are adaptations of earlier lectures, but the oral

106

diction characterized all the postnovel writings—the letters, occasional pieces, pen portraits, and the dialogue of the plays themselves. Actors have frequently remarked at the ease with which Shavian roles could be memorized—and of the difficulty in forgetting them once they were learned. Shaw wrote as he talked, lucidly and with an instinctive feel for musical line, his sentences structured to give the ring of the impromptu. The absence of any deliberate literary style, the use of easily understood words put together for absorption into the mind through the ear rather than through the eye, permits the auditor to maintain the Shavian pace despite demands of subject matter and the close logic of the dramatic debate. The prose reader has a similar aural experience: he seems to hear Shaw talking to him personally, face to face.

Shaw had no patience with cultivated literary style. If you have something to say, according to his credo, style will take care of itself. He once wrote that "in literature the ambition of the novice is to acquire the literary language: the struggle of the adept is to get rid of it." Of himself he said:

> I have no recollection of being taught to read or write ... The whole vocabulary of English literature, from Shakespear to the latest edition of the Encyclopedia Britannica ... is so completely and instantly at my call that I have never had to consult a thesaurus except once or twice when for some reason I wanted a third or fourth synonym.

Whether "deliberate overstatement" or unvarnished truth, the admission is no more remarkable than the fact that with the whole vocabulary of English literature at his call, Shaw never wrote a word that obliged the reader of average literacy to consult a dictionary. He never employed a polysyllable when a couple of monosyllables would do or slipped in a foreign word or phrase to add the color of italics to the page. He preferred the ordinary—even the homely—expression to the elegant one; words of French derivation are uncommon to his distinctly Anglo-Saxon vocabulary. Since his avowed purpose in life was to elucidate and persuade, his meaning had to be grasped at first hearing or reading. Consequently, his prose is free of nuance and subtlety, shadowy passages and ambiguities. It abounds in example and illustration, explained allusions and homey metaphor, its passages connected by everyday conversational phrases like "that is to say," "once for all," "that is just like us," "yet after all," "and please remember." He refers constantly to himself and to the reader: "Let me propose to you an experiment . . ." or, "If you shew what I have just written . . ." or, "Suppose that . . ." as a way of drawing the reader or listener into the argument, causing objections to form in his mind to which Shaw in the next passage or two will provide the rebuttal.

The beauty of Shaw's prose derives from its expansiveness, from the long melodic line of the sentences that swing about gathering similarities, forming contrasts and analogies and that come to a full stop in a literally breathtaking crescendo. Take as an example a typical passage from *The Intelligent Woman's Guide*. Notice the tremendous sweep of the concluding sentence. See also how Shaw shows up as hypocritical common practices of the idealist by the use of an ironic contrast to the we-us, that is, the Shaw-reader, point of view:

That is just like us. All the time we are denouncing Communism as a crime, every street lamp and pavement and water tap and police constable is testifying that we could not exist for a week without it. Whilst we are shouting that Socialistic confiscation of the incomes of the rich is robbery and must end in red revolution, we are actually carrying it so much further than any other fully settled country that many of our capitalists have gone to live in the south of France for seven months in the year to avoid it, though they affirm their undying devotion to their native country by insisting that our national anthem shall be sung every Sunday on the Riviera as part of the English divine service, whilst the Chancellor of the Exchequer at home implores heaven to "frustrate their knavish tricks" until he can devise some legal means of defeating their evasion of his tax collectors.

Shaw's prose is highly discursive; as he said of himself, he roamed at will through the pastures of thought. But unlike his character Sir Bloomfield Bonnington in *The Doctor's Dilemma*, who at the end of a flight of non sequiturs says, "I seem to have lost the thread of my remarks," Shaw's discursiveness never leaves the reader in a bramble of unfinished thoughts. Reading Shaw is rather like a sightseeing tour through the history of ideas, sociology, politics, and philosophy, the whole tour directed toward the end of making of the tourist a socialist and a vitalist, and if the sightseer sometimes feels that he has taken in more than he can hold, he knows at least where he has been and where he is at.

Shaw, the weaver of immense verbal tapestries, was a superb epigrammatist as well. Aside from those deliberately coined for inclusion in John Tanner's *"Revolutionist's Handbook"* at the end of *Man and Superman,* most of the Shavian epigrams are scattered throughout the prose and dialogue like brief summaries of preceding arguments. Some of Tanner's "wise sayings" have the neat flippancy of Oscar Wilde: "He who can, does. He who cannot, teaches"; or, "Folly is the direct pursuit of happiness and beauty"; or, "Decency is indecency's conspiracy of silence"; or, "When we learn to sing that Britons never will be masters we shall make an end of slavery." Often the Shavian epigram contains a reversal of a conventional idea; "I strive automatically to bring the world into harmony with my own nature"; "The law of change is the law of God"; It may consist of bringing two usually disparate ideas together, as in "What is virtue but the Trade Unionism of the married"; or "Trade Unionism is the capitalism of the working class." Some of his most memorable lines have the pungency and acuity of the true epigram; for example, Shotover's pronouncement in *Heartbreak House*: "Every drunken skipper trusts to Providence, but one of the ways of Providence with drunken skippers is to run them on the rocks"; or, for another example, Joan's poignant plea at the close of *Saint Joan,* "Oh God that madest this beautiful earth, when will it be ready to receive thy saints? How long, O Lord, how long?"

Much has been written on Shaw's dramatic technique, beginning with those who claimed that he had none and that the plays were badly disguised platform propaganda, to others like Eric Bentley who said that he had and took the trouble to analyze it and record the findings. During Shaw's fifty-six years of playwriting, each appearance of a play by him has been the occasion for renewing old controversies and mounting new attacks and counterattacks until finally with the arrival of *Geneva*—when the author was eighty-two—and of *Buoyant Billions*—when he was ninety-two—it was generally agreed that the power was waning and the battle over. The commonest objections were to the talkiness of the plays, to their lack of action, to their excessive length (Shaw warned producers not to cut a line: "Begin earlier, or change train schedules"), to their undramatic subject matter and to the contrariness of their author's opinions. None of these objections, however, was sufficiently compelling to constrain theatergoers from making Shaw the highest paid playwright the world has known. He gave them a new class of theatrical experience by replacing the emotionalism that arises from the senses with a different passion, no less moving, that has its source in the character's convictions and that strikes fire against equally passionately held counterconvictions. He was thus able to give to such undramatic subjects as sociology, politics, and religion the urgency and excitement that audiences had expected only to experience in shows of rape, murder, domestic intrigue, and romantic adultery.

Shaw's innovation was to endow the intellect with passion. Characters in his plays stand for something; and the defense of that something, whether the defeated world-weariness of a Hector Hushabye or the Christian optimism of a Lavinia, fires conflict as intense as anything ever produced by the theater's pathos merchants and, of course, is far more relevant. Shaw's characters admire or despise not each other but each other's opinions, which are promptly exhibited for challenge whenever two or more of them cross paths. "My procedure is to imagine characters," Shaw said, "and then let them rip." Marchbanks and Morell are alone for scarcely more than five minutes before they are ripping at each other over Candida. The weapons? Ideas. "I'll fight your ideas," vows Marchbanks. "I'll rescue her from her slavery to them: I'll pit my own ideas against them." In *Androcles and the Lion*, Lavinia and the Captain of the Guard, obviously attracted to each other, are at cross-purposes at once over the meaning of religion. She is on the way to the arena "with death coming nearer and nearer . . . and stories and reams fading away into nothing"—but not her capacity for dialectics. "A martyr," the Captain tells her, "is a fool. Your death will prove nothing."

LAVINIA: Then why kill me?
CAPTAIN: I mean that truth, if there be any truth, needs no martyrs.

LAVINIA: No, but my faith, like your sword, needs testing. Can you test your sword except by staking your life on it?

A minute or two later the issue is joined, he on the side of policy, she on the side of her own convictions:

CAPTAIN: Sacrifice then to the true God. What does his name matter? We call him Jupiter, the Greeks call him Zeus. Call him what you will as you drop the incense on the altar flame. He will understand.

LAVINIA: No. I couldn't. That is the strange thing, Captain, that a little pinch of incense should make all that difference. Religion is such a great thing that when I meet really religious people we are friends at once, no matter what name we give to the divine will that made us and moves us. Oh, do you think that I, a woman, would quarrel with you for sacrificing to a woman god like Diana, if Diana meant to you what Christ means to me? No; we should kneel side by side before her altar like two children. But when men who believe neither in my god nor their own—men who do not know the meaning of the word religion—when these men drag me to the foot of an iron statue that has become the symbol of the terror and darkness through which they walk, of their cruelty and greed, and of their hatred of God and their oppression of man—when they ask me to pledge my soul before the people that this hideous idol is God, and that all this wickedness and falsehood is divine truth, I cannot do it, not if they could put a thousand cruel deaths on me. I tell you, it is physically impossible.

The Captain is not persuaded, but he understands the ineluctable power of conviction. He concludes: "Yes: when all is said, we are both Patricians, Lavinia, and must die for our beliefs. Farewell." And as far as they know the courtship is over.

Lavinia is preparing to die in a Roman arena for her primitive Christian faith, but her arguments are of no time and no place. Change a word or two, and her lines could be spoken by half a dozen Shaw characters. Shaw's interest lay in the way people think far more than in what they think about, in what values they hold more than in the specific circumstance in which they are applied. In consequence, he has been charged with dragging historic personages (Napoleon, Caesar, Joan, Lavinia) out of their context, with taking liberties with facts and twisting incidents to suit his private purposes. The charge is unquestionably true; it is also irrelevant. Shaw did not write *Caesar and Cleopatra, Saint Joan, Androcles and the Lion, The Dark Lady of the Sonnets,* and *In Good King Charles' Golden Days* to provide London theatergoers with glimpses into an authentic past. He was interested in the similarities between past and present—differences would have been differences in fact, not in attitude—and like Shakespeare he employed language and conventions familiar to the listener to make the similarities pertinent. Joan died for essentially the same reasons Lavinia was heading for the arena: refusing to live by the conventional standards of the idealists in power. Caesar becomes a flesh-and-blood hero under Shaw's hand, not an inflated idiot of the traditional costume charade but a man of virtue coping with the stupidities, greed, and self-serving changelings which are the familiar workaday headaches of any conqueror, any president, any prime minister.

Androcles was first produced in the Kleines Theatre in Berlin in 1912. According to reports in the Berlin newspapers, the crown prince rose and left the house, unable to endure the exposition of autocratic imperialism given by the Roman Captain to his Christian prisoners. In referring to the incident in the appendix to the printed version of the play, Shaw expressed his gratitude at finding himself so well understood, but added, "I can assure him that the Empire that served for my model when I wrote Androcles was, as he is now finding to his cost, much nearer my home than the German one." So unused to allegory were modern theater audiences that he felt compelled to make the matter still clearer. ". . . my martyrs are the martyrs of all time," he wrote in the same appendix, "and my persecutors the persecutors of all time."

By imagining characters and "letting them rip," Shaw developed a loose, open-ended play structure in which the action from confrontation to crisis follows from the clash of characters—that is, the clash of their opinions—independent of external force or the suddenly revealed fact, the misunderstanding, or coincidence, customarily employed as plotting devices in the comic drama. He said that he avoided "plots like the plague," and, in the Scribian sense of "intrigue" with all its "postal arrangements, the telegraph arrangements, the police arrangements, the names and addresses," his plays are practically plotless. *Man and Superman*, for example, is simply a chase play interrupted by the debate of the dream scene; Tanner is pursued by Ann halfway across Europe until in the last act he is caught in the grip of the Life Force and succumbs. *Candida*, one of the tightest, best-made plays in any language, with powerful emotional crises at the end of acts 1 and 2, is activated by a declaration of love for another man's wife: Marchbanks, a young visitor in Parson Morell's house, announces that he is the true mate for Morell's wife, Candida. The husband is shaken but gives the youngster his chance alone with his wife (a scene in which the lover gets no further than the "gates of Paradise") and returns from delivering a lecture to hear Candida's verdict. She chooses her husband, and the lover departs.

Heartbreak House, written in the Chekhovian manner, has even less "plot" than *The Cherry Orchard*. Three hours of talk and nothing happens—except, as the bewildered tycoon Mangan puts it, starting to take off his clothes, "We've stripped ourselves morally naked, why not strip ourselves physically naked?" Nothing happens; even the bombs from a marauding Zeppelin miss the house. But as one by one the characters reveal their uselessness and emptiness, echoes of a world disintegrating beyond the lawns of Heartbreak House tremble ominously on the darkened stage.

Shaw's plays intrigue because of the unparalleled brilliance of the conversation, because the characters, all blessed with Shaw's forthrightness and lucidity, are personages whose experiences and judgments are clearly worth listening to, even when they hold to an un-Shavian point of view. That is the new element in the Shavian drama: controversy among people who have thought their way to conviction —or find their way to it in the course of the play. The businessman on the Shavian stage means an exposition of the business ethic; the parson, a definition of the meaning of religion; the prostitute, an analysis of how and why such pestilence as she represents infects the body of society. It may be "all talk," but it is talk raised to the level of a spectator sport.

Nonetheless, Shaw has disappointed many who grant the plays every other virtue by his reluctance to allow the tensions generated in the course of the action to reach a satisfyingly dramatic climax. Their objection is not so much to lack of action as to a promise of actions that do not come off. They say that the playwright, sometimes at the last moment, shies away from seemingly inevitable crises, or at least expected or desirable ones, into anticlimax, leaving the auditor with a feeling of letdown.

That such dampening of natural expectancies does not result from some structural defect of the playwriting but arises from a deliberate choice of direction governed by Shaw's "imagining things as they are," cannot soften the sensation of betrayal; for an awareness of the larger Shavian overview is not always operative in an audience left dangling at the frayed end of an irony. The reaction is less likely to be a sharp insight into the reality of life than a disgruntled suspicion that the whole thing was a hoax. For many auditors *Heartbreak House* ends on a crashing anticlimax. Through the darkness of the English night the ominous sound of the Zeppelin engines is heard slowly approaching. "Listen, what's that?" Ellie says in a tense voice. Everyone listens, each face following the sound until the machine is overhead. Hector Hushabye, bursting with heroics, turns on every light in the house. "We should be blazing to the skies!" he trumpets. But the monster passes over. The engine sounds diminish. The toolshed has been hit with Mangan in it, but otherwise nothing. "Go to bed, everybody," says Hesione. "The house is safe." "Perhaps they'll come back to-morrow night," someone ventures, and Ellie closes the play with, "Oh, I hope so."

Well, perhaps they will, but the audience will not be there. War-plane engines make a very compelling sound in the theater, but no *a posteriori* reflections on Shaw's implication that England will destroy itself from within and not expire in a romantic blaze of glory can compensate for the feeling of emotional letdown at the final curtain. The melodramatic device of roaring engines and whistling bombs has promised catastrophe in some form. The possible death of Mangan in the toolshed excites no sympathy. The audience has been emotionally encouraged into expecting that the lives of the characters will be affected in some way while they are still on stage so that the agony or the ecstasy of change can be experienced. In short, the melodramatic device is expected to deliver melodrama, and, of course, it does not. Indeed, it would be wholly un-Shavian if it did. As a dramatist Shaw would never employ accident as a causal agent in human affairs; it would be contrary to his philosophy to do so.

In most of Shaw's comedies the sexual drive provides at least some of the dramatic motive power. Many of the plays have courtship, love, or marriage as their central theme—*Candida, Overruled, The Philanderer, Arms and the Man, Getting Married.* And in one notable instance, *Man and Superman,* the play comes close to the origins of comedy as fertility rite, as the celebration of the virile young victorious over obstacles placed in their way by the old and impotent—although in this case the prime obstacle to the union seems to be the young man himself. The fact is that there are a great many lovers, or potential lovers, in the comedies of Shaw, which is hardly surprising in light of the importance he assigns to the biological drive and to the institution of marriage in his vitalist-socialist philosophy. What does surprise is that Shaw could have written as much as he did about sex—William Archer said his plays "reeked" with it—with so little expression of the *emotions* of sex. Not that we crave from Shaw suggestive bedroom scenes, the erotic, or the torrid. There is no touch of Frank Harris in G.B.S. He started as a playwright in the Victorian era, and in matters of taste and manners he remained a Victorian all his life. When *Mrs. Warren's Profession* was judged too "raw" for a London production at the time it was written, it was not because it was "sexy" or even titillating. It simply called a spade very distinctly a spade, which was quite enough to shock audiences for whom seduction scenes in adultery plays were a commonplace. When Shaw did set a scene in a lady's bedroom (as in *Arms and the Man*), he saw to it that the male intruder was too exhausted to think of anything but food and a good night's sleep, from which delightful and perfectly sound dramatic situation derives much of the humor and the subsequent plotting of the play. Where Shaw may be faulted (and I would not fall into the error of criticizing him for not writing plays he never intended to write) is in his refusal to probe into the feelings that are naturally aroused by mutual sexual attraction or to depict the actions of love that loving demands, not merely because such probings can always stimulate audience interest but also because lovers as flesh-and-blood real as Shaw's characters are in other respects must invariably come to such feelings and actions. Shaw appears deliberately to turn them off, to

115

deny them any moment of amorousness as though lovemaking were as far beneath an audience's contempt as the Ancients considered it in *Back to Methuselah.*

Shaw himself has admitted that whenever he was alone with a woman "she invariably throws her arms around me." But seldom do the ladies of the Shavian stage exhibit such shameless abandon, and when they try it, as Ann Whitefield does in the first act of *Man and Superman,* they are more likely to be rebuked than bussed. "Magnificent audacity," says Tanner, and the scene ends with her patting his cheek. Shaw himself once rebuked a "magnificent audacity" with a retort his admirers never tire of repeating:

> A certain foreign actress [Isadora Duncan], universally admired for her beautiful form, wrote to Shaw asking if he would consent to have by her a veritable wonderchild. "You have the greatest brain in the world. I have the most graceful body. Let us produce the perfect child." Shaw replied: "That's all very well, as you put it. But suppose the child had my body and your brain?"[6]

Shaw authenticated the anecdote.

Shaw's characters are never prudes. They certainly harbor no notions of sex as illicit or sinful. They do not reject the idea of sexual intercourse; they simply talk away the emotions that lead to it. Other ideas get in their way. Attitudes and preoccupations so filter the amorous impulse that when it finally makes its way into words or deeds its ardency has been screened out, and lovers end up debating the meaning of love instead of enjoying it. Shaw wrote one of his longest love scenes in *You Never Can Tell,* a play Archer miscalled "a formless and empty farce." Gloria is a woman of pronounced views— as most of Shaw's women are—and her "ideas" about love and marriage erupt in Valentine's face the moment he tries his hand at wooing her. Says Valentine, "How could that man have so beautiful a daughter?" Snaps Gloria:

> That seems to be an attempt at what is called a pretty speech. Let me say at once, Mr. Valentine, that pretty speeches make very sickly conversation. Pray let us be friends, if we are to be friends, in a

[6] Henderson, *George Bernard Shaw: Playboy and Prophet,* 705.

sensible and wholesome way. I have no intention of getting married; and unless you are content to accept that state of things, we had better not cultivate each other's acquaintance.

Nonetheless, Gloria has amorous feelings; she simply cannot bring herself to employ an amorous vocabulary. "I wonder," she says, "what is the scientific explanation of these fancies that cross us occasionally." And the love scene proceeds as a debate on the nature of emotion with Valentine at his wits' end trying to find a language of love that will not offend her preconceptions. She checks him at every turn. "I hope," she says, "you are not going to be so foolish—so vulgar— as to say love." He tries another tack:

> No, no, no. Not love: we know better than that. Let's call it chemistry. You can't deny that there is such a thing as chemical action, chemical affinity, chemical combinations—the most irresistible of all natural forces. Well, you're attracting me irresistibly—chemically.

"Nonsense," she retorts.

No matter how witty the dialogue the characters employ or how full of intellectual substance such confrontations may be, they generate no amorous tension and, as a consequence, reach no natural climactic culmination. They drift away or are frequently "interrupted" by other characters when the talk has gone on long enough. When Shaw allows his couple a degree of amorous tension, as he does in *Captain Brassbound's Conversion,* he manages to build into their natures the quality which will end their relationship not in union but in separation. "How glorious!" says Lady Cecily, as Brassbound departs at the end of that play, "how glorious. And what an escape." In *Candida,* Marchbanks goes out into the night. In *Arms and the Man,* Bluntschli will return "punctually at five in the evening on Tuesday fortnight" presumably to do his wooing, and in *Pygmalion* there is no wooing whatever, although Higgins' Galetea literally begs for it. In *The Apple Cart* the relationship between the King and his mistress turns out to be platonic; King Magnus finds release from the arduous labors of state not in his lady's arms but in her common sense. The Captain strikes the Shavian love note precisely after Lavinia has been saved from the arena at the close of *Androcles and the Lion.* "May I come and argue with you occasionally?" he asks her. "Yes, handsome Captain: you may," she replies. Sometimes one wonders how the Life Force ever gets off the ground.

The indifference of Shaw's characters to the romantic and erotic is, of course, Shaw's own indifference. He admitted to being a consummate philanderer with his pockets always "full of the small change of lovemaking," but the sexual aspects of Shaw's few love affairs ended quickly and, as he tells us, generally to his relief. "I am fond of women," he once wrote, "but I am in earnest about quite other things. . . . love is only diversion and recreation for me." Since Shaw could not be expected to write about "diversion and recreation," what we get are lovers who are in earnest about quite other things, which make for excellent talk and resounding anticlimaxes. "The ideal love affair," Shaw once told biographer Hesketh Pearson, "is one conducted by post."

During one of their many table talks Archibald Henderson asked his aging friend what he thought of the Nobel Prize awards and their influence. Shaw, who had no patience with prizes, honors, awards, or ceremonials of any other sort, delivered a predictable reply: ". . . the whole conception of prize-giving as applied to the fine arts is absurd," he said. "The Nobel business is a lottery open to all who have achieved a minimum of celebrity." He asserted to Henderson that the Nobel Prize committee

cannot recognize genius: it can only accept an established reputation and a very safe one: that is to say, an uncontroversial one. As the reputations of the greatest geniuses in literature are always matters of fierce controversy until they are dead, or at least very old and harmless, the greatest geniuses in literature are out of the running.

With no premonition of the irony of fate, Shaw placed himself firmly on the line: "The prize-winners," he said, "are like the modest hotels in Baedeker—'well spoken of.'" When in the following year, 1925, Shaw was awarded the Nobel Prize for Literature, Henderson had his moment of pleasantry, chaffing Shaw for being merely a writer of "established reputation" and not one of the greatest living geniuses. Shaw affected puzzlement. Since he had published nothing in the year 1925, he assumed it to be "a token of gratitude for a sense of world relief." Twenty-two of Shaw's major plays had appeared before the year of the award (only seven were to follow), including *Saint Joan, Back to Methuselah, Man and Superman, Candida, Pygmalion, Caesar and Cleopatra* and *Major Barbara*—any two or three of which might have earned a less controversial figure earlier approval of the prize committee had not Shaw's views on such "lotteries" been so well publicized. But the prize committee, to everyone's relief, was not rebuked for its audacity. Shaw graciously acknowledged the award in a letter to the permanent secretary of the Royal Swedish Academy. The prize money, however, was something else again; that he could not accept. Part of his letter to the secretary reads:

> My readers and audiences provide me with more than sufficient money for my needs; and as to my renown it is greater than is good for my spiritual health. Under these circumstances the money is a lifebelt thrown to a swimmer who has already reached the shore in safety. I, therefore, respectfully and gratefully beg the Swedish Royal Academy to confer on me the additional and final honor of classing my works as in that respect *hors concours*.

Since his refusal of the seven thousand pounds created an unforeseen and insoluable technical problem, Shaw accepted it for the split second that elapsed between signing a receipt for it and a trust deed which turned the money over to the Anglo-Swedish Literary Alliance, which at Shaw's suggestion had been organized by Baron Palmstierna to meet the emergency. The matter, of course, did not end there. The Shavianphobes had another field day, calling his rejection of the money a "cosmic publicity stunt." Others, impressed by Shaw's self-advertised wealth, tried their best to get their hands into his pockets. He was deluged by letters, many from Americans, begging for gifts and loans. After news of the award was made public, Shaw reported that

> some fifty thousand people wrote to me to say that as the greatest of men I must see that the best thing I could do with the prize was to give it to them. Instead, I gave it back. Then they all wrote again to say that if I could afford to do that, I could afford to lend them 1,500 pounds for three years.

As a defense against the panhandlers he reported to Henderson that he was "practising a complicated facial expression which combined universal benevolence with a savage determination not to save any American from ruin by a remittance of five hundred dollars." His final words on the whole extravaganza were: "I can forgive Alfred Nobel for having invented dynamite. But only a fiend in human form could have invented the Nobel Prize!"[7]

To follow Shaw's tracks through the pastures of his thought would of necessity produce a full critical biography. The man was constitutionally incapable of *not* having firm opinions on any issue that came to his attention from the most trivial to the world-important. He produced pamphlets, newspaper pieces, magazine articles, and radio talks by the score which range in subject matter from "How to Settle the Irish Question," "Common Sense About the War," "The Cinema as a Moral Leveler," "Actors on Acting," "The Jevonian Criticism of Marx," and "Neglected Aspects of Public Libraries" to "Why I Ought Not to Have Become a Drama Critic."

He had a great deal to say about prison reform, insisting that a "criminal" should not be punished but rehabilitated by giving him access to all the spiritual influences of his day, including good conversation, books, pictures, the opportunity for research, change of scene, marriage, and parentage. Of family planning he said:

> Birth control should be advocated for its own sake, on the general ground that the difference between voluntary, rational, controlled activity and any sort of involuntary, irrational, uncontrolled activity is the difference between an amoeba and a man.

He declared further that if he were a woman he would refuse to have a child for less than ten thousand dollars, that the burden of bringing up the children of the community should fall on the community and not on the individual, and that "a nation that will not guarantee the proper nurture of its children does not deserve to have them."

Shaw's interest in phonetics did not begin and end with *Pygmalion*. He devised a forty-two-letter phonetic alphabet, each letter representing one and only one sound. The purpose was to eliminate class accents, so that ultimately the chauffeur might marry the duchess, or

[7] *Ibid.*, 343.

the professor of phonetics the daughter of a dustman—if he was not too busy to consider the idea.

Another intense interest was printing and publishing, and in that his efforts were more influential. It was a mark of the low esteem in which the British and American public held its playwrights that plays were primarily published for the use of actors and provincial theater producers and not for the enjoyment of readers in their armchairs. Generally printed on cheap paper, with flimsy covers and scarcely readable print, the text interspersed with cryptic stage directions, the published play of the day was seldom a bookstore item. Shaw changed all that. He revised the acting version of his plays by writing readily understandable stage directions and lengthy character descriptions, chose the type and the paper, added a preface, and turned out a hardcover volume worthy of its content. Shaw's authorized complete works, published by Constable, composed in excellent type and printed on soft-colored paper in inexpensively priced volumes—are fine examples of the printer's art. Needless to say, when the new market opened to them, other playwrights followed suit.

Shaw gave to everything he did a seemingly inexhaustible energy, denying nothing he touched the full power of his enthusiasm, his brilliance, and, what is most remarkable considering the range of his coverage, his passion for detail. His insatiable interest in life could not be satisfied by any restriction narrower than life itself. He was a playwright for the same reason he was a pamphleteer and a Fabian essayist: to goad anyone who would listen to him into his way of thinking.

Although his histrionic flair found a happy outlet in dramatic form, drama was not his "calling" as it is with most playwrights and as it might be logical to assume it would be with a man who was responsible for some thirty major plays. Shaw was interested in art because it was one of man's enterprises and as such could be employed for life or against life. He was not interested in it for its own sake; for him, art was for God's sake. Henderson, who knew him as well as any man did, wrote that at times he felt "obsessed by the feeling that art has played a very secondary part in the life of this international publicist." Shaw himself, on the occasion of his seventieth birthday, asserted that he did not care a snap of his finger for his literary eminence compared with his pioneering work as one of the founders and organizers of the British Labour party.

Nonetheless, it is as dramatic artist and not as creative evolutionist or socialist theorist that Shaw has been acknowledged as one of England's greats. The plays continue to exercise their charm—especially those he wrote before 1930—although it is doubtful that they persuade audiences to Shaw's way of thinking any more than the prose works have done. G.B.S., the clever man for all occasions whom Shaw fashioned to gain a hearing, outsmarted his creator. The "privileged lunatic" took the place of the serious artist-philosopher in the public eye, and audiences still go to his plays to have their Shaw and dismiss him too, to enjoy the jester and ignore the prophet. Critic Egon Friedell has said of Shaw's playwriting that it was clever of Shaw to sugar his pill but it was even cleverer of the public to lick off the sugar and leave the pill alone.

On various occasions Shaw himself confessed that his game did not work. "I have got the tragedian and I have got the clown in me, and the clown trips me up in the most dreadful way," he lamented. "Not taking me seriously is the Englishman's way of refusing to face facts," Eric Bentley quotes Shaw, adding, "And by 'the Englishman' Shaw has always meant Monsieur Tout-le-monde." In 1932, speaking before the Fabian Society, Shaw said: "For 48 years I have been addressing speeches to the Fabian Society and to other assemblies in this country. So far as I can make out, these speeches have not produced any effect whatever." And again—with a touch of that self-deprecating humor that endeared but disarmed him—he announced: "I have solved practically all the pressing questions of our times, but . . . they keep on being propounded as insoluble just as if I had never existed."

There is something akin to tragedy here, although it might be considered somewhat presumptuous of Shaw to suppose that he could wash the world into paradise on a terrestrial flood of Irish rhetoric. World savers, if they are not executed by one means or another, generally end up with the world in much the same state in which they found it. But when Shaw says, "I have produced no permanent impression because nobody has ever believed me," we realize that he understood why his life was the failure he considered it to be. The clown simply was not taken seriously; and no matter how often he reiterated, "The real joke is that I am in earnest," and "Every jest is an earnest in the womb of time," the world he hoped to save took such remarks as merely more pieces of Shavian tomfoolery. If Shaw seemed not to take his ideas seriously (that is, solemnly), why should the audience? Was not Shaw's humor, as W. H. Auden said, his admission that his ideas were not true? A prophet with a sense of humor had never been heard of; a witty Savior was inconceivable.

Shaw was not oblivious to the negative response his wit could produce. Early in the twentieth century Tolstoi chided him for his levity in serious matters and warned him that his cleverness was self-defeating. In a letter to Shaw acknowledging the receipt of a copy of *Man and Superman*, Tolstoi wrote: "The first defect in it is that you are not sufficiently serious. One should not speak jestingly on such a subject as the purpose of human life, the causes of its perversion, and the evil that fills the life of humanity today."

There is more than a hint in the Russian's "you are not sufficiently serious" that Tolstoi, like many another, mistook Shaw's jesting manner for lack of dedication to the "grave questions" of humanity. Be that as it may, in his second "reproach" Tolstoi struck right at the mark.

> In your book I detect a desire to surprise and astonish the reader by your great erudition, talent and cleverness. Yet all this is not merely unnecessary for the solution of the questions you deal with, but often distracts the reader's attention from the essence of the matter by attracting it to the brilliance of the exposition.[8]

One is left to ponder what Tolstoi would have thought of the last act of *The Doctor's Dilemma*, Shaw's only "death scene," where, to Archer's indignation, Shaw refused to treat Dubedat's expiring "soberly, seriously, naturally, or in a word, with a straight face."

In *Back to Methuselah*, Shaw seemed to be taking Tolstoi's criticism to heart, but with only moderate success. There is still more fun in the Garden of Eden than the old Russian could have found appropriate. Shaw's literary method, "to take the utmost trouble to find the right thing to say and then to say it with the utmost levity," was not something he could put on and take off to fit occasions. G.B.S. was no

[8] Aylmer Maude, *The Life of Tolstoy: Later Years*, 461–62.

mask designed to gain a hearing behind which stood an exasperated "real" Shaw, unable to get the mask unstuck. The style was the man. For Shaw levity was inseparable from the right things he had to say. To many of his listeners, however, the two were incompatible. As a lady acquaintance once put it, summing up her reaction to Shaw's ideas: "Oh, pshaw!"

Besides mixing levity with the right thing to say, Shaw literally overturned the venerable institution of comedy writing by replacing the traditional targets for comic ridicule by a brand-new set of his own. The comic muse, gay as she is, had always been of a strictly conservative turn of mind. Her serious practitioners, from Ben Jonson onward, have generally stood in close support of the moral and social norm acceptable to the audience for which they wrote, the attack by their comic wit directed toward deviates from that norm, excesses or aberrancies which by common consent are considered undesirable for the continued well-being of the community. Most agreed-upon undesirables in Western culture have traditionally gathered under the label of the seven deadly sins: sloth, greed, lechery, and so on, and in various subspecies of them, such as hypocrisy, pretentiousness, affectation, and mendacity. In ridiculing human failings of this class, the comic playwright inhabits fairly safe ground, for not only does he appeal to the righteousness of his audience but also he knows that any member guilty of the excess or aberrancy under attack must laugh in public agreement and keep his secret to himself. If there is any therapeutic value to comedic art, it is that, through laughter at the stage symbol, private guilt may be exorcised and adjustment to the common norm effected. But even if comedy does little to correct human delinquency—and it would be difficult to prove one way or another—it reflects and bolsters accord on what a particular culture considers proper, right, and good and what it considers socially and morally distasteful. Molière (with whom Shaw has been frequently and erroneously compared) was, although occasionally misunderstood, a firm supporter of bourgeois morality. His comic attacks were of the typically limited sort: the ridicule of hypocrisy, avarice, hypochondria, pretentiousness, gullibility. When in *The Misanthrope* Shaw reached beyond simplicities and began to search the limits in which honesty and virtue can be socially useful, he experienced the sharp sting of public disapproval. Audiences sitting at a comic play do not relish being provoked into weighing values. They want their own judgments reaffirmed.

Shaw barged into the world of playwriting not to reaffirm the moral assumptions of his Victorian and Edwardian contemporaries but to disrupt them, to show them up for what he considered them to be: archaic, self-serving, and obstructive to social progress—in short, shibboleths of a complacent Philistinism and watchwords of an oppressive idealism. Shaw launched his comedic arrows not at the moral and social aberrant in his culture, but at the norm itself; that is to say, he put upon the stage for ridicule the very conventions that his audience lived by. In effect he proposed that his auditor should see himself as the fool, as the deviate from a norm that Shaw was busy constructing from the tenets of his own philosophy. Shaw ignored the traditional sins of comedy, substituting for them a catalogue of what he called the deadly virtues—respectability, conventional morality, filial affection, modesty, sentiment, devotion to women, romance, and the hard-work-leads-to-success principle of economics—that were, for all but a minority in his audiences, sacred cows. Shaw was the outsider, angered by the stupidities that others extolled as proper conduct, by the economic rudderlessness that others defended through the mystique of laissez-faire, by church going that concealed religious apathy or, worse, manifested belief in salvation from the skies, when Shaw knew as a certainty that man alone was responsible for his destiny. His enemy was the complacent Broadbent, the thinker of no thoughts, the believer of no beliefs except in the rightness of things as they are:

BROADBENT: I find the world quite good enough for me: rather a jolly place in fact.
KEEGAN: You are satisfied?
BROADBENT: As a reasonable man, yes. I see no evils in the world—except of course, natural evils—that cannot be remedied by freedom, self-government, and English institutions. I think so, not because I am an Englishman, but as a matter of commonsense.
KEEGAN: You feel at home in the world then?
BROADBENT: Of course. Don't you?
KEEGAN: (*from the depths of his nature*) No.

BROADBENT: Try phosphorus pills. I always take them when my brain is over-worked. I'll give you the address in Oxford Street.

The ridiculous on the Shavian stage are the Broadbents; they also occupy the seats in front of it. Discover yourself as absurd, Shaw's comedies said to them. Find yourself so ridiculous that you will laugh yourself out of thoughtless acceptance of things as they are into the "true joy of life" born of a "moral passion" to work for the purpose of the universe, to work for the good of the whole of society. It was too much for Shaw to expect. A man may acknowledge to himself the ludicrousness of his greed or lustfulness if the stage personification of it is sufficiently exaggerated to allow him to disclaim it publicly through laughter. But Shaw's characters are never exaggerations à la Molière. Shaw did not fashion caricatures; he put the Broadbents on stage very much as they really are. Nor did he ask Broadbent's alter ego in the stalls to have a laugh at anything as trivial as, say, Malvolio's pretentiousness which any pretentious Broadbent in the audience could find ludicrous without the temptation to self-loathing. Shaw put Broadbent's own ideas in front of him, his convictions, his sacred prejudices, his attitude toward all things in the world around him, and, what is more than Broadbent could have done, he gave them eloquence. That those ideas, convictions, and attitudes become ridiculous on the Shavian stage is not the result of dramatic hyperbole. When they are aired with Shavian eloquence and goaded by Shavian wit (that fine instrument vouchsafed him by the Life Force), they fall apart through their inherent weakness, causing Broadbent to be scandalized—if the magic works—that he ever could have held them in the first place.

But does the magic work? Does Broadbent emerge a Shavian realist, or does he leave the theater thinking Shaw a fool? The latter is more likely. Rarely can a man be ridiculed out of his convictions; ridicule serves rather to reinforce them. Shaw was under no illusions. He realized that the plays produce the effect of "all the characters being so many Shaws spouting Shavianisms and provoking first a lot of shallow but willing laughter and then producing disappointment and irritation."

In 1909, when Shaw was a young man of fifty-three, an editorialist in the *Nation* wrote:

126

> The time has come . . . when the insolent Shavian advertising no longer fills us with astonishment or discovery, or disables our judgment from a cool inspection of the wares advertised . . . The deep young souls who looked to him as an evangelist are beginning to see through him and despair.

What the writer could not know, of course, was that, after this notice of dismissal, a dozen of Shaw's major plays were still to come, a score of major essays, and the two volumes on socialism and politics. Yet it does not matter. A stark prophecy had been uttered: there were to be no more deep young souls to imbibe Shaw's teachings during the forty-one years left to him. Those whom he had offended by his tampering with their pet convictions shrugged him off as an amusing crank and went their ways undisturbed. For the rest he was the grand old clown who need not be taken seriously no matter how deftly he swung the bladder. He became a classic in his lifetime, venerable, safe, famous—and, for an author, comfortably rich.

More than fifty volumes of biography and criticism have appeared, as well as countless essays, commentaries, and reviews—and they still keep coming. There are Shaw societies in England, in America, and on the Continent (how he would howl if he knew), whose members continue to unearth and publish letters and occasional pieces that Shaw in his lifetime scattered over most of the civilized world. However, no new generation has felt his appeal. The disillusioned of the mid-twentieth century have turned not to Shaw, master iconoclast and institution destroyer, but to the soulful despair of Herman Hesse and the negativism of the new left. His works on Creative Evolution are not included in the curriculums of university philosophy or religion departments. Economic and political-science departments ignore him. Students of English literature are assigned a play or two, but for the most part English professors find him uninteresting. There is nothing for them to interpret; there is no mystery about him. He is scarcely acknowledged by sociologists or music historians, and in drama departments actors prepare his plays without bothering to notice what he has written on how to act in them. A few devoted Shavians in the university ranks offer semester courses on Shaw. Were it not for them, he might well be the most famous unread man in English literature. "I need inbunking, not debunking" he once said to Hesketh Pearson, "having debunked myself like a born clown."

History has still to present its verdict. Perhaps Pearson is right: the age he lived in will one day be known as the Shavian age. Maybe he will have the final laugh on Egon Friedell: Can generation after generation of playgoers lick the sugar off the Shavian pill without getting a bit of the pill stuck on their tongues? David Daiches, writing in the *New York Times*, seemed to think not. He wrote of Shaw's method of identifying the reader with the "fools, villains, hypocrites or slaves of mindless convention who are so often his chief objects of attack," and then stated: "And yet the reader has to accept this because he has been carried along by Shaw's persuasive rhetoric, and when the reader suddenly sees *himself* and not "them" as the fool or villain, it is too late for him to extricate himself from the implication."[9]

At the time of his marriage to Charlotte Payne-Townsend, Shaw developed an abscess on his instep that was diagnosed as necrosis of the bone. While he was recovering from that ailment, he fell down the stairs in their house in Halesmere and broke his left arm close to the wrist (temporarily holding up his work on Wagner which he had set himself as a honeymoon task). Shortly thereafter he fell from his bicycle and sprained his ankle. His doctors urged a change of diet. But Shaw was adamant. "Death," he said, "is better than cannibalism."

My will contains directions for my funeral, which will be followed not by mourning coaches, but by herds of oxen, sheep, swine, flocks of poultry, and a small traveling aquarium of live fish, all wearing white scarves in honour of the man who perished rather than eat his fellow creatures. It will be, with the exception of the procession into Noah's Ark, the most remarkable thing of the kind ever seen.

It did not happen quite that way. The animals he had not eaten were denied the opportunity to march. There was no procession and no "funeral." Shaw fell again while working in his garden at Ayot St. Lawrence a few weeks after his ninety-fourth birthday, fracturing his thigh. He died peacefully on Thursday, November 2, 1950. There was some notion of "ennobling" him by interment in Westminster

9 David Daiches, *New York Times Book Review*, October 25, 1970.

Abbey, but Shaw had his way, as he generally did. His body was cremated and the ashes mixed inseparably with those of his wife and inurned in the garden at Ayot St. Lawrence. No epitaph marks the spot, but something Charlotte once said will serve: "It is very hard," she said, "to feel quite sure that he is wrong."

JOHN GALSWORTHY

by Earl E. Stevens

For nearly twenty-eight years John Galsworthy followed the classic pattern of what the well-born young Englishman should and would do. The elder son of a wealthy London solicitor and director of companies, he was properly educated by private governesses; at Saugeen, the preparatory school at Bournemouth; at Harrow, where he proved to be a rather fine athlete; and then at New College, Oxford. Of the many sporting activities usually associated with his "set," Galsworthy enjoyed tennis, hunting, private theatricals, summer shooting in Scotland, horse racing, and a limited amount of gambling. At the university he read law, successfully played the role of the dandy, thought himself in love with Sybil Carr, a young singing teacher, and graduated with second honors in law. After being called to the bar in 1890, he enjoyed the life of a young man about London and continued unenthusiastically his readings in law. Because his interest in Miss Carr persisted, his father, finding her prospects unacceptable, decided that business matters required his son's presence in Canada. After the trip to Canada in 1891, John went on a long tour of Australia, New Zealand, and the South Sea Islands for the ostensible purpose of studying maritime law at first hand. While on this voyage Galsworthy came to realize that he and Sybil were not right for each other, and the affair was over. On his return to England he resumed his life about town and his law readings.

The predominant impression of Galsworthy during these years is that he was a typical, though rather retiring, handsome young man of the upper middle class. Except for the belief of some of his contemporaries at Oxford "that he was a very clever fellow with reserves of power," there was little indication of his future attainments. No challenge or cause had arisen as yet which necessitated his following any path other than the one of least resistance—the path of the gentleman dandy.

Although he dutifully continued doing what was expected of him, the London years from 1891 to 1895 were transition ones. Signs of discontent and sober questioning of his role, of his class, and of society itself began to appear. There are at least three factors which help to explain why and how Galsworthy broke free of the stultifying parochialism of his own class.

First, he was not interested in the conventional choices of a career in business or law, even though his father's influence and wealth would have practically guaranteed success. A career that did arouse his interest was that of a writer. In September, 1894, he wrote:

I do wish I had the gift of writing, I really think that is the nicest way of making money going, only it isn't really the writing so much as the thoughts that one wants; and, when you feel like a very shallow pond, with no nice cool deep pools with queer and pleasant things at the bottom, what's the good? I suppose one could cultivate writing, but one can't cultivate clear depths and quaint plants.[1]

The second factor concerns his personal discovery of the poor and their living conditions. He was given now and then the job of collecting rents for his father in the poorer districts. In this way he learned not only what life for the disinherited was but also that his family profited from such hopelessness. Unable to forget and unwilling to close his eyes, he developed a "fondness for wandering about at night in the poorer districts, listening to the conversations of the people, sometimes visiting doss-houses."[2]

The third factor gave Galsworthy a personal and immediate cause for rebellion and the crucial inspiration for a serious career in writing.

[1] H. V. Marrot (ed.), *The Life and Letters of John Galsworthy*, 97.
[2] *Ibid.*, 65.

From his two sisters Galsworthy was learning of the anguish that their cousin Arthur's wife, Ada, was enduring in her marriage. He had first met Ada in 1891 at a wedding party given in her honor at the home of his parents. They met again briefly during the cricket match between Harrow and Eton in 1893. Their third meeting occurred when Lilian Galsworthy was married to the painter Georg Sauter in 1894. The next meeting of Ada and Galsworthy took place during Easter week of 1895 at the railway station in Paris. He had come down to see off Ada and her mother. Amid the bustle, Ada had said to him, "Why don't you write? You're just the person!" Not long thereafter they were meeting one another as often as possible and were rapidly falling in love. They became lovers in September, 1895.

Knowing that Ada was extremely unhappy in her marriage to Arthur and that, as far as society cared, her plight was hopeless, Galsworthy completed his rejection of what the proper young Englishman should and would do. He was passionately in love with another man's wife; she had told him to write; with her love and encouragement he would try to please her, thereby fulfilling his wish and her command. The significance of these events to Galsworthy's career is made clear by Dudley Barker: "This unhappy marriage and the emotions it aroused in John Galsworthy are the foundation of all his writings. It turned him into the leading novelist of his generation; in particular, it was the direct cause and the very stuff of his first and best Forsyte novel, *The Man of Property*."[3]

The next nine years, 1895 to 1904, were later characterized by Galsworthy as "the spiritually stressful years of my life," and the reasons are not hard to find. Galsworthy and Ada were two people very much in love who had to forgo many of the expected joys of love because of the peculiarity of their situation. Believing that the scandal of divorce would cause Galsworthy's father great pain, they decided that, regardless of their own frustrations and personal desires, their relationship had to remain clandestine. Barker, doubting whether John's father was "quite so sensitive to scandal as is implied," suggested that young Galsworthy's almost total dependence on his father may have had something to do with their decision to keep silent. According to

[3] Dudley Barker, *The Man of Principle: A View of John Galsworthy*, 51.

Barker, the father could have been so difficult that a literary career would have been impossible.

Galsworthy's struggle to make himself a writer played a major role in these years of stress. He was not a born writer, and much of his early work is obviously apprentice work. He began by producing short descriptions of his travels, sketches, and short stories. In 1897, using the pseudonym John Sinjohn (John the son of John), he published his first book, a collection of ten short stories entitled *From the Four Winds*. His first novel, *Jocelyn*, came out in 1898. It was probably in 1899 that he discovered Ivan Turgenev and Guy de Maupassant. "They were the first writers who gave me, at once, real aesthetic excitement, and an insight into proportion of theme and economy of words." He studied them for their techniques and their craftsmanship. They, as well as Tolstoi, were to remain for him the writers who exerted the greatest influence on his own work, especially in matters of technique. Galsworthy's second novel, *Villa Rubein* (1900), was a better book because of what he had learned. The next year he published four long short stories under the title *A Man of Devon*. Of these early works Galsworthy permitted only *Villa Rubein* and the stories in *A Man of Devon* to be republished, but not until he had completely revised them.

There is much about *Villa Rubein* that is typical of many flowering romances. The youthful lovers are Christian Devorell, a young Englishwoman, and Harz, a struggling young Austrian painter who is an outsider because he is of the peasant class and because he had been involved while a student in illegal political activities. Less obvious, perhaps, is the exploration of the theme that one's desire for beauty and for passion can never be satisfied. One always wants more. This worship of beauty and the centrality of its role in men's lives is a theme that developed and persisted as a dominant motif throughout Galsworthy's work.

Another characteristic that developed was Galsworthy's use of irony in *Villa Rubein*. Uncle Nicholas Treffry drove Harz to the border and to freedom from the Austrian police because he was devoted to Chris. The exertion proved too much for him. On his deathbed Treffry learned that Harz, regardless of his own safety, had returned for Chris.

The gallant gesture of the old man had succeeded in becoming an unnecessary, even futile, extravagance.

In the *Man of Devon* two stories are of particular interest in the light of Galsworthy's future development. Both stories introduce what became his most famous subject—the Forsytes. In the earlier story, "Salvation of a Forsyte" (originally titled "The Salvation of Swithin Forsyte"), the major character is Swithin Forsyte, who is old and lonely and dying. As he, who has always enjoyed the best of everything, lies in bed savoring champagne, he recalls the only wild and youthfully foolish moment (when he was a comfortable thirty-eight) of his long life. Without quite knowing how it all came about, Swithin found himself involved with a girl named Rozsi and her Hungarian compatriots in revolutionary activities; at the moment when Swithin's excitement came perilously close to love and involvement in foreign entanglements, his Forsyte common sense saved him, and he fled back to his own kind. These wayward events took place over forty years before, and as he lies dreaming about them, he recalls once again his memories of Rozsi, and the thought that he lost something disturbs him greatly. In the end, Swithin Forsyte dies with a sigh "above the bubbles."

The other story in the *Devon* volume that uses Forsyte material is "The Silence." Completed shortly after the Swithin story, it introduces, though very briefly, old Jolyon Forsyte as the chairman of the board of the New Colliery Company. The main story is Pippin's; as a mine superintendent for the New Colliery Company in an alien land, he has been an outstanding success. Despite the isolation and the overwhelming responsibility, he has managed to survive against insuperable odds—a mine catastrophe, the forest, and the silence. The unwillingness of the London office to permit him the minor idiosyncrasy of not sending monthly letters of report finally drives Pippin to suicide: "a single instant of madness on a single subject!" When the board interviews Pippin's successor, old Jolyon, who has understood and sympathized with Pippin's difficulties, "was not there for once, guessing perhaps that the board's view of this death would be too small for him. . . ." Galsworthian irony provides a suitable context for developing some of the consequences of the business-is-business doctrine.

The publication of *A Man of Devon* brought the first phase (1895–

1901) of Galsworthy's new career to a close. Even though it is easy to agree with his evaluation of these works as "Kiplingesque, crudely expressed, extravagant in theme," it would be foolish to overlook what had been accomplished. In six years he had published two novels and two volumes of short stories; from his study of de Maupassant and Turgenev he had begun to develop clear insights into the writing of fiction. He had learned the value of irony, and he had discovered in his creation of the Forsyte world his abilities as a satirist.

The next five years (1901 to 1906) form what H. V. Marrot has called the "subterranean phase" of his developing career. Galsworthy worked quietly and steadily to improve his use of satire and irony. Continuing the development he had begun—the release of his satiric abilities in broaching the Forsytes—he undertook a major work which would fuse the new subject matter and the new technique. The work, a play entitled *The Civilised*, was not only his first attempt to treat the Forsytes full scale but it was his first major effort to write satire. The title itself suggests the irony implicit in the subject; by stating that the play deals with civilized people, the title raises the question, How do civilized people behave? In this particular instance the Forsytes exemplify their civilized behavior by their concern only with social respectability or with what people will say; beyond this veneer everything—ethics, morality, benevolence—is ordered and controlled for them by the doctrine of survival of the fittest.

As early as June, 1901, the play had taken some shape, but Galsworthy abandoned it not long thereafter, probably because he had tried to include too much in one work. Twenty-three years were to pass before Galsworthy had utilized all the ideas to be found in the play, and in the process he produced two novels (*The Island Pharisees* and *The Man of Property*), two plays (*The Fugitive* and *Old English*) and one long short story ("A Stoic").

Having discarded the play, he began work on his fifth book, a novel, around August, 1901. From his struggles to write this novel he learned how to handle effectively the device of the omniscient author. He worked on the novel for about three years and rewrote it three times. He first attempted to write from the first-person point of view of Ferrand, the young foreign vagabond who was in the eyes of society an outsider. Edward Garnett read the manuscript and told him to rewrite it because "its author was not sufficiently within Ferrand's skin." Galsworthy characterized the second version as "a hybrid between the young Pagan's [Ferrand's] adventures and the reactions they caused in his black-coated audience." Again Garnett told him to rewrite the novel. Of the third version Galsworthy said, ". . . it was rewritten entirely and became the spiritual adventures of a young black-coat among his own kind." This third version was published in January, 1904, as *The Island Pharisees*. Galsworthy was not satisfied even then, and when a new edition was issued in 1908, he revised the work drastically but still retained the point of view of Shelton, the young "black-coat."

With Garnett's help Galsworthy had discovered that he should not use the first-person viewpoint for characters of the lower classes and that he could use the omniscient-author convention skillfully when he restricted himself to presenting characters of the upper classes omnisciently. The material dealing with the world of the disinherited could be presented as seen or reacted to by the upper classes. The lessons he had learned in writing *The Island Pharisees* he consistently applied in his subsequent work.

As a novel *The Island Pharisees* is not completely satisfying because too frequently it seems to exist as an excuse for the satiric vignettes of the upper classes. The black-coat Shelton, finding himself entangled in the affairs of the young foreigner, begins to look at his own set from Ferrand's perspective. Shelton soon discovers that his criticisms of the smug self-righteousness of his own class make him unpopular, even with his fiancée, Antonia Dennant, of the Holm Oaks Dennants. By the end of the book Shelton comes to realize that his forthcoming marriage cannot work out and writes Antonia saying, "Our engagement is at an end by mutual consent."

Despite its weaknesses *The Island Pharisees* is significant because it is Galsworthy's first major independent work—independent in the sense of being distinctively Galsworthian and not imitative of other writers. The fact that he dropped the pseudonym he had been using and published the book under his own name indicates that Galsworthy recognized its importance to his career. As Galsworthy remarked, the novel serves as "an introduction to all those following novels which

136

depict—somewhat satirically—the various sections of English 'Society' with a more or less capital 'S'."

With the solid achievement of this novel behind him, Galsworthy could now turn all his creative efforts to completing the Forsyte novel. In this novel Galsworthy took up the main scheme of his abandoned play: property, a loveless marriage, and a helpless wife. Work on the novel was interrupted by the death of Galsworthy's father in December, 1904. Although both Galsworthy and Ada were deeply grieved by this loss, they realized that the seemingly interminable period of waiting—more than nine years—was at last at an end. Now they could defy society openly and endure divorce proceedings. They married on September 23, 1905, the day after the decree became final.

When the manuscript of the novel was completed in the spring of 1905, Galsworthy sent it to Garnett for comment. Garnett took strong exception to Bosinney's committing suicide after learning of Soames's violation of Irene and suggested two alternatives: let Bosinney be accidentally killed in the fog, or have him and Irene run off to Paris with the insouciance of youth. The vehemence of Garnett's reactions and his proposed alternatives led Galsworthy to revise the ending so that the truth of Bosinney's death was left ambiguous. It could have been suicide, it could have been accidental, or it could have been an inextricable combination of both possibilities. Leaving the question unresolved and unresolvable, Galsworthy increased the verisimilitude of the book by utilizing the same kind of ambiguity found frequently in life. The key to the mind of the Forsytes, according to Galsworthy, was the rejection of anything prejudicial to them. His portrayal of the Forsytes at the morgue rejecting the idea that Bosinney's death was suicide rings true precisely because there are at least two sides to the question; their repudiation of the idea of suicide has such an air of reasonableness that the reader can recognize them as people and not merely as victimized puppets of Galsworthy's satire.

During the exchange of letters between Garnett and Galsworthy regarding Bosinney's suicide Galsworthy expressed concern about what seemed to him to be an even more serious problem in interpretation. He feared that both Edward and Constance Garnett wanted him "to end the book with a palpable and obvious defeat of Forsyteism by making the lovers run away happily." In trying to justify ending

the book as he had, he discussed his use of the "negative method."
He wrote:

> To my mind (and I desire to defeat Forsyteism) the only way to
> do so is to leave the Forsytes masters of the field. The only way
> to enlist the sympathies of readers on the other side, the only way to
> cap the purpose of the book, which was to leave property as *an
> empty shell*—is to leave the victory to Soames. If I finish, as you
> would like me to finish, I merely add another to those many books
> which people regard Κυνήσον. To make success of "illicit love" is to
> invite mockery. . . .
> We both wish to produce the same effect, we both hate the For-
> sytes and wish their destruction. Your instinct tells you to do it posi-
> tively, you would leave them defeated; my instinct tells me that it
> can only be done by me negatively; I would leave them victorious—
> but what a victory![4]

He believed that a positive defeat of the Forsytes would have involved
the special pleading of a reformer. From his point of view such a novel
would of necessity be more propaganda than art.

He worked throughout the summer of 1905 on the final revisions of
The Man of Property, which was published on March 23, 1906.
Though he accepted Garnett's first alternative and enveloped Bosinney's death with uncertainty, he would not be moved concerning the
ending. The victory belonged to the Forsytes. The book was favorably
reviewed, though it is amusing to note that the *Spectator* reluctantly
remarked that it was "unacceptable for general reading." With this
novel, as Galsworthy realized, his name as a writer was made.

Before evaluating Galsworthy's accomplishments in *The Man of
Property*, it is helpful to consider his philosophy of art. The phrase is
pompous, even reminiscent of Polonius, and like Polonius at his best
may promise more philosophizing and less art, but it does refer to the
scattered and not always consistent statements made by Galsworthy
about his work. As one studies Galsworthy and considers the various
critical reactions, it seems likely that many of the widely repeated
opinions of Galsworthy as an artist derive from misunderstandings or
misconceptions about what he was trying to do. A review of his

4 Marrot, *The Life and Letters of John Galsworthy*, 169.

aesthetics should provide a basis for determining what he was striving to accomplish in his work.

A frequent criticism is that Galsworthy was either an unrepentant propagandist for social reform or a sociological reporter, or both. Virginia Woolf, for example, in her essay "Mr. Bennett and Mrs. Brown," has given what is probably the most famous and devastating criticism of the work of Galsworthy and of his two contemporaries, H. G. Wells and Arnold Bennett. She complained that their books were incomplete. "In order to complete them," she wrote, "it seems necessary to do something—to join a society, or more desperately, to write a cheque." Fancy writing a check for the liberation of the underdogs in Galsworthy's works or establishing a society for the enlightenment of the Forsytes so that they would be less concerned with material things!

In order to keep his creative work free from propaganda, Galsworthy used what he called the "negative method" because he was concerned with what he felt were essential differences between art and propaganda. In a letter to Frank Lucas dated November 27, 1910, he connected the matter of forcing goodness on the reader (propaganda) with the technique of the negative method. His comments are illuminating:

> I must talk to you some day on that question (the most worrying of all to the artist) of how far it is possible to force goodness on the consciousness of the reader or spectator except by the negative methods. I'm always conscious of being a pelican in the wilderness, and a dangerous one. For instance, *The Man of Property*, being a picture of the *soul*-destroying effects of property, is taken by nearly all readers as an indication that I would like to forcibly and *politically* remove from people their wives and property. This is crudely put, but you know what I mean—the political mind (nine-tenths of our minds) cannot abide a spiritual idea without translating it at once into facts. Whereas the very essence of a spiritual idea is that you mustn't force it by machinery from without, but must let it germinate, until it forces the fulfilment from within.[5]

In this statement Galsworthy has made a clear distinction between propaganda—forcing an idea or attitude on the reader's consciousness—and art—presenting a spiritual idea, such as the soul-destroying

[5] *Ibid.*, 687–88.

effects of property, and letting it germinate into its own fulfillment in the reader's mind. Apropos of this difference between art and propaganda, Galsworthy believed that the novel was the best medium for communicating because by its very nature the novel

> is the great fertiliser, the quiet fertiliser of people's imagination. You cannot appreciate and weigh the influence it has, except in the case of novels frankly propagandistic, which, paradoxical as it may seem, have (in my opinion) the least real influence. To alter a line of action is nothing like so important as to alter or enlarge a point of view over life, a mood of living. Such enlargement is only attained by those temperamental expressions which we know as works of art and not as treatises in fiction-form.[6]

Of first importance for Galsworthy was the consideration that a work of art effect its purpose of giving revelation and delight. There should be no special pleading for any particular reforms that the artist may have in mind, for insofar as a work partakes of being a treatise it fails as a work of art. Inculcating goodness or ethical values in the reader should be done indirectly by enlarging the reader's view of life and by awakening his imagination. In his own handling of ethical values, as Galsworthy wrote to his sister, Mrs. R. E. Reynolds, on October 5, 1917: "I always have used the negative method—(I suspect because I *can't* use the other)—deliberately, from the hatred of preaching; from a sort of natural disgust at setting up to being a preacher on a lofty moral plane." In the same letter and elsewhere he iterated that as a creative artist he wished to avoid all party labels, thereby remaining uncommitted and impartial so that he could freely impugn redundancy or excess wherever he found it.

In short, because of his own temperamental dislike of preaching and because he rejected the propagandistic as the antithesis of art, he used the "negative method." What he meant by the phrase is best indicated by the following:

> The artist is no schoolmaster, can claim no teacher's temperament, and no direct function. His contribution (not inconsiderable) to social and ethical values must be by way of the painting of character and environment. But such painting may, so far as ethics are con-

[6] *Ibid.*, 720.

cerned, take either of two forms—the negative, quasi-satiric, which shows what men might be, by choosing defective characters and environments and giving their defects due prominence; or the epic, which shows what men might be, by choosing heroic characters, or earthly paradises, and stressing their virtues and delights. A novelist, like his readers, is disposed by Nature to one of these methods or to the other—occasionally to both. Realists and satirists practise the first, romanticists the second.

. . . I speak, no doubt, with the partiality of a practitioner—but to me the negative form seems far the more effective. Most of the great characters of fiction, certainly nearly all who have contributed to ethical values—Don Quixote, Sancho, Hamlet, Lear, Falstaff, Tom Jones, Faust, D'Artagnan, Sam Weller, Betsy Trotwood, Micawber, Becky Sharp, Major Pendennis, Bel-ami, Irina, Bazarov, Anna Karenin, have been conceived and painted in that manner. Readers do not like being led by the nose, any more than novelists . . . like leading them; they prefer to deduce for themselves, rather than to be shown the shining example. However it may be in life, in fiction the heroic too soon cloys the palate.[7]

If to this quotation is added a summary of Galsworthy's "A Novelist's Allegory" (written in 1908), a reasonably complete picture of his philosophy of art emerges. Unfortunately a summary cannot do justice to the charm and artistry of the essay, but the general purport of the allegory can at least be established.

The story is that of an old man, Cethru, who had been ordered by his prince, Felicitas, to carry a lantern through a street known as the Vita Publica. It is Cethru's duty to aid passers-by as they traverse the dark street. As time passes, Cethru succeeds in irritating various citizens because he has done nothing but carry the lantern through the street; he will not reassure them that all is well in front of their homes. Obediently doing his duty even gets him into trouble with the authorities; on one occasion as he is carrying his lantern he becomes involved in three different criminal charges: (1) the light from his lantern shines upon a girl drowning; a young man seeing her plight rescues her but in the process ruins his clothes and catches a fever; Cethru is charged with vagabondage; (2) the lantern makes it possible for the watchman to see three footpads, and in attempting to

[7] John Galsworthy, The Works of John Galsworthy, VII, xi–xii.

arrest them, he is severely beaten; Cethru is charged with complicity in the assault; (3) a wealthy merchant, Pranzo, is sickened at the sight of a beggarwoman and her children foraging for garbage; Cethru was charged with inciting rebellion and anarchy. When arraigned, Cethru's only comment is "Can I help what my lanthorn sees?" Finally, just as the judges are ready to pass sentence, a young advocate rises and speaks in the old man's defense:

> And when, Sirs, this pale flame [of the lantern] has sprung into the air swaying to every wind, it brings vision to the human eye. And, if it be charged on this old man Cethru that he and his lanthorn by reason of their showing not only the good but the evil bring no pleasure into the world, I ask, Sirs, what in the world is so dear as this power to see—whether it be the beautiful or the foul that is disclosed? . . . For Sirs, the lanthorn did but show that which was there, both fair and foul, no more, no less. . . . And I would have you note this, Sirs, that by this impartial discovery of the proportions of one thing to another, this lanthorn must indeed perpetually seem to cloud and sadden those things which are fair, because of the deep instincts of harmony and justice planted in the human breast.[8]

In these paragraphs the strong emphasis Galsworthy placed on the writer's assiduous regard for truth can hardly have escaped notice, for to him reality (however pleasant or unpleasant) was the touchstone of life as well as of art. To his way of thinking this reality required both the physical and the spiritual—the spiritual without the physical was impossible. Illustrative of their inseparability is Galsworthy's statement: ". . . all claim that there is some mysterious way of apprehending the Universe and God other than through the mentality and emotions of the human being (that is, through the senses and their higher products) is inadmissible. . . ." Needless to say, he always portrayed these elements inextricably bound together.

Truth thus being the basis of his art, the artist, like the scientist, has to be impartial in his investigation of it—as Cethru's lantern shone on everything without regard for the consequences. A concomitant aspect of art for Galsworthy was its impersonal quality; art was not concerned with the author's personality. While keeping his own personality out of his work, the novelist should permit his novels to evoke the

[8] *Ibid.*, 191–92.

flavor or essence of their creator. Because a true vision of reality is colored by the seer, Galsworthy believed that both the vision and the coloring should be evident. In this way the work would have "the essential novelty of a living thing." Relevant to this point is his observation that the artist's temperament will supply all the necessary moral and meaning. In *The Forsyte Saga*, to look ahead briefly, Galsworthy made the coloring evident by his use of satire and lyricism. The major emphasis being on the Forsytes and their materialistic philosophy, he developed this subject matter satirically. The treatment of Irene and the philosophy of beauty he presented lyrically. He gave expression to his own artistic temperament by using satire and lyricism in this way, and he controlled his presentation of the *Saga* by relying on the negative method.

The final element in his aesthetics is concerned with the relativity of truth. Since truth is relative, its reflection in art must accordingly be relative. Neither can be dogmatic, for neither can discover an absolute answer. In reflecting truth, art is ever concerned with achieving perfection, just as truth itself is striving for perfection. Galsworthy the man and Galsworthy the artist subscribed to this ultimate faith in balance and harmony, or what he has called "Perfection for Perfection's sake."

To him the creative principle itself was cosmic: "This impulse to create is itself the Good—the God. . . . God is the joy of making things for ever, good, bad, or indifferent, but good for choice." The universe or first cause manifested the urge to create and in this manifestation was like an artist, and man the artist emulated the divine principle. Although perfection for perfection's sake was an unobtainable goal, still it was worth striving for.

A corollary of this creed was his belief that the worship of art or the cult of beauty—which was to Galsworthy another way of saying, "A higher and wider conception of the dignity of human life"—had made possible man's emergence from the animal man into the human man. Galsworthy succinctly characterized the artist when he wrote: "Is not the artist, of all men, foe and nullifier of partisanship and parochialism, of distortions and extravagance, the discoverer of that jack-o'-lantern— Truth; for, if Truth be not Spiritual Proportion I know not what it is?"

The main points of Galsworthy's philosophy of art may be sum-

143

marized as follows: Art attains its purpose of revelation and delight when it is able "to alter or enlarge a point of view over life, a mood of living" or when it increases the reader's "power to see." Art fails insofar as it is blatantly didactic or propagandist. For Galsworthy the artist's job was to present life as he honestly saw it, whether pleasant or unpleasant, in an impartial, self-effacing manner, and in his own work he employed the negative method as best suited to his temperament.

It should now be possible to discuss and evaluate *The Man of Property* on its own terms. The novel focuses on the Forsytes, an upper-middle-class family of propertied and professional wealth. Their world is one of the comfortable tangibles of existence: no sentiment, for sentiment does not pay. But property, social position, a suitable return on one's investment, and self-preservation—in short, triumphant materialism—do pay. Accustomed to mastery in their affairs, the Forsytes are unprepared for the discovery that beauty and passion are forces that are not always amenable to the rules of a materialistic, possessive world. Galsworthy described the theme of the work in these words: ". . . our earthly paradise is still a rich preserve where the wild raiders, Beauty and Passion, come stealing in, filching security from beneath our noses."

The novel opens as the Forsytes in their highest efflorescence gather at Old Jolyon's "at home" to celebrate June's engagement to the young architect Philip Bosinney. Because the occasion is an important social event for the family, all but two of the important Forsytes—Uncle Timothy and Young Jolyon—are present. By their absence these two Forsytes define the polar limits of the Forsyte world.

Timothy, who outdoes all the other Forsytes in his Forsyteism, is absent ostensibly because he fears he might catch diphtheria. He is characterized by his isolation even from the other Forsytes as a result of carrying his version of their creed of self-preservation too far. Certain that an economic recession is bound to come, he has sold his share in a profitable publishing company during a time of prosperity and invested the quite conspicuous proceeds in three per cent consols. By this act he had at once assumed an isolated position, no other Forsyte being content with less than four per cent for his money; and this isolation had slowly and surely undermined a spirit perhaps better than commonly endowed with caution. He had become almost a myth—a kind of incarnation of security haunting the background of the Forsyte universe. He had never committed the imprudence of marrying, or encumbering himself in any way with children.

At the other extreme is Young Jolyon, who had repudiated Forsyte principles fifteen years before when he deserted his wife and child and ran off with a foreign governess.

These two Forsytes exemplify the extremes which circumscribe the Forsyte world, and the struggle between these extremes—pure Forsyteism versus non-Forsyteism—supplies the basis for the action of *The Man of Property* and ultimately for the entire *Forsyte Saga*.

The novel utilizes two plots to tell its story of the impact of beauty and passion on the Forsyte world. The main plot concerns Old Jolyon, the head of the family, and Forsyte family unity. Jolyon, faced with the increasing loneliness of old age, has found Forsyteism insufficient to his needs. Desiring something more than wealth and position to answer to his heart's emptiness, he turns to his son, Young Jolyon, and Young Jolyon's family for comfort and companionship. The subplot concerns Soames and his unhappy marriage to Irene. Though irresistibly attracted by beauty, Soames is incapable of appreciating it for its own sake. Whether it be a painting, a wife, or a house, he has to own it because it is valuable as an investment. When Irene discovers that she does not and cannot love Soames, she asks for her freedom. Divorce being contrary to Forsyte principles, Soames refuses. In his own way he loves and admires her, and he is willing to endure a great deal if she will fulfill even minimally her role as his wife. She resents bitterly her husband's desire to own her, and she falls in love with Bosinney, the young architect who is designing Soames's new country home at Robin Hill.

In the main plot Old Jolyon becomes increasingly irritated by the fact that Soames's difficulties with Irene are interfering with his affairs. June, his granddaughter, has lost Bosinney to Irene because Soames has been unable to manage his wife. Old Jolyon's anger at further instances of what seem family interference prompts him to censure the family for its meddling. Soames, not understanding Irene's behavior but suspecting her interest in Bosinney, informs her that he intends to ruin Bosinney because the architect has exceeded the financial limits agreed upon for decorating the house. Irene's persistent refusal to be a wife to him finally drives him to the desperate act of raping her. Later Soames wins his case against Bosinney and returns home to find that Irene has left him. Only later do the Forsytes learn that Bosinney has been killed in the fog. Irene, having nowhere else to go, returns to Soames. The novel ends as Young Jolyon, sent as an emissary from Old Jolyon to Irene, has the door slammed in his face as Soames announces, "We are not at home."

The way Galsworthy handled the love affair in the subplot shows how carefully he managed his materials to gain the maximum effect. Up to the point in the subplot when Irene locks Soames out of the bedroom because of his threat to ruin Bosinney, the subplot has focused completely on the difficulties Soames has been having with the house at Robin Hill; consequently, his difficulties with Irene (including the love affair with Bosinney) have remained in the background. Presenting the lovers in this oblique way kept the primary emphasis on the more commonly accepted connotation of property, that is, property in the sense of material possessions such as houses and bank accounts. And for the Forsytes that is where the emphasis belonged. A fuller and more direct treatment of the affair would have detracted from the main concern of the novel—Forsyteism.

In perspective, the movement of the novel from its beginning—Old Jolyon's "at home" to its conclusion, Soames's "we are not at home"— has illustrated how disturbing beauty and passion can be in a possessive world. The logic justifying the two plots is probably to be found in the fact that *The Man of Property* has shown how two kinds of love, paternal and sexual, have succeeded in destroying the unity of the family and have destroyed in all but name the marital relationship between man and wife.

From the beginning of *The Man of Property*, Galsworthy is in effective command of his material. His satire is certain, as the following quotation shows:

When a Forsyte was engaged, married, or born, the Forsytes were present; when a Forsyte died—but no Forsyte had as yet died; they did not die; death being contrary to their principles, they took pre-

146

cautions against it, the instinctive precautions of highly vitalized persons who resent encroachments on their property.

The phrasing suggests the overassertive self-righteousness of persons who would tolerate no tampering with their principles or property. Moreover, their amusing if startling attitude toward death (the idea of considering one's body as part of one's property may be eccentric, but it is not absurd) is memorable. The Forsytes, who provide rich and varied opportunities for the satiric, are such vitalized personages that they are real enough and large enough to provoke satire without being overwhelmed by it.

Galsworthy used the omniscient-author convention with deliberate care so that the handling of the material would enhance the artistic effect. The point of view was restricted mainly to the Forsytes, members of a class whose outlook he shared. Un-Forsytean characters like Irene or Bosinney are presented only indirectly, that is, as seen through the eyes of the Forsytes. But Galsworthy as author was not limited to the Forsyte vision; he encircled it and could look into it from outside. Therefore, occasionally he commented from his own larger, omniscient point of view. Yet he tried to minimize the effect of such intrusions by relating comment in the third person as impersonally and unobtrusively as possible, thereby making his role inconspicuous.

The tendency of readers to take sides in the enduring struggle and favor either Irene or Soames, while probably a tribute to Galsworthy's ability as a creator of character, is likely to involve the reader in judgments which are at best tangential. To take sides is to risk losing the "perception of the simple truth, which underlies the whole story, that where sex attraction is utterly and definitely lacking in one partner to a union, no amount of pity, or reason, or duty, or what not, can overcome a repulsion implicit in Nature." Throughout the novel he remained deliberately impartial: each is guilty, each is a victim. He said simply, "I have not attempted to set up Irene or Bosinney, because I have not attempted to set up Soames."

The publication of *The Man of Property* tells but half the story of Galsworthy's literary achievement in 1906. Just as Ada Galsworthy's suggestion persuaded him to attempt writing, so also did her advice that he attempt playwriting meet with success. It was perhaps due to her influence that Galsworthy first tried to put the Forsyte material into dramatic form as *The Civilised*. Despite his failure in that instance, Ada's persistence and a recommendation from Garnett in the autumn of 1905 that he write a play for Granville Barker and J. E. Vedrenne, managers of the Court Theatre, were ultimately successful. Galsworthy's immediate response to Garnett's suggestion was an unequivocal refusal; nevertheless, he began working on a play in January, 1906. Within six weeks he had completed *The Silver Box* and sent it to Barker and Vedrenne. Barker and George Bernard Shaw read it the next day and accepted it on the following day. As Galsworthy said, it was "probably a record for a first play." Its opening performance on September 25, 1906, at the Court Theatre brilliantly inaugurated Galsworthy's career as an important dramatist.

The publication of one of his greatest novels in March was thus followed by the production in the professional theater of his first play, and before the year was out he had completed his next novel, *The Country House*. Moreover, his marriage to Ada had freed him from a compromising social position, and he was free to explore a new field for his creative abilities.

Spurred on by the consciousness of what he had achieved and confident of his abilities, Galsworthy was able to produce in the years 1906 to 1910 a substantial body of work of high artistry. In 1908 he published *A Commentary*, a volume of essays of social comment. He wrote four full-length plays—*Joy* (produced in 1907), *Strife* (produced in 1909), *The Eldest Son* (produced in 1912), and *Justice* (produced in 1910). He wrote three novels: *The Country House* (1907), *Fraternity* (1909), and *The Patrician* (completed in 1910 but not published until 1911). He produced a number of miscellaneous and critical pieces, and his revisions of *Villa Rubein, A Man of Devon,* and *The Island Pharisees* became on occasion almost rewritings.

In addition to his work as a novelist, dramatist, and essayist, he had become a public man who gave generously of his money, time, and energy to various crusades and charities. Two of his major crusades during the years 1906 to 1910 concerned the unsuccessful attempt to abolish play censorship and the successful crusade for prison reform, to meliorate the punishment of prisoners by solitary confinement. Throughout his life he continued to support many causes; in fact, his steady and active commitment to the service of others was such an integral part of Galsworthy that no discussion of him would be just which did not mention some of his humanitarian activities: "sweated industries" (minimum wage), woman suffrage, divorce-law reform, slaughterhouse reform, slum clearance, anti-vivisection of dogs, and the P.E.N. Club. Galsworthy customarily gave away half of his income, but during World War I he increased his private contributions to about three-fourths of his income, and, in addition, the royalties he earned from everything he published during the war were given to various war and relief funds. One of his last gifts was a trust fund for the P.E.N. Club, set up with the Nobel Prize money, a sum of more than nine thousand pounds. Although the total amount of money he gave is incalculable, the figure would obviously run to thousands of pounds.

As indicated above, during the years 1906 to 1910 Galsworthy enjoyed an impressive creative period. Four aspects of his writings of this period will indicate his development in literary technique, characterization, and social philosophy.

While Galsworthy was finishing the revisions of *The Man of Property*, he became interested in writing two novels which would serve as sequels to it. The sequels would explore through character rather than story "the utter disharmony of the Christian religion with the English character," a theme that had been manifest in *The Island Pharisees* and *The Man of Property*. As he worked on the first sequel, to be called *Danae*, certain of his characters—Mr. Pendyce, the spaniel John, and Mrs. Pendyce—ran away with the book, and in the end a quite different novel resulted; it was published on March 2, 1907, as *The Country House*. With the change from *Danae* to *The Country House*, Galsworthy dropped the idea of the two sequels to *The Man of Property*.

Although the idea of direct sequels was discarded, however, it is significant to note that his novels from *The Island Pharisees* through *The Patrician* form, as it were, indirect sequels in that they are related thematically; their focus is on presenting satiric portraits of four sections of upper-class English society. *The Island Pharisees* began the series with a satiric, generalized portrait of that society; *The Man of Property* dealt specifically with the propertied, professional class; *The*

Country House, the landed gentry; *Fraternity,* the intelligentsia; and *The Patrician,* the aristocracy.

The second aspect of his work concerns his accomplishment as a dramatist. During his career he established himself as a major playwright by writing twenty full-length plays, eight of which were important successes in their own day. Drama, perhaps because of its public nature and because of its frequent need to be contemporary, seems to be a very difficult genre in which to achieve lasting success or fame. Whether Galsworthy's achievements in drama will warrant as much as a passing footnote may be debatable, and yet considerable merit is to be found in a number of his plays. His most important dramas include *The Silver Box, Strife, Justice, The Skin Game, Loyalties,* and *Escape,* for they were critical successes in their own time. There are other plays, however, such as *The Foundations* and perhaps *A Family Man,* which, while not well received at the time, merit reconsideration.

Galsworthy described in some detail what seemed to him to be distinctive about his dramatic technique. He acknowledged that the scenes in his plays and his novels were similar because in both he tried to create an "intensely exact and actual reproduction of people talking, and the room or what not in which they talk." He called his method the "actual brickwork technique" and remarked that it refused "from end to end to take *any liberty at all with perfect naturalness and actuality of expression.*" The success of this technique depended on "absolute fidelity"—a fidelity which put "a great strain on invention and device" and which ruled out "wit (not humor) and lyricism, except such as . . . [was] implicit in the theme." Galsworthy believed that such a technique put "a special kind of grip of the audience that no other technique"[9] would achieve.

Two scenes—one from *Strife* and one from *Justice*—come to mind as examples of Galsworthy's ability to realize his dramatic effect. In both scenes he achieved the impact, paradoxically, by total silence. In *Strife* the scene is the climactic one in which the two enemy leaders—Anthony, chairman of the company, and Roberts, the strike leader—have been newly deposed because of their unwillingness to compromise.

[9] Rudolf Sauter, *Galsworthy the Man: An Intimate Portrait,* 153.

When the two men confront each other, the stage directions read as follows:

ANTHONY rises with an effort. He turns to ROBERTS who looks at him. They stand several seconds, gazing at each other fixedly; ANTHONY lifts his hand, as though to salute, but lets it fall. The expression of ROBERTS' face changes from hostility to wonder. They bend their heads in token of respect. ANTHONY turns, and slowly walks towards the curtained door. . . . ROBERTS remains motionless for several seconds, staring intently after ANTHONY, then goes out into the hall.

This moment of recognition says more by its silence and suppressed gestures than many a scene can manage with a flurry of words and action.

The scene from *Justice*, act 3, scene 3, may well be the most famous scene in all Galsworthy's plays. Falder—young, weak, and a first offender—is enduring the rigors of solitary confinement (at the time all English prisoners served at least three months of solitary confinement). The stage directions describe his reactions:

. . . he begins pacing the cell, moving his head. He stops again at the door, listens, and, placing the palms of his hands against it with his fingers spread out, leans his forehead against the iron. Turning from it presently, he moves slowly back towards the window, tracing his way with his finger along the top line of the distemper that runs around the walls. He stops under the window, and, picking up the lid of one of the tins, peers into it, as if trying to make a companion of his own face. It has grown very nearly dark. Suddenly the lid falls out of his hand with a clatter—the only sound that has broken the silence. . . . There is a sharp tap and click; the cell light behind the glass screen has been turned up. The cell is brightly lighted. FALDER is seen gasping for breath.

A sound from far away, as of distant, dull beating on thick metal, is suddenly audible. FALDER shrinks back, not able to bear this sudden clamour. But the sound grows, as though some great tumbril were rolling toward the cell. And gradually it seems to hypnotise him. He begins creeping inch by inch nearer to the door. The banging sound, travelling from cell to cell, draws closer and closer; FALDER's hands are seen moving as if his spirit has already joined in this beating, and the sound swells till it seems to have entered the

151

very cell. He suddenly raises his clenched fists. Panting violently, he flings himself at his door, and beats on it.[10]

The dramatic effect of this scene is unforgettable and indicates the power and imagination that Galsworthy at his best could use to involve the audience in his drama. The very fact that this scene of terrible silence had such an impact probably accounted for the widespread belief that the play was primarily a propaganda piece against solitary confinement. In this perspective it is important to note Galsworthy's statement that "*Justice* tried to paint a picture of how the herd (in crude self-preservation) gore to death its weak members—with the moral of how jolly consistent that is with a religion that worships 'Gentle Jesus!'" Concerning prison reform Galsworthy remarked, "The public—bless them—take it for a tract on solitary confinement (which incidentally it was—but only incidentally!)."

One of Galsworthy's distinguished novels, *Fraternity*, written during this period, illustrates a third aspect of his work. Distinctively Galsworthian both in its strength and in its weaknesses, the novel possesses a corrosive quality that continues to haunt the reader's memory long after the novel has been finished.

Shadows, the title originally planned for this novel, suggests one important motif to be found in the novel: the poor are shadows of the prosperous and secure. But the major emphasis of the novel is on the meaningfulness of brotherhood in the comfortable if troubled world of the Dallisons. In portraying their world, Galsworthy relies on a schematic pattern which seems too artificial, too balanced, and even too representative of various opinions or ideas. Such carefully planned patterning often occurs in Galsworthy's work and weakens the overall effect because the reader rightly tends to resent what seems to be obvious and artificial manipulation. A brief review of the novel illustrates this weakness and at the same time indicates the power of the novel to haunt the memory.

Hilary Dallison and his wife, Bianca, represent the arts; he is an author, she a painter. Although they are not on good terms with one another, they remain together because it is the civilized thing to do. Both suffer from severe cases of overintellectualized refinement and as

---

[10] Galsworthy, *The Works of John Galsworthy*, XIX, 98–99.

a consequence find it impossible to express human, even vulgar, needs and desires. Paralysis of the will overrides all. The denial of all that is human and meaningful is perhaps most sharply defined by their dog Miranda, who finds not a brave new world of people but a perfect world with a perfect artificial dog:

> ... Miranda found what she had been looking for all her life. It had no smell, made no movement, was pale-grey in colour, like herself. It had no hair that she could find; its tail was like her own; it took no liberties, was silent, had no passions, committed her to nothing. ... Suddenly she slithered out her slender grey-pink tongue and licked its nose. The creature moved a little way and stopped. Miranda saw that it had wheels. She lay down close to it, for she knew it was the perfect dog.

The Stephen Dallisons, in contrast, enjoy a reasonably contented family life. Stephen, Hilary's younger brother, is a successful barrister; Cecilia, his wife, is Bianca's older sister and an accomplished wife and mother; and Thyme is their charming grown daughter. Thyme and her cousin, young Martin Stone, spend a great deal of time together. Martin is known as "The Sanitist" because he is studying to be a doctor and believes, therefore, that such measures as proper sanitation and the like will provide the answers to mankind's problems. Thyme tries to help him in his work in the slums.

Sylvanus Stone, the father of Cecilia and Bianca, is the voice of the prophet crying in the wilderness for universal brotherhood. Formerly a brilliant natural scientist, he suffered from a serious illness when he was seventy and during his convalescence has turned with all the perseverance of a monomaniac to the idea of the brotherhood of all, becoming a latter-day combination of Saint Francis and Don Quixote. His whole life is now spent writing his *Book of Universal Brotherhood.* Although he is ascetic, gentle, well-intentioned, and rather admirable, his obsession makes him incapable of alleviating the distress of others; he can only sympathize with their sufferings, as the miserably unhappy Bianca discovers when she comes to him for help.

Two lesser characters, Mrs. Tallents Smallpeace and Mr. Purcey, serve to round off the world of the Dallisons. Mrs. Smallpeace is "secretary of the League for Educating Orphans who have Lost both

Parents, vice-president of the Forlorn Hope for Maids in Peril, and treasurer to Thursday Hops for Working Girls." Purcey, a junior partner in a banking house, spends his spare time driving around in his A.1 Damyer, perhaps as suitable an occupation for this self-confident Philistine as can be imagined.

The principal inhabitants of the world of shadows are Ivy Barton, or the Little Model, the Hughs family, and Joshua Creed, formerly a butler but now reduced to selling newspapers. Ivy Barton is a young woman from the west country; she enters the Dallison world by serving as a model of a woman of the streets for Bianca's painting *The Shadow*. Knowing that she is sexually attractive, the Little Model sets her cap for Hilary, who, because of his estrangement from Bianca, is vulnerable. With little to lose, Hilary is tempted for a few hours to go away with Ivy and live abroad; but, recognizing that their life together would be impossible, he gives her £150 and leaves. Being a practical young woman, she has a good cry and then carefully puts the money in a secure place.

Various solutions for mankind's problems are explored in the novel: the poor like the Hughses and the Little Model survive as they can; Hilary intellectualizes everything to the point that he is incapable of action; Stephen sends checks to his favorite charities; young Martin's remedy is better health measures; Stone expounds the theme of brotherhood; and Thyme tries to help Martin but finds she cannot face the squalor.

At the end Hilary has left the country, never to return to Bianca. That night Bianca—proud, miserable, and, except for her father's company, alone—sits brooding in her bedroom, haunted by a vision of the Little Model; feeling the need for fresh air, she goes to a window overlooking the garden. Unexpectedly, a shadow moves in the garden and she overhears her father talking to the universe, confessing his failure to "discover to my brothers that they are one. I am not worthy to stay here. Let me pass into You, and die!" To the night he calls out, "Brothers!" A policeman passing by hears the voice and uses his lantern to search "for those who had been addressed. Satisfied, apparently, that no one was there, he moved it to right and left, lowered it to the level of his breast, and walked slowly on." A visionary's cry in the night for brotherhood addressed to no one is an effective image to express the impossible ideal of fraternity.

The fourth aspect of Galsworthy's work in this period concerns the shifting pattern found in his writings. While still at work on *The Patrician*, Galsworthy observed that it was less satiric than the others of the series; he said, in fact, that there had been as the series progressed a continuing decrescendo in the satiric and an increasing attempt for the lyric and the beautiful. As one possible explanation of this development he suggested that there is so much that one can't express in the dramatic form that one tends naturally in the novel to make up to oneself and write out one's feeling for beauty more and more in the novel form." The shift from the satiric to the lyric is one of his important characteristics as an artist. His whole literary career can be described in terms of this shifting pattern; Galsworthy himself epitomized his career in three sentences: "My early work was certainly more emotional than critical. But from 1901 came nine years when the critical was, in the main, holding sway. From 1910 to 1918 the emotional again struggled for the upper hand; and from that time on there seems to have been something of a 'dead heat.' "

Galsworthy devoted most of 1911 to drama and the theater. In the succeeding year he published his first volume of poems, *Moods, Songs, and Doggerels*. His work as a poet is not memorable; too frequently the poems seem pallid, labored, and banal. Other representative works of this lyrical period include *The Inn of Tranquillity* (1912)—a collection of short pieces "which has for main object the rendering of mood, feeling, philosophy, and atmosphere, rather than the telling of a tale"; novels—*The Dark Flower* (1913), *The Freelands* (1915), and *Beyond* (1917); and plays—*The Mob* (finished in 1913 and first produced on March 30, 1914) and *A Bit o' Love* (finished February 26, 1914, and first produced on May 25, 1915).

Galsworthy was profoundly shocked by the horrors of World War I. Having reached his forty-seventh birthday shortly after the outbreak of war and too old for military service, he felt that he was probably of more use to the war effort by writing and by giving all that he could afford. In November, 1916, he and Ada went to France, where they worked for several months at a hospital for injured French soldiers.

The amount of time and effort he spent in wartime duties is undoubtedly partly responsible for the artistic decline noted in some of his works written during the war. This artistic decline probably explains the poor reception given *A Bit o' Love* and *The Freelands*.

In 1916, however, Galsworthy showed signs of regaining his artistic powers. In that year he wrote three of his finest and most famous long short stories—"A Stoic," "The Apple Tree," and "The Juryman." Not long thereafter, in the second quarter of 1917, he resumed his treatment of the Forsytes with the composition of "Indian Summer of a Forsyte." Another long short story, "The First and the Last" (written in 1913 and 1914), was included with these four stories and they were published as *Five Tales* on July 25, 1918.

The fact that he followed the decline of his powers with a return to the genre of long short story and to the Forsytes seems strikingly parallel to his development in the years 1901 to 1906. In accord with his predominant concern for the lyric, he wrote a lyrical tale of Old Jolyon's death. Just as the short story dealing with Swithin released his satiric abilities and led him on to *The Man of Property*, so the "Indian Summer of a Forsyte" seems to have released both his lyric and satiric abilities and led him on to the completion of the *Saga*. In both periods, he used the long short story as the form by which he attained a high level of artistic achievement, and in both periods he used the Forsytes as the springboard for more complete treatments of his subject matter.

It was just three days after the publication of *Five Tales* that he first conceived the idea of making *The Man of Property* the first part of a series of novels and short stories to be known as *The Forsyte Saga*. Galsworthy tells of the experience in his notebook:

> We stayed on at Wingstone till the end of August, during which I began the Second Part of *The Forsyte Saga*, to be called *The Second Flowering*. The idea of making *The Man of Property* the first volume of a trilogy cemented by *Indian Summer of a Forsyte* and another short episode came to me on Sunday, July 28th, and I started the same day. This idea, if I can ever bring it to fruition, will make *The Forsyte Saga* a volume of half a million words nearly; and the most sustained and considerable piece of fiction of our generation at least.[11]

As he says, he began working on the second volume immediately. There were the usual myriad interruptions to his work on the *Saga*. In April, 1918, he had undertaken the editorship of *Reveille*, a magazine published for the benefit of disabled soldiers, and he remained the editor until February 1, 1919, when he and Ada left England for a lecture tour of the United States. Throughout this period he was at work on the Forsytes. The second novel was completed by early November, 1919, and was published on October 22, 1920, with the new title *In Chancery*. The second interlude, "Awakening," was published on November 18, 1920.

He began work on the final volume, *To Let*, in January, 1920, while touring Spain, and had finished it by October 20 of that same year. With its publication he had reached a pinnacle of achievement. The appearance in 1922 of a one-volume edition of the *Saga* made him for the first time a popular writer and brought his work into the best-seller category.

The idea of continuing *The Man of Property* with two sequels, it will be recalled, had been Galsworthy's earlier intention. That plan did not work out, however, and the novel *Danae* was transformed into *The Country House*. A further exploration of Forsyte materials, nevertheless, remained in his mind; in his letters he made several references to a continuation using Young Jolyon and Old Jolyon, and in his preface to *Five Tales* for the Manaton Edition he remarked ". . . as for 'Indian Summer'—I knew I should write it some day, soon after 'The Man of Property' came out in 1906." Thus in 1918, with "Indian Summer" continuing *The Man of Property*, the pattern for the rest of the *Saga* fell into place—satiric novel, lyric interlude, satiric novel, lyric interlude, and satiric novel.

The end of *The Man of Property*, had showed the family unity of the Forsytes shattered by the struggle between property and beauty. "Indian Summer" begins almost five years later, in 1892, and tells of Old Jolyon's serene and rich enjoyment of the pleasures of living as his life draws to an end. Because of its idyllic tone and its subject matter, the story functions as a lyrical interlude between *The Man of Property* and *In Chancery*. Old Jolyon as the family patriarch has rejected Forsyteism and become a convert to a worship of beauty. His love of

[11] Marrot, *The Life and Letters of John Galsworthy*, 443.

beauty for its own sake without any material reward has won Irene's affection, but this victory for Old Jolyon, in sharp contrast to Soames's defeat, is not without cost. Love of beauty must be paid for—one must be willing to give of oneself. Old Jolyon finds the presence of beauty worth striving for, even at the cost of overexertion, and the result is his death. Such a sacrifice for something immaterial is, of course, the antithesis of Forsyteism. This short story thus makes clear the reason for the opposition between beauty and property. Because the love which has developed between Old Jolyon and Irene has succeeded in allying beauty to Jolyon's branch of the family, the remainder of the *Saga* will be concerned with the struggle between the lineage that admires beauty and the "man of property" and his descendants who wish to own it.

The second novel, *In Chancery*, opens in 1899, seven years after "Indian Summer." Whereas *The Man of Property* is relatively simple with only one subplot, *In Chancery* is more complex. The main plot concerns the fact that Soames's Forsyteism is incomplete because he lacks an heir. His desire for an heir makes it necessary for him to regain Irene or, as a last resort, to obtain a divorce so that he can marry again. There are four subplots: Soames's sister, Winifred, faced with the loss of her property when her husband runs away with a Spanish dancer, tries to free herself from being in chancery either by getting a divorce or by persuading her husband to return; Soames's efforts to regain Irene make him and Young Jolyon rivals for Irene's affection; Val, Winifred's son, quarrels with Jolly, Young Jolyon's son, because Val is in love with Jolly's sister; and Timothy's extreme Forsyteism is threatened by various developments on the family level—divorces and feuds—and on the national level—the Boer War.

The greater complexity of *In Chancery* is consistent with the subject matter of the novel, the basic theme of which is that Forsyteism continues to flourish because it has learned to accommodate itself to changing conditions in society. The Forsyte attitude has changed "from self-contented and contained provincialism to still more self-contented if less contained imperialism . . ."; and the possessive instinct is no longer found in the collective form represented by Forsyte 'Change. Family unity has been shattered. The spirit of possession flourishes on the smaller scale of the separate families and individual members. Unable to own others, the emphasis shifts and becomes self-centered. The connotations of the title—the Court of Chancery, litigation, the unavoidable and expensive court costs, and, figuratively, an awkward situation—foreshadow the greater complexity of the novel. Court cases are usually in the nature of a fight and the pugilistic connotation of the phrase "in chancery" is present in all the subplots: two involve divorce cases; one involves the continuing feud between the two families, including an actual fight between Val and Jolly and also their subsequent fighting in the Boer War; and one involves the reactions on Forsyte 'Change to the Boer War.

Soames's efforts to escape the trap of being married to but separated from Irene culminate in a scene of comic irony, when Soames is read a description of himself as Irene's guilty lover. The irony of the situation lies in the truth of the accusation. In the struggle between Soames and Irene he was the guilty lover; his inability to give of himself and his need to own her drove Irene from him. Soames obtains a divorce and marries Annette, a French girl.

At the end of the novel all Soames's hopes for an heir are seriously threatened when Soames learns that Annette's condition was critical. He has to choose between Annette and their child. Knowing that Annette will probably be unable to have any more children, Soames, rather than face the future without an heir, decides to risk Annette's life to save the baby's life and hopes that Annette will survive. Fortunately events turn out well, and he succeeds in attaining the one thing necessary to fulfill his Forsyte desires—he had an heiress, Fleur, for his fortune.

The next link in the *Saga* is the lyric interlude "Awakening." The action takes place in about six hours on a late afternoon in July, 1909. Jon, the eight-year-old son of Irene and Young Jolyon, discovers the importance of beauty in his life. Jon's awakening to the importance of beauty, while not directly affecting the Forsytes themselves, has repercussions on his own Forsyte world of childhood—a world richly encumbered with all that money can buy. Finding that this world does not protect him from loneliness, Jon turns to his mother, who opened his eyes to the world of beauty. His conversion has carried the *Saga* one step further in its development; just as the possessive instinct has continued in the successive generations, so, too, the admiration of beauty has lived on. By implication, Jon's discovery contains the possibility that his adherence to beauty can have more direct repercussions on the Forsytes in the future.

To Let, the final novel of the Saga, continues the struggle between Forsyteism and beauty. The conflict between Soames and Young Jolyon and Irene bursts forth again, the fuel being supplied by the romance between Forsytes of the younger generation—Fleur and Jon. Soames, as the exemplar of Forsyteism, dominates the main plot. There are three subplots: Young Jolyon and Irene, fearful of any relationship with Soames's family, try to keep Jon ignorant of the past; Fleur and Jon, defying the past, fall in love; and the Timothy material focuses on Forsyteism in an advanced state of senility and second childhood.

Soames tries to keep Fleur away from Jon and ignorant of the past, just as Young Jolyon and Irene try to do with Jon, but the very fact that there is something forbidden about their relationship prompt Jon and Fleur to go on seeing one another until they fall in love despite parental disapproval.

Soames's Forsyte nature has been modified as a result of previous experiences: "His possessive instinct, subtle, less formal, more elastic since the War, kept all misgiving underground." His inability to control events in To Let develop cumulatively in three stages: (1) he recognizes his helplessness concerning Annette's carryings-on and accepts it because he is indifferent to her; he has had as much of her as he desired, and he does not want a scandal; (2) Soames's helplessness regarding Fleur is of much greater moment, for he has learned to "put up with things" to keep her affection; and (3) he is more than helpless in the relationship between his family and Young Jolyon's because his very presence would arouse forces which would work actively against him; the fact that he is the obstacle preventing any rapprochement with Jolyon's family is of greatest moment because it endangers his relationship with Fleur, and for the first time in the Saga Soames had been forced to admit that he himself was the cause of the alienation between possessiveness and beauty.

Fleur, headstrong and tenacious like her father, is determined at all costs to have Jon, and, also like her father loses everything as a result. From the very beginning Fleur takes the lead, using deception to get what she wants, whatever the cost. Jon follows her lead reluctantly, for he strongly disapproves of double dealing. To get what she wants Fleur even lies to Jon and continues to ride roughshod over others. Soames goes to see Irene in an effort to settle the business between Fleur and Jon. Believing that he is not likely to see Irene again, Soames asks her to shake hands "and let the past die." Irene refuses, and when Jon sees his mother's aversion, he has his first real understanding of the suffering wrought by an unhappy marriage. This insight, his knowledge of Fleur's possessiveness and her stratagems—convince him that marrying Fleur would not bring happiness. He realizes that Fleur is, after all, a Forsyte like her father. Stung by Jon's rejection, Fleur marries young Michael Mont on the rebound.

The end of the old Forsytes comes with the death of Uncle Timothy. After the funeral Soames unexpectedly passes Irene and turns to see her once more. "She, too, was looking back. Suddenly she lifted her gloved hand, her lips smiled faintly, her dark eyes seemed to speak. It was the turn of Soames to make no answer to that smile and that little farewell wave. . . . He knew what she had meant to say: 'Now that I am going for ever out of the reach of you and yours—forgive me; I wish you well.' "

Several days later Soames goes to Highgate Cemetery to inspect the family vault. In his melancholy he muses about the past and looks into the future. He suspects that the possessive instinct of the Forsytes is dying out; the fourth generation is not interested in making money. Instinctively, Soames is convinced that the attacks on property will in time dissipate and new avenues for the possessive instinct will be found: "What though the board was up, and cosiness to let?—some one would come along and take it again some day."

Much has changed in the Forsyte world since Old Jolyon's days, which opened *The Man of Property*, and *To Let*, which closed on the world of Forsyteism at ebb tide. Timothy is dead, and his house on Bayswater Road is "to let"; Young Jolyon is dead, his watercolors are for sale, and Robin Hill is "to let." Fleur has lost Jon, and the long struggle between Irene and Soames has culminated in her farewell salute—a salute which can be friendly because she is at last completely free of Soames and his world. Soames's refusal to acknowledge the salute indicates that he completely understands the meaning of her gesture. The Forsyte philosophy seems clearly out of step with the temper of the times. Despite these facts, which indicate that the principles of Forsyteism are "to let," Soames remains serene, convinced that after the interval of destructive change has passed the principles of Forsyteism will return when the time comes to rebuild.

Whatever the ebb and flood tides of Forsyteism, the *Saga* has dramatized the eternal nature of the conflict between Irene and Soames. Regardless of changes in social philosophies or in ways of life, the fact remains that beauty will always arouse the Forsyte desire to possess.

A critical observation frequently made about the *Saga* is that the character of Soames changes as the story progresses. He is something of a villain in *The Man of Property*, but he becomes more heroic and likable as the *Saga* continues. To question this view may be unorthodox, but, in the light of the foregoing discussion of some of the major aspects of the *Saga*, it is reasonable to suggest that the view of Soames's villainy or heroism needs to be qualified.

The change in Soames's character is perhaps less a change and more of a realization of the good qualities that he possesses as a Forsyte. As early as *The Man of Property* the virtues of Forsyteism were clearly enunciated, and these virtues were consistently portrayed throughout the *Saga*. Young Jolyon in his discussion with Bosinney diagnosed Forsyteism and pointed out that the Forsytes were

> half England, and the better half, too, the safe half, the three per cent half, the half that counts. It's their wealth and security that makes everything possible; makes your art possible, makes literature, science, even religion, possible. Without Forsytes, who believe in none of these things, but turn them all to use, where should we be?

Their philosophy of triumphant materialism—property, possession, profit—while important, is also stultifying, because it limits appreciation of the spiritual, the beautiful, and the intangible to its material value or use. The Forsytes have to own, to enslave; Soames as the representative Forsyte remains true to these principles throughout the *Saga*. In the final analysis both the material and the spiritual are indispensable, but there must be a balance or proportion between them.

Barker argues that Galsworthy, in the continuation of the Forsytes with "Indian Summer," betrayed the "whole Forsyte theme." He main-

tains that Galsworthy used this long short story as a retreat from the
bitter ending of *The Man of Property* and that the result was a blunting
of the satire and tragedy.[12] In the context of the complete *Saga*, the
view that "Indian Summer" betrays the Forsyte theme is not very convincing. Despite its lyricism "Indian Summer" sets up clearly the basis
for the continuing struggle in the *Saga*.

Writing to André Chevrillon on November 8, 1921, Galsworthy
commented that with the completion of the *Saga* he was somewhat at
a loss, and he went on to say that he felt he was not yet done with
Fleur. Within a year he had begun the first volume of a new trilogy,
ultimately titled *A Modern Comedy*. The first volume, *The White
Monkey*, was published at the end of October, 1924. The second
volume, *The Silver Spoon*, was started in December, 1924, and was
published on August 26, 1926. Two years later, on July 12, 1928, the
third novel, *Swan Song*, was published.

A Modern Comedy continues the story of the Forsytes from 1922 to
the death of Soames in 1927 and like the *Saga* utilizes the same ar-
rangement—satiric novel, lyric interlude, satiric novel, lyric interlude,
and satiric novel. In *To Let*, Soames learned that he had to keep his
misgivings underground and that he had to put up with things to keep
Fleur; in *A Modern Comedy* Soames continues this course. Fleur takes
over the role of possessiveness in the struggle between Forsyteism and
beauty and passion. *The White Monkey* presents "a picture of modern
youth in all its irreverence." Fleur remains self-centered and willful
and yet not totally committed to any course of action. She wants both
the stability provided by her husband Michael and the excitement provided by Wilfrid Desert's attentions. Her tenacity keeps her from
giving up a good thing—Michael—and the novel ends as she gives birth
to the eleventh baronet.

The lyric interlude "A Silent Wooing" resumes the story of Jon as he
discovers his love for Anne Wilmot.

In *The Silver Spoon*, Soames's Victorian anger at Marjorie Ferrar's
betrayal of Fleur's hospitality by calling Fleur a snob and a nobody is
taken up by Fleur with a vengeance. In the lawsuit that follows, Fleur,
like her father in his earlier experiences as a Forsyte, wins the suit but
loses the victory.

[12] Barker, *The Man of Principle: A View of John Galsworthy*, 182–84.

Soames, in the interlude "Passers By," discovers that Irene, Jon, and Jon's wife, Anne, are staying at the same hotel in Washington, D.C., at which he, Fleur, and Michael are registered. So as not to disturb sleeping dogs, Soames sees to it that the two families remain unaware of one another. The disturbing presence of beauty is, nevertheless, again manifest.

In *Swan Song*, Fleur decides that she wants Jon at any cost, now that he and Anne have returned to England. She finally succeeds in seducing him in the coppice at Robin Hill, but the consequences are disastrous. Jon refuses to continue the relationship without telling Anne. He flees, leaving Fleur alone and defeated. When Fleur learns that Jon is lost to her forever, she becomes indifferent whether she lives or dies. Soames, knowing what has happened, takes her home. That night Fleur unwittingly starts a fire in Soames's picture gallery. When Soames sees Fleur's life endangered by a falling picture, he rushes to save her at the risk of his own life. Fleur promises Soames on his deathbed that she will be "good."

Fleur has learned perhaps the real limits of possessiveness in her futile efforts to make Jon hers, and Soames, the "man of property," has learned for the first time to give of himself and by this sacrifice has transcended the limits of Forsyteism.

Galsworthy's last major work, the trilogy *End of the Chapter*, did not continue with the Forsytes. Instead, although Fleur and Jon Forsyte appear, the major emphasis is on the Charwell family. R. H. Mottram suggests that Galsworthy switched to the Charwells because "he may have felt somehow constrained to correct the very full use he had made of his paternal heritage by turning to his other side, and setting his final trilogy in an atmosphere of those very much older and originally landed . . . maternal relatives."[13] The first novel, *Maid in Waiting*, was published in November, 1931; the second novel, *Flowering Wilderness*, appeared in November, 1932; and the final volume, *Over the River*, was published posthumously in October, 1933.

Unlike its predecessors, this trilogy does not contain lyrical interludes between the novels. Most critics generally believe that these three novels, though well done, are not Galsworthy at his best. One

[13] R. H. Mottram, *For Some We Loved: An Intimate Portrait of Ada and John Galsworthy*, 269.

reason may have been the fact that the concerns of the Forsytes and the Charwells had begun to seem irrelevant. Important concerns in this last trilogy are Hubert Charwell's possible misconduct as a British officer when he shot a half-caste Indian in Bolivia and Dinny Charwell's serious involvement with Wilfrid Desert despite the fact that Desert had converted to Islam at gunpoint. Such matters may have seemed worn out when more serious events were involving men's minds—the Great Depression, the rise of Hitler in Germany, and the role of the fascists in Italy.

The crowning honor of Galsworthy's career came on November 10, 1932, when it was announced that he had been awarded the Nobel Prize for Literature. His health was so precarious that he was unable to travel to Sweden to receive the prize. Grave signs of serious trouble began to appear: the dragging of one leg, the gradual loss of speech, and anemia. His death, caused by a tumor, occurred on January 31, 1933.

The Nobel award was given to Galsworthy "for his distinguished art of narration which takes its highest form in the *Forsyte Saga.*" Recognizing that Galsworthy had "aimed at capturing feeling and imagination," Anders Österling, of the Nobel committee, pointed out in the presentation that the two trilogies, the *Saga* and the *Comedy,*

together form an unusual literary accomplishment. The novelist has carried the history of his time through three generations, and his success in mastering so excellently his enormously difficult material, both in its scope and in its depth, remains an extremely memorable feat in English literature—doubly remarkable, if we consider that it was performed in a field in which the European continent had already produced some of its best works.

At the time the award seemed an appropriate culmination to an exceptionally successful literary career. As novelist, playwright, essayist, and short-story writer, Galsworthy had earned an international reputation as one of the important literary masters of the twentieth century.

Following his death in 1933, his reputation began a sharp and steady decline. Nearly four decades have passed, and there has been little serious critical interest in his work. The generally accepted view remains: Galsworthy is hopelessly dated. The eclipse has been almost total.

The reputation of nearly every major writer undergoes a period of reaction during which interest in his work declines. In time, however, renewed interest makes possible a reassessment of the author's permanence. In Galsworthy's case one is struck by the fact that renewed interest and reassessment seem to have been postponed indefinitely. The problem then is to explain why Galsworthy, who had been considered an author of major importance, could be dismissed so quickly.

First, Galsworthy's reputation at the time of his death was greatly inflated. The overpraise of his own day has probably had a great deal to do with the indifference that has flourished ever since. Second, much of his success had come about because of the widely held notion that he was a sociological critic, a reformer of man and institutions, and a disturbing chronicler of the contemporary. Third, in matters of technique Galsworthy was old-fashioned. He worked within the traditions of the Victorian novel, slightly modifying for his own purposes some of its more cumbersome characteristics. Fourth, his works, moreover, reflected a philosophy that also seemed old-fashioned. The code of behavior was that of the gentleman, the ideals of a humanitarian—tolerance, understanding, compassion, and reason—in short, all that made for human dignity. Fifth, both in range and in subject matter he was limited. Although he frequently used representatives of the lower classes, he was most familiar with the milieu of the upper classes; the worlds he created were seen through the eyes of the wealthy and the privileged.

Though these comments indicate the serious inadequacies in his work, the same points taken together do not prove conclusively that Galsworthy's work is without merit. To admit that Galsworthy's reputation was greater than his talents warranted does not mean that one should disregard his real but limited achievements. To judge him as a sociological critic is to misjudge him. Concerning the last three points, the fact that Galsworthy was a product of his time should not preclude a proper evaluation of his work. Within the tradition in which he was working, he handled his materials with considerable skill and deliberate artistry. What he said of his work—"If my work has any mission, it is only as a plea for proportion, and for sympathy and understanding between man and man"—can hardly be dismissed as irrelevant because he expressed these ideals in a context now thought to be old-fashioned.[14]

Now that the Victorian age is beginning to be considered as a period deserving study rather than scorn, its various spokesmen will be found worthy of serious consideration or reconsideration, whichever the case may be. In this light John Galsworthy will come to be recognized as the last important Victorian novelist, one whose work will carn for him a secure place as a novelist.

[14] John Galsworthy, *Glimpses and Reflections*, 38.

BERTRAND RUSSELL

by Irving Polonoff

Upon learning that Bertrand Russell received the Nobel Prize, the casual reader of today might infer that Russell had been awarded the prize in mathematics as co-author of *Principia Mathematica* with A. N. Whitehead (though there is no prize in mathematics) and for his many contributions to mathematical logic, or perhaps the Nobel Peace Prize for his efforts during the 1962 Cuban missile crisis or the Sino-Indian dispute or for his other activities on behalf of peace. Of course, either conclusion would be wrong. Although one could argue the merits of a possible Nobel Peace Prize to Russell, most points in his favor for that award would relate to his activities after 1950, the year the award was made.

There is no special category for contribution to philosophy or even to belles lettres in the strictest sense. The Nobel Prize in Literature was intended by Nobel to honor authors of idealistic tendency whose works exemplified the moral force of literature. The term literature was to be construed widely to include not only works of fiction but also other writings which through their form and manner of presentation possess literary worth. It was the Nobel Prize in Literature that was awarded to Bertrand Russell. The citation reads: "in recognition for his varied and significant writings in which he champions humanitarian ideals and freedom of thought."

The announcement that he had won the prize reached Russell on

November 10, 1950, just before he delivered a lecture on "Mind and Matter" at Princeton University to a large audience. Albert Einstein was among the scholars who rose to applaud him in the standing ovation at the end. Russell told reporters: "I am very pleased to receive the Nobel Prize. It is one of the two great honors I have received. The other is the Order of Merit of the British Empire." On December 10 Russell was in Stockholm to receive the prize, and he delivered his Nobel lecture, "What Desires are Politically Important," on December 11.

Writing some eighteen years later in the third volume of his *Autobiography*, Russell recalled the occasion:

When I was called to Stockholm, at the end of 1950, to receive the Nobel Prize—somewhat to my surprise, for literature, for my book *Marriage and Morals*—I was apprehensive since I remembered that exactly three hundred years earlier Descartes had been called to Scandinavia by Queen Christina in the wintertime and had died of the cold. However we were kept warm and comfortable and instead of snow we had rain, which was a slight disappointment. The occasion, though very grand, was pleasant and I enjoyed it.

The remarkable thing about this recollection is that neither the Nobel jury's citation nor the presentation by Anders Österling, secretary of the Swedish Academy, singled out the book *Marriage and Morals* (1929) for special mention, although Österling's presentation did mention such specific books as Russell's *History of Western Philosophy, Human Knowledge,* and *Sceptical Essays* and the essay "My Mental Development" in *The Philosophy of Bertrand Russell.*

Nobel's will stipulates that the award is to be based on the laureate's greatest service to mankind during the preceding year. This injunction is clearly difficult to adhere to. The Nobel juries' citations often connect the award with a single work but frequently depart from this procedure, making more general remarks reflecting a larger view of an author's achievements. This varying practice generates false impressions not only in the public at large but even among the laureates about the specific works considered as grounds for the award. The remarks during the presentation add to the laureate's impressions of the reasons for the award. Österling used the occasion of the presentation of Russell's prize to note the two hundredth anniversary of the award to Jean-Jacques Rousseau of the prize offered by the Academy of Dijon for his essay responding to their question "whether the arts and sciences have contributed to improve morals." Österling drew a parallel between the Swedish Academy's award with that of the Academy of Dijon, noting that Russell was chosen to be rewarded for his philosophical works because they are of service to moral civilization and answer to the spirit of Nobel's intentions.

It is perhaps the remarks on that occasion which prompted Russell's recollection that the enlightened Swedish Academy had recognized the merits of the book *Marriage and Morals*. This is the work which, together with *Education and the Modern World* (1932), had figured so largely in the case against Russell in 1940, in which he was judicially pronounced unworthy to be professor of philosophy at City College of New York. The infamous decision of Justice Joseph McGeehan directed the Board of Higher Education of the City of New York to rescind and revoke the appointment of Bertrand Russell as professor of philosophy in the college. In the decision he agreed with the petitioner that "Mr. Russell has taught in his books immoral and salacious doctrines" and supported this claim by citing passages from *Marriage and Morals*. "Considering Dr. Russell's principles," McGeehan asserted, "it appears that not only would the morals of the students be undermined, but his doctrines would tend to bring them, and in some cases their parents and guardians, in conflict with the Penal Law." Russell must have felt himself publicly vindicated when he heard his philosophical works described by the secretary of the Swedish Academy as of service to moral civilization. One can understand the pardonable error in Russell's later hazy recollection that the Nobel Prize had been awarded to him for his book *Marriage and Morals*.

Alfred Nobel, no doubt, had intended his prizes to go to worthy young or middle-aged men or women to free them from financial concerns so that they might devote themselves fully to their projected works. As Naboth Hedin has observed, "The prize has often come to a man fairly established in Letters, an author whose earnings have already made him independent, and it has come as an accolade to a career which has already reached its peak or passed it." Things are seldom what they seem to be on the surface, however. Bertrand Russell was seventy-eight when he received the prize and was certainly established as an author. Yet he did not consider himself financially free. The award associated with the prize was an important contribution to his income and of considerable help in freeing him for further work. Russell reports in his *Autobiography*:

> 1950 beginning with the Order of Merit and ending with the Nobel Prize seems to have marked the Apogee of my respectability. It is true that I began to feel slightly weary, fearing that this might mean the onset of blind orthodoxy. I have always held that no one can be respectable without being wicked but so blunted was my moral sense that I could not see in what way I had sinned. Honors and increased income which began with the sales of my *History of Western Philosophy* gave me a feeling of freedom and assurance that let me expend all my energies upon what I wanted to do.

What followed were two decades of productive writing, increased involvement in international affairs, and work to promote peace.

The circumstances of the 1950 Nobel Prize in Literature award were unusual in two respects. The 1949 prize was withheld until the following year, when it was awarded to William Faulkner for his contribution to American fiction. The awards to Faulkner and to Russell were announced simultaneously. Both were popular awards, well received by the press and public at large. The *New York Times* editorialized on November 11, 1950, under the caption "Nobel Bedfellows," that Bertrand Russell was a strange companion for Faulkner but well deserving of the prize. Anyone who could make *A History of Western Philosophy* fascinating was certainly a "literary" genius. "It is good," the editorial adds, "to see a true liberal get his reward in these partially totalitarian and reactionary days." Thanks to the Nobel award, Russell received better treatment from the press than he had before or has since—but then he never put much stock in its opinions about him.

The other unusual circumstance of the awards arose from the fact that 1950 was the fiftieth anniversary of the Nobel Foundation. The foundation was in a retrospective mood, reflecting upon the half century years of its activity, reviewing the pattern of its choices, and estimating whether they had fulfilled the intentions of the founder. The book *Nobel: The Man and His Prizes* (1950), edited by the foundation, was one outcome of that review. Another was the selection of

Bertrand Russell as the anniversary-year literature laureate. The search for the 1950 prizewinner provided a challenge to the Swedish Academy. The Nobel Institute of the Academy perceived the occasion as an opportunity to prove itself in regard to its image of Alfred Nobel and his intentions and to allay the various criticisms which had been directed against it over the years. Usually the selections had been along purely literary lines. On the rare occasions on which the prize juries had departed from these considerations—as in the nomination of Rudolf Eucken in 1908 and of Henri Bergson in 1927—their choices had met with less general approval. In the selection of Eucken equivocation about the ambiguity of the term "idealistic" in its technical and popular meanings may have played a part in recognizing his work on spiritualistic-idealistic metaphysics as qualifying in the category designated by Nobel's phrase "works of idealistic tendency." In 1950 the jury's clearer understanding of Alfred Nobel's personal hopes helped clarify the humanitarian intention of the phrase. By the same token, direct consideration of Nobel's personality and aspirations figured more intimately in the estimation of Bertrand Russell's qualifications by the Academy than it had in previous choices and perhaps in subsequent ones. This is attested to by Österling's remarks in the presentation when he asserted that

> Russell's philosophy may be said in the best sense to fulfill just those desires and intentions that Alfred Nobel had in mind when he instituted his Prizes. There are quite striking similarities between their outlooks on life. Both of them are at the same time sceptics and Utopians, both take a gloomy view of the contemporary world, yet both hold fast to a belief in the possibility of achieving logical standards for human behavior. The Swedish Academy believes that it acts in the spirit of Nobel's intention when on the occasion of its fiftieth anniversary of the Foundation it wishes to honor Bertrand Russell as one of our time's brilliant spokesmen of rationality and humanity as a fearless champion of free speech and free thought in the west.

There is little doubt that the spirit of Nobel's intention was carried out by the Academy's choice, but the mixed motives of honoring the memory of Alfred Nobel and lauding Bertrand Russell were further confused in this statement. The enthusiastic remarks coupling their beliefs and outlooks on life seem preposterous. The reality of Nobel's generosity regarding the disposition of his estates after death and his adherence to his rule, "I'd rather take care of the stomachs of the living than the glory of the departed," speaks for itself. But how can one forget that in his youth his major activities were devoted to laboratory research work and then to his factories and building his estate? When did he put his career on the line? When did his desire for peace lead him to use his considerable prestige and power to decline participation in the actual production of armament? How can his vaguely pro-fessed hopes for peace be regarded as more than lip service? Was his remark to Bertha van Suttner an instance of utopianism or of self-deception, no better than an excuse to continue production when he said, "My factories may make an end of war sooner than your con-gresses. The day when two army corps can annihilate each other in one second, all civilized nations, it is to be hoped will recoil from war and discharge their troops."

There is a vast difference between the outlook of the industrialist with clandestine dreams of peace and that of the aristocratic rebel. Russell was not one to ignore present realities in the name of vague future possibilities. He would not shunt onto others choices he had to make for himself. He acted in accordance with the free-thinking principles he proclaimed, not shirking his responsibility, even when the consequences were severe or his activities met with general dis-approval. He would not avoid his obligations by pinning his hopes on a later and better generation to do the work, when the work needed to be done right now. Fearless, outspoken, and rational, Russell was willing to break the law if his basic principles demanded it, and he was willing to pay the legal penalty for his nonconformist views and actions. This characteristic was best illustrated by his pacifist activities during World War I.

By 1914, Bertrand Russell, then forty-two years of age, was an in-tellectual figure of considerable stature and achievement. He was a Fellow of the Royal Society; the author of many erudite articles and a half-dozen learned books, including *The Principles of Mathematics*; the co-author of *Principia Mathematica*; past president of the Aris-totelian Society (1911); and lecturer at Trinity College, Cambridge. He had an international reputation as a mathematical logician and philosopher. His theory of descriptions and his theory of types were much discussed. He was highly regarded and much sought after as a lecturer in Paris at the École des Hautes Études Sociales, in Oxford at the university as Herbert Spencer lecturer, in Boston as Lowell lecturer at Harvard. After the declaration of war in August, 1914, by which time many of his erstwhile pacifist friends had changed their minds, Russell remained consistent. In a letter to the London *Nation* (dated August 15, 1914) he wrote:

> Against the vast majority of my countrymen, even at this moment, in the name of humanity and civilization, I protest against our share in the destruction of Germany. . . . Those who saw the London crowds, during the nights leading up to the Declaration of War saw a whole population, hitherto peaceable and humane, precipitated in a few days down the steep slope to primitive barbarism, letting loose, in a moment, the instincts of hatred and blood lust against which the whole fabric of society has been raised. . . .

Russell, writing more than forty-eight years later in his *Autobiography*, recalled how the prospect of the disaster of war filled him with horror, but what he found even more horrifying was the fact that more than 90 per cent of the population delighted in the prospect of carnage:

> I had to revise my views on human nature. . . . I had supposed that most people liked money better than almost anything else, but I discovered that they liked destruction even better. I had supposed that intellectuals frequently loved truth, but I found here again that not ten percent of them prefer truth to popularity.

Yet through it all he was tortured by his own patriotic feelings. "Love of England is very nearly the strongest emotion I possess and in appearing to set it aside at such a moment, I was making a very difficult renunciation."

Russell remained steadfast in his pacifism. He was one of the original members of the Union of Democratic Control, an organization in the forefront of the antiwar movement, and he established a branch at Trinity College, where he was lecturing on mathematical logic. He wrote a letter to President Woodrow Wilson urging him to adopt the role of peacemaker, and he became involved with the activities of the No Conscription Federation. The purpose of the federation was to fight conscription by parliamentary means and to resist military service if conscription was enforced. It was in this organization that the life and values of the humble schoolmaster Ernest Everett, conscientious objector, and of the eminent Bertrand Russell intertwined. A leaflet was written and distributed by the federation protesting Everett's sentence to two years at hard labor for refusing to disobey the dictates of conscience. Six men were arrested and imprisoned for distributing the leaflets. When he heard of this event, Russell refused to remain silent and wrote a letter to the *Times* which appeared on May 17, 1916. He asserted: ". . . I wish to make it known that I am the author of this leaflet and that if anyone is to be prosecuted, I am the person primarily responsible."

The response was swift. On June 5, 1916, Russell was charged and found guilty of "making in a printed publication 'statements likely to prejudice the recruiting and disciplining of His Majesty's forces.' " The fine was one hundred pounds. Russell refused to pay the fine; as a result, books in his rooms were seized and sold. On July 11, 1916, the council of Trinity College voted to dismiss Russell from his teaching post. "It was agreed unanimously that, since Mr. Russell has been convicted under the Defence of the Realm Act, and his conviction has been confirmed on appeal, he be removed from his lectureship in the college." Some members of the faculty were ashamed of the action, but the story did not come to light until G. H. Hardy's pamphlet *Bertrand Russell and Trinity* was printed for private circulation in 1942.

Russell left Trinity College and continued his pacifist work during 1917. His second encounter with the authorities occurred when he wrote an article, "The German Peace Offer," for the federation newspaper, the *Tribunal*, on January 3, 1918. Embedded in the article was this sentence: "The American Garrison which will by that time be occupying England and France, whether or not they will prove efficient against the Germans, will no doubt be capable of intimidating strikers, an occupation to which the American Army is accustomed at home."

Again the response was quick. On February 11, 1918, Russell was tried, found guilty, and sentenced to six months' imprisonment on the charge of "having in a printed publication made certain statements likely to prejudice His Majesty's relations with the United States." He was incarcerated in Brixton Prison until September, 1918.

The same independent spirit and the sense of urgency to face present realities were evident in Russell's alertness to tendencies in philosophy which needed to be challenged. This vigilance is perhaps best illustrated by his criticism of the philosophical views of Henri Bergson, who was to become a Nobel Prize winner in literature in 1927 and was on that occasion praised for his theory of intuition, which had influenced the thinking of his time. The remarks made during the presentation ceremony referred to

> the great vogue of Bergsonianism at the beginning of the twentieth century, . . . a heartening counterbalance to materialism, . . . it has been compared to the influence of Schelling's philosophy a hundred years earlier. Unmistakably, it was in harmony with the spirit of Alfred Nobel.

Early in the century Bertrand Russell had perceived the popularity of Bergsonism as posing a danger to the philosophical movement of his time. By advocating "intuition" against "intellect," it seemed to sanction appeals to irrationality. It appeared to do so on scientific grounds by attempting to justify its claims in the quasi-scientific terminology of evolutionism. This, to Russell, specious appeal to biological theory needed to be exposed. Feasible alternatives for keeping philosophy on a more secure path needed to be displayed. Russell used the 1914 Lowell Lectures at Harvard to sketch the line of thought which he had been developing, juxtaposing it to Bergsonian and other current tendencies. He proposed examples of how philosophy might be pursued in a more truly scientific way by following a logical analytic method. These lectures formed the basis for his book *Our Knowledge of the External World, as a Field for Scientific Method in Philosophy.* Russell's contention was that propositions are true because they relate to what there is and not because, were they believed, they would help us survive. Bergson's reduction of the intellect to the status of an instrument in the biological struggle for survival subordinates the concern for truth to other values. Russell was convinced that reliance upon intuition means a willingness to accept quick, unanalyzed convictions which are least deserving of uncritical acceptance. Philosophy is more consonant with the will to doubt than with William James's will to believe. Writing before August, 1914, Russell remarked in *Our Knowledge of the External World*:

> The barbaric substratum of human nature, unsatisfied in action finds an outlet in imagination. In philosophy as elsewhere, this tendency is visible; and it is this rather than formal argument, that has thrust aside the classical tradition for a philosophy which fancies itself more virile and more vital.

The classical tradition is the child of the Greek belief in reason and the medieval belief in the tidiness of the universe. Russell recognized that the classical tradition had become stultified and needed criticism. This was especially true of the form the tradition had taken in the thought of its most articulate recent exponents, F. H. Bradley and John McTaggart. F. H. Bradley's *Appearance and Reality* had revived the Eleatic doctrines of monism, which treats reality as One Absolute and regards the life of experience as appearance. Couched in a Hegelian idiom employing logic of negation, this aspect of the tradition needed to be modified. The correction had to come from a revised logic, a logic adapted to analyzing experience rather than to tracing out contradictions designed to show the purported unreality of prima facie experience. This kind of metaphysical philosophy was, to Russell fundamentally mistaken.

It is, Russell agreed, perhaps best to make a new beginning, but the direction taken by Nietzsche, Bergson, William James, and the pragmatists was to be avoided. The popularity of their doctrines blinded them to much that is important for a true understanding of the universe. It is interesting to observe the arch-modernist that Russell is reputed to have been cautioning his restless contemporaries to take heed: "Something of Hellenism must be combined with the new spirit before it can emerge from the ardor of youth into the wisdom of manhood."

The claim is sometimes made that *Our Knowledge of the External World* signaled the beginning of the antimetaphysical phase of modern analytical philosophy. To infer that this work denies the possibility of metaphysics would be in error. Indeed, it proclaims a metaphysical doctrine of its own, logical atomism. Russell makes it explicit that "ultimate metaphysical truth . . . can be discovered," but it will take the joint efforts of dedicated thinkers, "those who are willing to combine the hopefulness, patience, and open-mindedness of science with something of the Greek feeling for beauty in the abstract world of logic and for the ultimate intrinsic value in the contemplation of truth."

Russell drew a sharp distinction between the advocacy of ethical norms or social outlooks and the practice of philosophy in the scientific manner. He did not advocate an ethical neutrality as some readers think, but urged that "the ethical interests which have often inspired philosophers must remain in the background." This procedure was not recommended not to withhold information from the reader but to avoid special pleading for a private preference and to appeal to criteria of intellectual adequacy. However, "some kind of ethical interest may inspire the whole study but none must obtrude in the detail or be expected in the special results which are sought." The long-range commitments to pursuing philosophy in this way are difficult to sustain. They require an uncommon dedication to intellectual integrity and honest inquiry and a sustained loyalty to the value of truth. The value of truth is not to be compromised or subordinated to the Platonist's concern for the good or the pragmatist's concern for the useful. As Russell explained:

> In order to become a scientific philosopher, a certain peculiar mental discipline is required. There must be present first of all the desire to know philosophical truth and this desire must be sufficiently strong to survive through years when there seems no hope of its finding any satisfaction. The desire to know philosophical truth is very rare . . . in its purity, it is not often found even among philosophers. It is obscured sometimes . . . particularly after long periods of fruitless search . . . by the desire to think we know.

Not even Russell could live up to the ideal he portrayed in this passage, which occurs near the end of *Our Knowledge of the External World*, but it is clearly an ideal which he had aspired to reach in his own philosophical career. Perhaps it was during moments of encounter with his intense young student Ludwig Wittgenstein that the forty-two-year-old Russell had glimpsed what a philosopher might be. Wittgenstein, then twenty-three, had made a strong impression upon

Russell by his grasp of difficult theoretical issues and by the cogency of his criticisms. In a letter to Ottoline Morrell, written in 1916, Russell referred to the time before the composition of *Our Knowledge of the External World*:

I wrote a lot of stuff about the theory of knowledge which Wittgenstein criticized with the greatest severity. His criticism . . . was an event of first rate importance in my life, and affected everything I have done since, I saw he was right and I saw that I could not hope ever again to do fundamental work in philosophy. My impulse was shattered, like a wave dashed to pieces against a breakwater. I became filled with despair.

In his *Autobiography* Russell noted that he soon got over this mood. His letter continues: "I had to produce lectures for America but I took a metaphysical subject, although I was and am convinced that all fundamental work in philosophy is logical. My reason was that Wittgenstein persuaded me that what wanted doing in logic was too difficult for me" (this from the author of *The Principles of Mathematics* and co-author of *Principia Mathematica!*).

So there was no really vital satisfaction of my philosophical impulse in that work and philosophy lost its hold on me. That was due to Wittgenstein more than to the war. What the war has done is to give me a new and less difficult ambition which seems quite as good as the old one. My lectures have persuaded me that there is a possible life and activity in the new ambition.

Russell may have had negative feelings about his work in composing *Our Knowledge of the External World*, but its lucidity, brilliance, and probity are merits which speak for themselves. There is irony in the fact that Rudolf Carnap, the leading logical empiricist, singled out this book of Russell's as a most influential work in his own intellectual development:

In my philosophical thinking in general I learned most from Bertrand Russell. In the winter of 1921 I read his book *Our Knowledge of the External World*. Some passages made an especially vivid impression on me because they formulated clearly and explicitly a view of the aim and method of philosophy which I had implicitly held for some time.

179

In 1940, Russell returned the compliment when he acknowledged in the Preface to *An Inquiry into Meaning and Truth*: "I am, as regards method more in sympathy with the logical positivists than with any other existing school. I differ from them, however, in attaching more importance than they do to the work of Berkeley and Hume." Of course this agreement as regards method did not mean that Russell had become a logical positivist, although he shared with them their penchant for translating complexes into terms of empirically preferable minimum vocabularies. It was a technique which could trace its ancestry to Russell's earlier injunction to analytical philosophers: "Wherever possible substitute logical constructions for inferred entities." Russell had come to understand that the resolution of incomplete symbols was a process which did not necessarily entail metaphysical consequences. The process could be detached from his presumption of the reality of logical atoms or any other metaphysically simple beings. The technique of resolution remains effective when joined with the nonmetaphysical reduction of the special vocabulary of various sciences to expressions couched in terms of the minimal vocabulary, a set of words in which no one word can be defined in terms of others in the set.

Nevertheless, Russell did not share the logical positivists' antimetaphysical bias. He did not agree with them in the view that logic does not provide a basis for any metaphysics. A metaphysical question remains concerning how logical categories of language correspond to the nonlinguistic world with which language deals. In addition, Russell held the view, which would be anathema to the positivists, that a proposition may be true although one can see no way of obtaining evidence either for or against it. He remained loyal to the classical ideal that "truth" is the fundamental concept and that "knowledge" must be defined in terms of "truth" and not vice versa. Pure empiricism is an appealing philosophy, but it has its limits, as Russell intimated in *An Inquiry into Meaning and Truth* (1940) and as he made explicit in *Human Knowledge* (1948). These limits are clearly evident in the need to admit principles of nondeductive inference if scientific knowledge is to be possible.

Russell had remained consistently logical and analytical in his approach to philosophical inquiry ever since his earliest encounter with his fellow undergraduate G. E. Moore. Together they helped diminish the stature of monolithic Absolute Idealism as an intellectual doctrine and substituted a pluralistic timeless world of Platonic ideas in its place. In his essay "My Mental Development," in *Philosophy of Bertrand Russell* (1946), he detailed their rebellion against Bradley, who had argued that everything common sense believes in is appearance. In reaction to this doctrine they went to the opposite extreme claiming everything is real which common sense supposes real. Ever since then, G. E. Moore has remained an adherent to the primacy of common sense in judging knowledge claims. His philosophical analyses have been phrased in nontechnical terminology and refer to the immediacy of individual experience.

For Russell it was not common sense but scientific knowledge which came to occupy the central position. Philosophy, if it is to be significant, must be closely linked to the results of scientific inquiry. Competent philosophy does not shun the mastery of the truths of logic, mathematics, and the factual sciences for the arbitrary reason that they are technical and difficult to grasp. It is not surprising to find that Russell deplored the trend to ordinary language philosophy in English academic circles after World War II. He made some telling criticisms of this tendency within philosophy in the amusing essay "The Cult of 'Common Usage.'" This essay was written in the early 1950's and is included in *Portraits from Memory and Other Essays*. Russell formulated the doctrine to which he took objection in the following way: "It maintains that the language of daily life with words used in their ordinary meanings, suffices for philosophy, which has no need of technical terms or of changes in the signification of common terms." He cites several objections which he has to this doctrine. It is insincere, an excuse for ignorance, and smug. It trivializes philosophy and tends to perpetuate the muddle-headedness of common sense. The insincerity lies in the pretense that common usage is what these ordinary language adherents believe in. It is not the common usage observed by careful empirical methods, but something more cliquish. As Russell put it: "What they believe in is the usage of persons who have their amount of education, neither more nor less. Less is illiteracy, more is pedantry, . . . so we are given to understand." The excuse for ignorance resides in the fact that adherents to the doctrine may thereby absolve themselves from acquiring a knowledge of mathematics and the sciences. The charge of smugness derives from the misguided presumption that they obviously speak on behalf of the common man when they present their own version of common sense. In connection with the charge that this conception of philosophy trivializes the pursuit, in *Portraits from Memory*, Russell tells this priceless story:

> These philosophers remind me of the shopkeeper of whom I once asked the shortest way to Winchester. He called to a man in the back premises: "Gentleman wants to know the shortest way to Winchester." . . . "Winchester?" an unseen voice replied. . . . "Aye." . . . "Way to Winchester?" . . . "Aye." . . . "Shortest way?" . . . "Aye." . . . "Dunno." He wanted to get the nature of the question clear, but took no interest in answering it. This is exactly what [this] modern philosophy does for the earnest seeker after truth. Is it surprising that young people turn to other studies?

There is an undeniable social dimension to scientific knowledge which makes it public knowledge. But in Russell's view public knowledge is a construction which contains less than the sum of private knowledge possessed by individuals. In *An Inquiry into Meaning and Truth* Russell disagreed with those logical positivists who claim that there are no absolutely primitive propositions for science and contend that the set of propositions accepted as basic and true are so called by virtue of the historical fact that they are accepted as such by the scientific community. These positivists are concerned with sifting opinions of the best authorities in order to determine the standard scientific opinions of the time and their organization in a structure of knowledge. The crucial distinction between knowledge and opinion rests in a logically significant order which can bring the set of loosely held opinions to systematic unity as knowledge. Russell characteristically insisted on a more individualistic basis to knowledge. Individual men of science are not engaged merely in comparing each others' opinions. They make observations and conduct experiments on the basis of which they may reject unanimous opinions. Thus new knowledge may arise which is at first purely personal and private. This is why observation and experiments are undertaken—so that perceptive experience may take place in the context of these activities, which brings new knowledge to the perceiver. Public knowledge is an abstract or epitome of private knowledge in Russell's view:

All theory of knowledge must start from "what do I know?" not from "what does mankind know?" For how can I tell what mankind knows? Only by (a) personal observation of what it says in the books it has written, and (b) weighing the evidence in favor of the view that what is said in the books is true. If I am Copernicus, I shall decide against the books.

In the last analysis it is only the individual who can be the critic and the knower. The source of critical insight or adequate knowledge lies directly in the conscious awareness of the private subject. For this reason Russell reminded his contemporaries that too many of them had forgotten about the arguments of Descartes and Berkeley.

How characteristically Russellean these doctrines are. The defiant nonconformist will not be intimidated by scientific or philosophical orthodoxy any more than he will be by the social or political establishment or its police force. It is all of one piece; underlying his many variations of doctrine, the basic themes of staunch independence, of defiant individualism, and of devotion to truth remain constant. It is not the specious individualism which can be coupled with claptrap about free enterprise and private initiative but an individualism which has encountered defeat at the hands of exponents of freedom. Russell knew from bitter experience how little comfort it must be to be told that one is at liberty to hold any opinions one pleases and that the holding of controversial opinions is not punishable by law and then to be refused employment because one is thought wicked for holding unorthodox beliefs. Russell was not naïve, but if ever he had been it would have been knocked out of him by the action of Cambridge University and the British courts during World War I. He knew how such refusal of employment in a highly industrialized state amounts to a rigorous form of persecution. He had spoken on these issues many times, but perhaps never more cogently than in his Conway Memorial Lecture, *Free Thought and Official Propaganda* (London, 1922).

If his philosophy at times seemed tainted with subjectivism, it is not because he was a bourgeois individualist, as some doctrinaire Marxists may claim, but because it may be linked to his recognition of the core

183

of loneliness which he recognized within himself and other persons and to which he addressed himself. Writing in the essay "My Mental Development" (1943) in *The Philosophy of Bertrand Russell* (1946, edited by P. A. Schilpp), Russell admitted that much of his published work reflects a subjective bias. However, readers were cautioned not to infer from this that his philosophy is subjective:

> In some respects, my published work, outside mathematical logic does not completely represent my beliefs or general outlook. Theory of knowledge, with which I have been largely concerned has a certain essential subjectivity; it asks "how do I know what I know?" and starts inevitably from personal experience. Its data are egocentric, and so are the earlier stages of its argumentation. I have not, so far, got beyond the earlier stages and have therefore seemed more subjective in outlook than in fact I am. I am not a solipsist, nor an idealist; I believe (though without good grounds) in the world of physics as well as in the world of psychology. But it seems clear that whatever is not experienced must if known be known by inference.

In his next book, *Human Knowledge: Its Scope and Limits* (1948), Russell discussed those principles of inference which justify valid inferences from experience to the world of physics. He enunciated five general postulates of scientific inference which turn out to be of a kind which cannot be based on experience, although they are needed to justify specific scientific inferences. This result goes beyond the limits which empiricists would set. The doctrine thus enunciated seems to have a Kantian ring to it and might lead casual readers to think that Russell had returned to the modified form of Kantianism he had espoused in his early *Essay on the Foundation of Geometry* (1897). This conclusion would be mistaken. Russell's procedure may seem somewhat akin to a transcendental analysis which considers scientific knowledge as given and seeks to determine the pervasive judgments which make it possible. However, Russell had set himself the more limited goal of justifying induction. The set of five postulates is offered as asserting antecedent probabilities authorizing inductive inferences based on reasoning from frequently recurring runs of events. Needless to say, Russell did not attempt anything like an a priori transcendental deduction or justification when the question of how we know these postulates or minimum assumptions is raised. Instead, he answered in a manner reminiscent of Hume—that the concept of knowledge is not as precise as many philosophers would like to think and that its roots are embedded in unverbalized animal behavior. On logical grounds the minimal assumptions are to be treated as basic.

From a psychological point of view Russell was prepared to assert that such assumptions are the end product of an analysis which is a stage in "a long series of refinements which starts from habits of expectation in animals, such as that what has a certain smell is good to eat." Does this mean that Russell had reverted to an outlook which he had previously condemned in Bergson and the evolutionists? Not at all; he never denied the biological basis of human thought and action. The easy inferences whereby those thinkers concluded from false doctrines or weak analogies of animal behavior the existence of nonexistent human powers are as invalid now as they were then. In *Human Knowledge*, Russell was presenting a much more subtle, though seemingly simpler, doctrine than those philosophers had ever offered.

Russell's impulse to be flippant and clever may often mislead us into thinking that what he had to say is less profound than it actually is. Consider his injunction in *An Inquiry into Meaning and Truth*: "a man possessed of intellectual prudence will avoid such rash credulity as is involved in saying 'there's a dog' " when all he can truthfully claim is "there is a canoid patch of color." Russell reminded the reader that, as the films do today, perhaps the physiologist of the future will be able to stimulate the optic nerve in the way necessary for seeing a dog, and added, "I have gathered from the works of Bulldog Drummond that contact of a fist with the eye enables people to see the starry heavens as well as the moral law." How shaky the Kantian system must be after a blow like that. Or consider Russell's remarks in his much-read book *The Problems of Philosophy* (1912), an excellent introduction to the subject and still widely used as a college textbook: "The man who has fed the chicken every day throughout its life at last wrings its neck instead, showing that more refined views as to uniformity of nature would have been useful to the chicken." How shaky is anyone's philosophical confidence after a thought like that. Russell did not proceed to belabor the point with jargon about the problem of induction or its justification, but added, "Our instincts certainly cause us to believe that the sun will rise tomorrow but we may be in no better

position than the chicken which unexpectedly has its neck wrung."
We are distraught, and our predicament is not lessened, though we
understand the peril.

The irrepressible joy in uttering the well-turned phrase was with
Russell from his earliest days. Consider the article "Recent Work in
the Philosophy of Mathematics," in the issue of *International Monthly*
dated October, 1901. Here we find his famous definition of mathematics: "the subject in which we never know what we are talking
about, nor whether what we are saying is true"—a remark which gains
the quick approval of many a reader perplexed by mathematics but not
aware that what is being asserted is literally correct. Within a mathematical system, derived terms are defined in terms of primitive undefined terms, and derived propositions are proved on the basis of
unproved assumptions containing these undefined terms.

This spirit did not desert Russell even when, incarcerated in Brixton
Prison for the first time, he sat penning *An Introduction to Mathematical Philosophy* (1918): "It is the object of mathematical philosophy to put off saying what 'zero,' 'number,' or 'successor' mean as long
as possible." This remark is not Russell's confession of a desire to avoid
the task which is the very one that he had embarked upon to exemplify
the logistic thesis, but it is an accurate description of the process undertaken. Terms left undefined in mathematics, especially in arithmetic,
could be defined in terms derived from logical theory. Giuseppe Peano
had systematized arithmetic on the basis of five postulates containing
"zero," "number," and "successor" as undefined terms. The logician's
task was to display the logical terms which could define Peano's
primitive terms, thereby giving them meaning in logical theory. It was
an objective which came at the end, not at the beginning, of inquiry,
as Russell's remark literally says. It was the successful work in *Principia Mathematica* which supported the claim of logicism that mathematics is reducible to logic. *An Introduction to Mathematical
Philosophy* was intended to be a popular work which summarized the
results of that project. In the last chapter Russell remarked that
mathematics and logic, which hitherto had been entirely distinct dis-
ciplines, were now more closely joined. "They differ as boy and man:
logic is the youth of mathematics and mathematics is the manhood
of logic."

Russell's wry verve was displayed over the years again and again in learned articles, popular and academic books, lectures, interviews, and occasions of pomp and glory. Never the prude, never the prig, his sense of fun remained undiminished. At seventy-eight, in the middle of his Nobel lecture, he confided that "the Devil has many forms, some designed to deceive the young, some designed to deceive the old and serious. If it is the devil that tempts the young to enjoy themselves, is it not, perhaps, the same personage that persuades the old to condemn their enjoyment?" The profile of the author which emerges from Russell's popular writings before 1950 is one of an acute, learned, irreverent, sharp-witted, free-thinking, emancipated libertarian—an iconoclast with compassion.

It is not always apparent to occasional readers of his more erudite philosophical books that there had been a consistency to Russell's method of inquiry ever since his abandonment of Absolute Idealism. The consistency is there to be discerned. He sought to free himself and his readers from the captivity of misleading myths. Foremost among these myths was the belief that there are *permanent* "things" with changing "appearances." It may have seemed a bizarre delusion to be offended by such an initially plausible doctrine and truly Quixotic to challenge its validity. It was clearly a challenge worthy of Russell. Armed with his "principle of abstraction"—perhaps better called the "principle which dispenses with abstraction"—he attacked nonexistent metaphysical entities intent upon demolishing them. In addition to this goal was his conviction that a word taken in isolation need not have meaning, even though that word might contribute to the meaning of the sentence in which it occurs.

Pursuing this idea, Russell developed his theory of descriptions, which provided him with a method of dealing with sentences containing descriptive phrases. Thus such sentences as, "The present king of France does not exist," can be regarded as true or false without implying that the phrase "the present king of France," embedded in the sentence refers to anything in particular. This technique of logical translation helped him to answer such questions as, "What is it that does not exist?" thereby aiding the exposure of metaphysical pseudo-entities as fictions.

First, such obvious contenders as "golden mountains" and "round-squares" fell, but then came classes and other purported beings. The next step was to devise a method of defining incomplete symbols by their uses, resolving these symbols into other preferable ones. By treating symbols for classes as incomplete symbols, Russell abolished the notion that classes were self-existing real beings. Since cardinal numbers had been defined as classes of classes, it could only be concluded that numbers were pseudoentities, not real beings. This conclusion swept away the age-old belief deriving from Pythagoras that numbers are ultimate realities.

Under the influence of Whitehead, Russell went on to deal in like manner with points of space, instants of time, and atoms of matter. He outlined a method for reinterpreting statements in which these terms occur into statements which say as much but contain references only to events. Thus, he said, we are freed from the illusion of believing in the metaphysical reality of discrete points, instants, or atoms. Events are real; points, instants, and atoms are logical constructions of events. The key symbols of mathematics and physical science have been shorn of spurious metaphysical references. Finally the symbols of everyday discourse, "rock," "flower," "table," "person," need reinterpretation. They are not permanent things with changing appearances, but the changing aspects taken collectively to constitute things are themselves real. "All aspects of a thing are real whereas the thing is a mere logical construction."

Little did the general reader suspect the extent of unorthodoxy and iconoclasm of which Russell was capable in the theoretical domain as in the practical. A few of his contemporary philosophical readers did glimpse some unity in the wide scope of his writings as logician, philosopher, and social critic. Hans Reichenbach, writing about Russell in 1928, offered this note of appreciation.

> He who is ready to overthrow the oldest tradition in logic and to uncover the illusory nature of ancient ideals will also look with more freedom at the ideals of bourgeois ethics and not be afraid to give up values which those who are tradition bound are unable to renounce.

How poignant are these words, from the days of the Weimar Republic, applauding Russell for his basic consistency: "The way Russell lives

188

his philosophy is his greatest contribution to our times so deeply torn between thoughts and deeds."

Russell was well known to Continental philosophers interested in logic and in mathematical and scientific philosophy. His social and political writings were generally recognized as of another class, somewhat eccentric and not to be taken too seriously. In fact, he was the least insular of British philosophers. As we have seen, his university studies had brought him into contact with the writings of Kant and Hegel. After graduation he spent some time in Paris and Berlin, where he studied Marxist and socialist doctrines. His first book, *German Social Democracy* (1896), augments the lectures he delivered at the London School of Economics earlier in 1896. He was frequently invited to review works written in French or German for learned journals. During 1899 he was absorbed in a study of Leibniz' writings and lectured on that topic as a substitute instructor for J. McTaggart's class. *A Critical Exposition of the Philosophy of Leibniz* (1900) was published a year or so before works on the same topic by Ernst Cassirer (*Leibniz' System*, 1902) and by Louis Couturat (*La Logique de Leibniz*, 1901). Russell was thrilled to discover that his own novel view of the logical basis of Leibniz' metaphysics was supported by the scholarly work of Couturat. Cassirer held a more traditional view, with which Russell disagreed. The departure in Leibniz' studies evident in his own and Couturat's work was a considerable contribution to philosophical scholarship in its own right. Their line of inquiry was of a nature which needed to be encouraged in the scholarly world. Couturat initiated a correspondence with Russell, and they maintained contact until Couturat's death in 1914.

For a time Russell continued to take an interest in Leibniz and in other studies in the history of philosophy, but he soon abandoned Leibniz scholarship. He had more urgent tasks of his own to perform in the cause of renovating logic. This task brought him into further contact with Continental thinkers—Gottlob Frege, Georg Cantor, Giuseppe Peano, Henri Poincaré, and Alexius Meinong, to name a few. It is now well known that, were it not for the fact that Bertrand Russell featured the important thought of Frege and his work *Begriffschrift* (1879), they would have long languished in the obscurity to which it had been confined by European intellectual circles and not become a part of the world-wide philosophical scene in which Russell was so important a figure.

By 1950 Russell's cosmopolitanism was evident to all. He had lectured, taught, and traveled in Britain and in many parts of Europe, China, North America, and Australia. The lectures he was invited to deliver often formed the basis for many of his books. In addition to the 1914 Lowell Lectures, the lectures delivered at the University of Peking were incorporated in *The Analysis of Mind* (1921); the William James Lectures at Harvard University became *An Inquiry into Meaning and Truth* (1940); lectures sponsored by the Barnes Foundation of Philadelphia were incorporated in *The History of Western Philosophy* (1945), and the B. B. C. Reith Lectures became *Authority and the Individual* (1949). His journalistic writing on a wide variety of subjects had appeared as occasional pieces in many popular magazines. Some of these essays reappeared in anthologies such as *Sceptical Essays* (1928), *In Praise of Idleness* (1935), and *Unpopular Essays* (1950). Works such as *Bolshevism: Practice and Theory* (1920) and *The Problem of China* (1922) were the outcome of visits to the Soviet Union and then to China. Russell was disappointed with what he saw in Soviet Russia, but enthralled by China. The book about China contains a brief but remarkable epitome contrasting Chinese and Western civilization. He came to love the Chinese people during the year he spent among them and recognized the problem of sustaining their ancient civilization in the face of the military forces arrayed against them. He spoke often thereafter of having gained a habit there of thinking in terms of long stretches of time which provided him with a sustaining perspective in the years ahead.

In addition to his journalistic efforts on behalf of peace, internationalism, woman suffrage, liberalism, and special political topics, Russell wrote a number of expository and popular books on social and political theory before 1950. The most noteworthy works in this group are *Principles of Social Reconstruction* (1916), *Freedom and Organization, 1814-1914* (1934), and *Power: A New Social Analysis* (1938). Russell did not regard these works as contributions to erudite social or political philosophy. He made it explicit that the first of these books was not intended as a theoretical contribution but had a practical purpose. He was regarded as advocating anarchism when his concern was with promoting liberty. He was even accused of holding the gloomy view that there is an "ineradicable impulse to war." In the "Reply to Criticisms" in *The Philosophy of Bertrand Russell* (1946) he tried to correct such misconceptions. "What I have said is that people whose lives are unhappy or thwarted are apt to develop hatreds and impulses toward violence, and that, under our present social system, there are very many such people." In case the sense of professionalism among academic philosophers was offended, Russell reminded such readers that he wrote for a larger audience. "I did not write *Social Reconstruction* in my capacity as a 'philosopher'; I wrote it as a human being who suffered from the state of the world, wished to find some way of improving it, and was anxious to speak in plain terms to others who had similar feelings."

Bertrand Russell had a remarkable gift for putting technical matters simply and explaining crucial points cogently without recourse to jargon. His *ABC of Atoms* (1923) and *ABC of Relativity* (1925) were valuable additions to the popular literature on science. Readers were fortunate to have so expert a guide to help improve their understanding of recent scientific developments. The importance of promoting an understanding of the role of science in our culture was always keenly felt by Russell, and he did not hesitate to use his gifts of expression to serve the purpose of general education of the reading public. His well-written little book *Icarus, or the Future of Science* (1924) presents a gloomy prospect of the interactions among science, industry, and nationalism. It takes off from a previous work in the same series by J. B. S. Haldane. *Daedalus* (1924), written in the latter's pre-Marxist days, conveyed an optimistic message. Needless to say, Russell did not regard the existence of science as an unmixed blessing. On the whole, the intellectual impact of science upon the prevailing world view has been beneficial, but the power which science has granted men for gratifying their desires is another matter. The outcome will depend upon the extent of kindliness which men can generate toward one another, for only kindliness can save the world. The dilemma at this point, as Russell recognized, is that, even if we were to know how to produce kindliness, we would not do so unless we were already kindly.

"Icarus having been taught to fly by his father Daedalus was destroyed by his rashness. The same fate may overtake the populations whom modern men of science have taught to fly."

The prospects were not reassuring, but Russell was not driven to despair. There would be something unseemly about such a response. He had often expressed the attitude that there is something feeble, even contemptible, about a man who cannot face the perils of life without the help of comfortable myths, and he made no exception for himself. There was work to be done. Within the next few years he turned to brighter prospects, the hope of educating children to develop their kindly impulses. Together with his wife, Dora, he established a school at Beacon Hill and became its headmaster. During the twenties and thirties and even thereafter, the thoughts expressed in the conclusion of *Icarus* remained important considerations for Russell:

> Science has not given men more self-control, more kindliness or more power of discounting their passions in deciding upon a course of action. It has given communities more power to indulge their collective passions, but, by making society more organic, it has diminished the part played by private passions. Men's collective passions are mainly evil; for the strongest of them are hatred and rivalry directed towards other groups. Therefore at present all that gives men power to indulge their collective passions is bad. That is why science threatens to cause the destruction of our civilization. The only solid hope seems to lie in the possibility of world-wide domination by one group, say the United States, leading to the gradual formation of an orderly economic and political world-government. But perhaps in view of the sterility of the Roman Empire, the collapse of our civilization would in the end be preferable to this alternative!

Russell held high hopes for an educational process which was reasonably permissive and devoid of regimentation and authoritarianism. The ideal education would promote individuality in a context of freedom. The process must begin in early childhood and provide an environment in which the child is helped toward maturity as a cultured individual who could judge himself and his community justly and act accordingly. Russell had written a plea for the child as the vital factor in modern education as early as 1916. His major works on educational topics were written just before and during the time he was associated with Beacon Hill School (1927 to 1935): *On Education Especially in Early Childhood* (1926) and *Education and the Social Order* (1932). This was also the period during which he wrote *Marriage and Morals* (1929) and *The Conquest of Happiness* (1932). The former expressed his condemnation of the stultifying prudishness which hampers healthy sexuality and advocated a point of view which is in keeping with the sexual revolution that has occurred in English and American circles since that time. Russell had been concerned with the social and intellectual issues regarding sexual freedom since 1915, when Lady Ottoline Morrell introduced him to D. H. Lawrence.

The total lack of priggishness and false pride in Russell's character was evident in his willingness to write a book like *The Conquest of Happiness*. It was not addressed to highbrows, and he avoided profound philosophy or erudition. It came straight from the heart in remembrance of his own moments of boredom and anguish and sprang from an impulse to do something about helping unhappy people become happy. It is clearly not a book which a "professor" would write, or one which Russell would advise the novices among them to write.

On the subject of style, Russell's first ambitions were more florid and rhetorical. The much-reprinted essay "A Free Man's Worship" (*The Independent Review*, December, 1903) has a Miltonian ring to it, a style which he came to deplore. Style, he believed, must be an intimate expression of the personality of the writer if it is to be any good, but it does not succeed unless the writer's personality is interesting. Russell's style succeeds on his own criteria. Aldous Huxley, writing in appreciation of Russell, remarked that there are three kinds of censorship: political, economic, and stylistic. The first two are easily recognized. Stylistic censorship is closer to the communicator and derives from his inability to communicate because of his misuse of his native language. Huxley's encomium to Russell was that he had fought against political and stylistic censorship, for he who had made the difficult analyses and had had the deep ideas never became their stylistic censor.

On the other hand, there have been some philosophers, among them George Santayana, who have held the opinion that, although Russell wrote on many topics, he is only worth reading when he is really abstract. Even Russell at times held such a view of his own work.

Aside from the wrongness of Russell's judgment concerning the merits of his writing, the parallel he drew between Leibniz and himself is interesting. There are many similarities in their theoretical interests in logic, mathematics, and philosophy; in addition, Leibniz was perhaps the philosopher with whose writings Russell was most familiar. Over the years, as Russell sharpened his views of the relation between his own theoretical work in logic and philosophy and his practical writings aimed at influencing action, he came to a clearer awareness of the kind of man and philosopher he understood Leibniz to have been. His view was not complimentary to Leibniz as a human being, although he retained his high regard for him as an intellectual. Perhaps this tells us more about Russell than it does about Leibniz.

In 1937, writing in the Preface to the second edition of *The Philosophy of Leibniz*, Russell remarked on the cogency of Leibniz' work in logic and in his application of logic to the solution of metaphysical problems. It is as if Leibniz had perceived that logic was the essence of philosophy in his more serious work. Russell observed that as Leibniz grew older "he forgot the good philosophy which he had kept to himself," a reference to Leibniz' unpublished manuscripts, "and remembered only the vulgarized version by which he won the admiration of Princes and even more of Princesses." In 1944 Russell wrote of Leibniz:

> His intellect was highly abstract and logical; his greatest claim to fame is as an inventor of infinitesimal calculus. One may read Spinoza in order to know how to live, but not Leibniz. Locke is at least as important as founder of philosophical liberalism as he is as the founder of empiricist philosophy.

It is clear what values Russell was seeking to discern in the philosopher to whose writings he had devoted so much thought and study.

We are now in a position to understand how much these values were Russell's own. The goals he set for himself as theoretician and human being were what he would have been pleased to find in his studies of the abstract thinker he admired. Instead, he believed that he had found a mind divided within itself—courtier by day, philosopher by night. In the same essay, "Reply to Criticisms" (1944), Russell commented:

194

Some of Leibniz' private reflections . . . suggest that at times he himself saw through his own theology. I think he had moments of insight which he felt to be inconvenient and therefore did not encourage. He was insincere toward himself as well as toward his public . . . a similar problem arises in some degree as regards most philosophers, but in the case of Leibniz it is most acute.

In *A History of Western Philosophy* (1945), Russell reasserted his harsh judgment of Leibniz and seems to have warmed to the task.

Leibniz was one of the supreme intellects of all time but as a human being he was not admirable. He had, it is true the virtues that one would wish to find mentioned in a testimonial to a prospective employee; he was industrious, frugal, temperate and financially honest. But he was wholly destitute of those higher philosophic virtues that are so notable in Spinoza. His best thought was not such as would win him popularity and he left his records of it unpublished in his desk. What he published was designed to win the approbation of princes and princesses.

Byronic Russell was the aristocratic rebel who wrote defiantly for the masses, not for princes and princesses. His publishers were members of the established bourgeois press who welcomed a dissident voice which spoke in civilized cadences even when angry, never raucous, never strident. Is it a merit to seek this kind of popularity under such patronage and regard it a demerit to seek it under royalty? At times Russell was the victim of his own generous impulses, permitting various publishers and their editors who had their eyes on the market to compile mismatched collections of his essays and release previous works under new titles. The time was soon to come when Russell, too, would succumb to the lure of a prize presented by royal academicians on behalf of a bourgeois industrialist legator.

Russell's evaluation of Leibniz' motives does less than justice to this important philosopher. Although Russell analyzed Leibnizian writings carefully, his estimate of Leibniz' intentions reflects a facile conception of what constitutes the historical context of thought. He paid insufficient attention to the concrete conditions of Leibniz' milieu. A more detailed knowledge of the material conditions in the social, economic, and political circumstances of the thinker and his actions in the matrix of possible alternatives could have led Russell to a more judicious appraisal. This comment on the shortcomings of Russell's method of historical inquiry is not to be construed as implying that he lacked concern for considering the social circumstances under which thought is produced. The criticism turns rather on the probity of his analysis.

Russell's treatment of Leibniz is a typical instance of his approach to the larger subject of intellectual history. A *History of Western Philosophy* purports to show the development of philosophy in the context of the social conditions in which it occurred. Valuable as the book is in its exposition of ideas and its sketches of the lives of philosophers, it is nevertheless disappointing in the way it deals with the social background and how that background relates to the philosophers and their ideas. The delineation of the social conditions goes on alongside accounts of the ideas and the philosophers who developed them, but the intimate connections between these factors is not elaborated. Russell asserted that his purpose was "to exhibit philosophy as an integral part of social and political life: not as the isolated speculation of remarkable individuals but as both an effect and a cause of the character of the various communities in which different systems flourished."

It is a much more difficult task to show the reciprocal interaction of social, political, and philosophical factors than would appear on the surface. Russell succeeded in outlining possible connections in a few cases but failed to sustain this theme throughout the book. The early 1940's, during which time Russell was most actively involved in composing *A History of Western Philosophy*, were trying years for him. The sting of ostracism in a foreign land, deprived of income, a temporary association with the A. C. Barnes Foundation, financially dependent upon the whim of an erratic benefactor, victim of a breach of contract, a lawsuit for redress of grievances—considering these events one finds it remarkable that Bertrand Russell succeeded in completing the book. No doubt the need to finish it and deliver it to his publishers as soon as possible was, in fact, the cause of some of the minor infelicities in composition. The task was a grand one, his effort was valiant, and the spirit with which he approached the subject was generous. His desire, as he put it in the Preface, was to help his readers to a "sympathetic comprehension of philosophers in relation to the times that formed them and the times that they helped to form." How poignant and yet how characteristic of his indomitable spirit it is to find him saying in the Introduction, ". . . to teach how to live without certainty and yet without being paralyzed by hesitation, is perhaps the chief thing that philosophy, in our age, can still do for those who study it."

This remark is one of the two quotations which the secretary of the Swedish Academy, Österling, selected some five years later to characterize Russell in the presentation speech formally requesting Russell to accept the Nobel Prize for Literature from the hands of the king of Sweden. Occasions of prize presentation tend to be stuffy and the rhetoric somewhat stilted, but Österling's remarks struck the right note. He characterized *A History of Western Philosophy* as a work containing "passages which give us an idea of how he himself might like us to regard his long and arduous life." Österling went on to cite a highly appropriate passage drawn from Russell's remarks about the pre-Socratic philosophers:

In studying a philosopher the right attitude is neither reverence nor contempt, but first a kind of hypothetical sympathy, until it is possible to know what it feels like to believe in his theories, and only then a revival of the critical attitude which should resemble, as far as possible, the state of mind of a person abandoning opinions which he has hitherto held.

Of course it is much more difficult to treat one's contemporary in that way.

By 1950 the earlier Russell had in some ways become a historical figure to a number of younger philosophers. They read his works on logic and theory of knowledge but shunned the others. They had become strangely out of sympathy with his bold views and wide-ranging approach and sought the comforts of meticulous analyses in the quiet precincts of university seminars. Intellectual confrontation had been transformed into controlled genteel debate, and irritation was displayed as private nervousness. G. E. Moore was to be emulated, Ludwig Wittgenstein's "Blue Book" and "Brown Book" were circulated with precaution and secrecy to the favored few, but Russell's later writings were ignored. Bertrand Russell was again battling the academy and its new and younger intellectual establishment.

The alienation was there, and the attitudes and the posturings were evident, but the crucial differences were never explicitly formulated and debated. It is the stray remark that gives readers a clue to what was going on. The later Wittgenstein was to be revealed to the public for the first time in 1947, before his *Philosophical Investigations* were published in 1953. Russell made his intention clear that he wrote not for the exclusive few but for the larger reading public. On this issue he was on the side of the people. The very first paragraph in the Preface to *Human Knowledge* makes his position clear:

These pages are addressed not only or primarily to professional philosophers but to that much larger public which is interested in philosophical questions without being willing or able to devote more than a limited amount of time to considering them. Descartes, Leibniz, Locke, Berkeley and Hume wrote for a public of this sort, and I think it is unfortunate that during the last hundred and sixty years or so philosophy has come to be regarded as almost as technical as mathematics. . . . Philosophy proper deals with matters of interest to the general educated public, and loses much of its value if only a few professionals can understand what is said.

In this context we can understand how cogent were the considerations of the Nobel jury and how well Bertrand Russell deserved the Nobel Prize for Literature. The award not only honored a great man but also added the prestige of the award to the kind of writing which is directed at informing the public about philosophical topics. Österling summarized the point admirably:

It is not his achievements in special science that the Nobel Prize is primarily meant to recognize. What is important from our point of view is that Russell has so extensively addressed his books to a public of laymen and in doing so, has been so eminently successful in keeping alive the interest in general philosophy.

The speech "Politically Important Desires" which Russell delivered when he accepted the prize, showed him in his best form as lecturer. As might be expected, Russell was his usual witty, intransigent self, making no concessions to the occasion, delivering an incisive piece of plain speaking. The theme and thought of the lecture were an extension of work in progress since 1945. While he had been thinking on topics related to the composition of *Human Knowledge*, Russell had written several chapters with the idea of including a discussion of ethical knowledge in the book. Finally he decided against including them because he remained unsure of the sense in which ethics may be regarded as knowledge. Later on he incorporated those essays, together with the Nobel lecture, in *Human Society in Ethics and Politics* (1954).

Russell arrived at the view, expressed in *Human Knowledge*, that the sources of our beliefs are more deeply rooted in our animal behavior than most philosophers have suspected. The connection with animal behavior is even more obvious as regards action and impulses to action in moral and political matters. Russell pointed out in his lecture that politics is concerned with herds, not individuals, and that the sources of individual moral actions are desires and passions, not reason. "Reason is not a cause of action but only a regulator." Ideologies are rallying points whereby groups are generated among people. The hostility created by conflicting ideologies has more to do with the rivalry of groups and herd feeling than with the ideas at issue.

According to Russell, it is falsely believed that those who urge rationality deny a role to emotion and passion. Quite the contrary, reason is correctly advocated as reliable in the choice of means to desired ends. If men were to desire their own happiness as ardently as they desire the misery of their neighbors, says Russell, things would improve rapidly. Champion of humanity though he was, he had few illusions about man's collective behavior. "We love those who hate our enemies—if we had no enemies there would be very few people whom we should love." His analysis was cogent, but his remedies were few. The suggestion that we treat the soil, or Mother Nature, as the enemy and struggle to get the better of her has an unecological tone to it. Nature needs our care, not our animosity. In many ways Russell is still close to John Stuart Mill and nineteenth-century utilitarians. Perhaps he is more sophisticated when he asserts:

Much that passes as idealism is disguised hatred or disguised love of power. When you see large masses of men swayed by what appear to be noble motives, it is well to look below the surface and ask yourself what it is that makes these motives effective.

199

After all the pessimism, he cannot end without striking an optimistic note: ". . . the main thing needed to make the world happy is intelligence, . . and intelligence is a thing that can be fostered by known methods of education."

During the next two decades Russell became increasingly involved in antiwar movements, devoting his writing skills and his personal prestige to promoting peace. In the early fifties Russell was writing in a new and unexpected genre, perhaps stimulated by the award for literature: a short novel, *Satan in the Suburbs* (1954), and some brief stories and moral fables, *Nightmares of Eminent Persons* (1954). The few books on philosophical topics published subsequently were mainly compilations of essays written earlier.

Wisdom of the West (1959) was a briefer and more carefully edited history of philosophy. Russell intended it to serve as a reminder to the forgetful in an age of fierce specialism not to forget their intellectual debts to their forebears. Russell himself had been an important figure in promoting modernism and initiating a new way of pursuing philosophy. Logical-analytical inquiry can proceed by the collective efforts of individuals producing piecemeal results. Russell, whose earlier advocacy of scientific methods in the field had provided a rationale for increased specialism in philosophical studies, had now come to deplore some consequences of the trends he had set in motion. He was especially irked by the low level of philosophical literacy among some practitioners:

> The prevailing view that philosophers need know nothing about anything is quite certainly wrong. Those who think that philosophy really began in 1921, or at any rate not long before, fail to see that current philosophic problems have not arisen all of a sudden and out of nothing.

Over the years Russell remained something of an enigma even to himself, writing and rewriting accounts of his development. The set of "events" constituting Bertrand Russell needed description and review. Some philosophers culminated their works in comprehensive efforts at unity, weaving their thoughts together in grand and abstract systems. Russell was against such efforts in principle and avoided them in practice. In spite of his commitment to analytical methods in philosophy, he was not of a mind to escape from the concrete world in which change must be wrought. Consistent with his principles, Bertrand Russell, philosopher and author, found the form for culminating the events of his life and thought not in logical reconstruction but in autobiography. If for no other reason than his mastery of prose style, the three volumes of *The Autobiography of Bertrand Russell* are a fitting monument to a Nobel honoree in literature, who some years earlier had received the Nobel Prize "in recognition of his varied and significant writings in which he champions humanitarian ideals and freedom of thought."

WINSTON S. CHURCHILL

by Amos C. Miller

T<small>HE ANNOUNCEMENT OF THE AWARD</small> of the Nobel Prize for Literature to Sir Winston Churchill in October, 1953, came as no surprise. Over a period of fifty-five years he had written twenty-seven books, most of which had received high praise from critics. For several years before, he had been a leading candidate for a Nobel prize, and support for him in the Swedish Academy had risen sharply since the publication of *The Second World War,* the final volume of which appeared in November, 1953.

In making the presentation of the award, Siegfried Siwertz, a distinguished writer and member of the Swedish Academy, observed how seldom it is that the attributes of a great writer are combined with those of a statesman and warrior. But Churchill, he said, was "a Caesar who has the gift of Cicero's pen." The speaker emphasized the high quality of Churchill's biographical and historical work and the power of his oratory as the principal reasons for the award. He mentioned Churchill's biographies of his father, Lord Randolph Churchill, and of his ancestor, John Churchill, Duke of Marlborough; the biographical sketches in *Great Contemporaries*; *The World Crisis,* Sir Winston's account of World War I; *My Early Life*; and the autobiographical narrative of his career until 1902. Siwertz also commented favorably on one of Churchill's earliest works in the field of military history, *The River War.*

In evaluating Churchill as a writer, Siwertz referred to the vigor and impetuosity of his style. These qualities, he said, were a clear reflection of Churchill's own dynamic and uncomplicated personality. Siwertz also spoke of Sir Winston's skill in describing military and political conflict. He remarked upon Churchill's talent as a word painter, which gave "a marvellous coloring" to his battle scenes. Noting particularly Sir Winston's participation in many of the events he described, Siwertz stressed the fact that the intimate blend of the subjective and the objective in Churchill's books added to their vividness and authenticity. In addition, Siwertz praised Churchill's capacity to delineate human character, which, he said, was well demonstrated in the biography of the Duke of Marlborough.

Siwertz concluded by observing that behind Churchill the writer was Churchill the orator and that from this fusion of oratorical and literary technique came the sharp and pungent phraseology that appears so frequently in his books. "Churchill's mature oratory," Siwertz said,

is swift, unerring in its aim and moving in its grandeur. There is the power which forges the links of history. Napoleon's proclamations were often effective in their lapidary style. But Churchill's eloquence in the fateful hours of freedom and human dignity was heartening in quite another way. With his great speeches he has, perhaps, himself erected his most enduring monument.

Unable to attend the presentation of his award in Stockholm on December 10, 1953, Sir Winston sent his wife to read his speech of acceptance. In it he struck a note that was both modest and somber. "I am proud," he declared, "but also, I must admit, awestruck at your decision to include me. I do hope you are right. I feel we are both running a considerable risk and that I do not deserve it. But I shall have no misgivings if you have none." These remarks must have sounded odd coming from a man who had never been known for his modesty, but there can be no doubt about his sincerity. Despite his long experience and success as a writer, Churchill had always been humble regarding his ability in that sphere. When his friend T. E. Lawrence presented him with a copy of *Seven Pillars of Wisdom*, he remarked that his own writing was that of a mere journalist.

Unlike many Nobel Prize winners, Churchill gave no personal credo on the profession of writing, nor did he offer any reflections upon the state of contemporary literature. Instead, he presented the Academy with a forbidding appraisal of the world scene:

We have entered upon an age of storm and tragedy. The power of man has grown in every sphere except over himself. Never in the field of action have events seemed so harshly to dwarf personalities. Rarely in history have brutal facts so dominated thought or has widespread individual virtue found so dim a collective focus.

Against this grim background Churchill saw hope for mankind in the idealism that motivated Alfred Nobel

He has left behind him a bright and enduring beam of culture, of purpose and of inspiration of which it stands in sore need. This world-famous institution points a true path for us to follow. Let us therefore confront the clatter and rigidity we see around us with tolerance, variety, and calm.

The views expressed in this speech reflected the assessment of a great statesman who perceived the dangers which then threatened a world that had only recently emerged from the second great war of the twentieth century. They also indicated a pessimism that was natural in a man almost eighty years of age who had suffered a stroke a few months earlier and who still bore the burden of leadership of his country. Yet the mood was, to some extent, characteristic of Churchill. Beneath his outward optimism there had always been a vein of pessimism that became more pronounced as he witnessed in the Western world the emergence of a society with whose values he had little sympathy.

Indeed, in some respects, it was rather curious that he should have received the Nobel Literary Prize in 1953, because his ideas and mode of expression ran counter to the trends of the time. The other English recipients in the period following the World War I—Shaw, Galsworthy, and Russell—made their reputations, in varying degrees, as critics of the social order in which they lived. This was even more true of such American winners as Sinclair Lewis, Eugene O'Neill, T. S. Eliot, William Faulkner, Ernest Hemingway, and John Steinbeck. All these men, of course, preserved some of the values of the past, but in the main they reflected the disillusionment and sense of despair characteristic of the post–World War I generation. They tended to look upon conventional society and morality as corrupt and decadent. In their view man had little control over his destiny and external forces.

Churchill, on the other hand, was the living embodiment, as a writer and as a man, of the relatively secure, self-confident Victorian and Edwardian ages, which had been destroyed by World War I. Throughout life he accepted nearly all the values and goals of the dominant classes of this prewar society. He believed that personal ambition and the pursuit of worldly success by honorable means were the right and duty of every man. He opposed determinism and was convinced that each individual, by means of self-discipline and effort, could creatively shape his own environment. The energetic and pur-poseful life he had led since early youth represented the fullest ex-pression of these ideals. As Siwertz said, "Churchill was heart and soul a late Victorian who has been buffetted by the gale, or rather one who chose of his own accord to breast the storm."

One must not press this point too far, however. In part of his mind Churchill was well aware that courage and initiative alone are not enough. He believed that in human existence and in human nature itself there are malevolent forces which can defeat the most resolute efforts a man may make. Indeed, at times he was afflicted by feelings of hopelessness concerning himself and the world in which he lived. According to the English psychotherapist Anthony Storr, it was by learning to master this sense of despair within himself that Churchill developed his remarkable courage. From a literary point of view it occasionally invested his writing with an irony and pessimism that resembled the outlook of many authors of the 1920's and 1930's with whom Churchill differed so sharply in most other respects.

Despite these undercurrents, the overriding attitudes in Churchill's mind were those common among Englishmen of his class before 1914. He held that there were certain unalterable values—loyalty, honor, courage, and devotion to duty—which were obligatory for men and nations alike. He was an ardent patriot and, during most of his career, an imperialist. Though a champion of liberal principles of individual freedom and constitutional government, he was fundamentally a con-servative who adhered to the idea of a hierarchial society in which

205

leadership was exercised by a gifted and cultured elite. In his method of writing and speaking, Churchill was a traditionalist who molded his style on that of the great literary craftsmen and orators of the eighteenth and nineteenth centuries.

To discover the source of Churchill's inspiration as a writer, we must look to the circumstances of his childhood. Neglected and ignored by his parents during his early years, Winston found compensation in the development of a highly colored imagination. His imaginative faculties were amply stimulated by his environment. He was born at Blenheim, the magnificent residence of the dukes of Marlborough, the first of whom had been granted the estate for his great victory over the French in August, 1704. He also had before him the career of his brilliant father, who while still a young man had risen to such power and influence in the Conservative party that he dared to challenge its leaders. By fatal miscalculation, however, he brought upon himself not only defeat but the ruin of his political life. This event took place when Winston was only twelve years of age, and it made an indelible impression upon him. Politics and war became the chief interests of his existence, and they were linked in his mind with a profound sense of Britain's past. This consciousness was, of course, intensified by Churchill's awareness that he belonged to a family and to a class that had taken an active part in shaping his country's development as a nation. He felt the history of England as part of his very flesh and blood. In precisely the same way he assumed an inherent right and obligation to play a leading part in its making.

Moreover, he came to see both present and past in terms of a dramatic contest between good and evil in which men endowed with exceptional courage, ardor, and intelligence must assume leadership in order to ensure the triumph of the good. This was a vision of life and of history from which he drew his literary inspiration. It was also the driving force behind his career.

Anthony Storr believes that these attitudes arose because of his parents' neglect of him. To combat the recurrent depressions resulting from it, he became determined to win from the world, through high achievement, the approval denied him in childhood. He developed an overpowering ambition and a conviction that he was destined to fulfill a glorious mission. Robert R. James remarked that Churchill "is always playing a part in an heroic drama, and that he himself is his most astonished spectator."[1] The life of action became the primary outlet of his creative energies. Closely related was the desire to give literary expression to that life, and above all to his own role in it. In Churchill's writing there would also appear an awareness of the tragic possibilities of life that may well have resulted from his childhood experiences, as well as from his father's disastrous career and early death.

After he had achieved success and recognition in the world, Churchill took pleasure in describing his backwardness as a schoolboy, thereby, no doubt, intending to emphasize the contrast with his later achievements. But even then his teachers noted his veneration for the English language and his love of history. From one of his teachers, Churchill later recalled, he "got into my bones the essential structure of the ordinary English sentence, which is a noble thing."

While serving as a cavalry officer in India following graduation from Sandhurst, Churchill set to work to repair the deficiencies of his education. During the long hot afternoons before time for polo, he read in many fields: history, politics, philosophy, economics, and religion. He also began to acquire experience in writing, first as a war correspondent and then as an author. Two historians who exercised strong influence on him were Edward Gibbon and Thomas Macaulay. In the works of both writers there is a pronounced rhetorical quality based upon classical models, and they also possess an eloquence, a sense of the sound and rhythm of the English language, and a clarity which Churchill greatly admired. Gibbon's style is characterized by long, intricately constructed, finely balanced sentences. The drama and excitement of historic events are vividly portrayed, but over Gibbon's entire narrative there is a majestic spirit in which qualities of irony and of detachment are closely intermingled. Like the author of the *Decline and Fall*, Churchill learned to avoid monotony by skillfully varying the tone, structure, and length of his sentences. He also acquired the dramatic sense, the stateliness, and the irony of Gibbon, though he seldom attained Gibbon's calm aloofness.

Macaulay's style, on the other hand, is crisp and forceful. Its vigor is enhanced by the use of sharp antitheses in sentence structure. As he developed his own capacities for literary expression, Churchill sought

[1] Robert Rhodes James, *Churchill: A Study in Failure, 1900–1939*, 19.

to achieve a fusion of the styles of these two writers, but he also achieved a humor, a descriptive power, and an aptitude for pungent comment that were distinctively his own. To develop his talent for description, Churchill consciously and painstakingly cultivated the art of observation so that he could depict accurately and clearly what he had seen and heard.

Even more important, his imaginative power enabled him to reconstruct events and personalities of the past and to transmit them vividly and realistically to the reader. In this process he was assisted by a keen visual sense, which he employed for the creation of imagery, especially metaphors derived from the sights and sounds of the natural world. He also enjoyed using anecdotes. These he called "the gleaming toys of history," and he related them frequently and effectively to bring a situation or a character more sharply into focus. But Churchill's chief attribute was his vitality. He was the fighter and leader who learned how to express in literary form the life of action. His writing, as Siwertz said, was infused with a "resolute impetus" in which "every word is half a deed."

Churchill's literary work began with *Savrola*, which he began writing in 1897 while he was in India but did not complete and publish until 1900. An adventure story set in the fictitious country of Laurania, the book resembled Sir Anthony Hawkins' *The Prisoner of Zenda*, which had appeared only a few years earlier. In this simple story Churchill displayed much of the facility for the swift, forceful narrative that distinguished his later writing. Devoting a major portion of the book to an account of the fighting between the forces of the democratic party and the army of Molara (the would-be dictator of Laurania), he portrayed the suspense, movement, and violence of war with graphic realism.

This book is of particular interest because the leading character was obviously young Churchill himself. An aristocrat in taste and manner, Savrola had Churchill's daring and self-confidence, the same sense of destiny, the conviction that he would play a great part in the world, and the determination to test his powers to the utmost. These qualities gave a vibrating intensity to his style.

By the time *Savrola* was published, Churchill had produced four other books: *The Story of the Malakand Field Force, The River War,*

London to Ladysmith, and *Ian Hamilton's March*. All of them concerned military actions in which he had been personally involved. Of these works the first two are the most important. Although Churchill was acting as a newspaper reporter as well as a soldier, his accounts *The Malakand Field Force* and *The River War* were more than mere journalistic narratives of military campaigns from a personal standpoint. They marked his initiation as a historian. In *The River War* Churchill described Gordon's state of mind during his last days under oiogo by the Sudanese rebels:

> To the military anxieties were added every kind of worry that may weary a man's soul. The belief that he was abandoned and discredited, that history would make light of his efforts, and perhaps never know of them filled his mind with a sense of wrong and injustice which preyed upon his spirit. The miseries of the townsfolk wrung his noble, generous heart. The utter loneliness depressed him. Yet he was sustained by two great mental and moral stimulants: his honor, his faith as a Christian.

This passage reveals Churchill's tendency toward idealization. Early in the book he made clear his own awareness that Gordon was an egocentric and unstable individual, but his imagination was caught by the courage with which the general met his death, and in the end he overstressed the nobility of Gordon's character.

The Malakand Field Force and *The River War* gained considerable public acclaim for Churchill and established his reputation as an author. Eighty-five hundred copies of *The Malakand Field Force* were sold; both the Prince of Wales and the prime minister, Lord Salisbury, read and enjoyed it. Critics were especially favorable toward *The River War*. The *Daily Mail* praised the balanced and judicial character of the book. While paying tribute to Churchill's style, however, the reviewer observed that the author sometimes became overly grandiose: "Mr. Churchill, having the *Decline and Fall* up his sleeve, forgets that only the great occasion justifies the music of the organ."[2]

By 1900, Churchill was able to turn his undivided attention to politics, which was to become the chief occupation of his life. He had used his military profession and even, to some extent, his writing as a means

[2] Randolph S. Churchill, *Winston S. Churchill*, I, 443.

for gaining the public attention which was essential to begin a career in politics. His journalism, his books on war—especially *London to Ladysmith,* in which he described his escape from an enemy prison camp during the Boer War—provided the necessary personal publicity, and in the summer of 1900 he was elected to the House of Commons as a Conservative member. Just as war had hitherto provided an impetus for his writing, so now politics became an inspiration. Indeed, the clash of parties and personalities in Cabinet and Parliament offered his imagination much the same kind of stimulus as war.

His personal involvement in political life was all the keener because of his painful memories of his father's tragic career. Less than six years before Winston entered Parliament, Lord Randolph had died at the age of forty-six, a pitiful and broken man whose mind had been destroyed by disease. Winston had loved his father devotedly, despite the almost invariable coldness with which the latter had behaved toward him. In fact, Winston's admiration for and desire to emulate his father almost became an obsession. Many people who had known Lord Randolph were astonished at the extent to which his son resembled him in speech, mannerisms, and dress. More important, Winston was determined to vindicate his father's name and to fight for the ideals which his father had sought unsuccessfully to achieve. These aspirations led him to rebel against the Conservative party hierarchy as Lord Randolph had done. They also provided the inspiration for the biography which Winston wrote of his father.

Published in 1906, *Lord Randolph Churchill* received almost universal praise at the time it appeared, and even after an interval of more than fifty years the book is still rated highly. Churchill devoted a major portion of his book to the years 1880 to 1886, when Lord Randolph made his rapid ascent to power in the Conservative party and in the government. Many believed that he was soon destined to become prime minister. Then, because of disagreement on what he regarded as an important matter of policy, Lord Randolph resigned from the Cabinet. By this reckless act he reduced himself to complete political impotence. Hitherto one of the most powerful men in the country, he was ostracized by his own party and a permanent outcast from public life.

In relating these events, Churchill showed himself an accomplished master of political as well as military narrative. All the issues in which his father had been involved—the struggle for control of the Conservative party, Irish home rule, foreign policy, social reform—were elucidated with vigor and clarity. He knew how to keep all the threads of a complex story firmly in hand so that the reader is never at a loss, and at the same time he moved the narrative ahead at a swift pace.

One of the most admirable features of Churchill's biography was the extent to which he avoided extreme partisanship on his father's behalf. He showed the enormous enthusiasm that Lord Randolph aroused among the people through his personal magnetism and brilliant oratory. He brought out clearly his father's qualities of charm, courage, and vitality. On the other hand, his references to Lord Randolph's recurrent fits of depression indicate that Winston was aware to some degree of the neurotic side of his father's personality. As the English historian Maurice Ashley has pointed out, the very aloofness with which Lord Randolph treated his son probably enabled the latter to gain a certain detachment about him. Churchill did not shirk the fact that his father's arrogant behavior toward colleagues, his impatience, and his occasional want of judgment were major factors in precipitating his downfall.

Well balanced and perceptive as it is in many ways, Churchill's book does not provide a complete understanding either of his father or of his political associates. This was not entirely Sir Winston's fault. Because the book was published only ten years after Lord Randolph's death, a number of his leading adversaries were still alive. Discretion did not permit Churchill to tell the full truth about some of the situations he described. In addition, a good deal of information about Lord Randolph has come to light since the publication of Churchill's book which was not known to him at the time he wrote it. There can be no doubt, however, that Churchill's judgment was colored by filial admiration. Robert Rhodes James, Lord Randolph's most recent biographer, makes it clear that he was neither as high principled nor as consistent as his son believed. Moreover, Churchill's book affords little insight into the psychological bases of Lord Randolph's behavior. He made no attempt to explain the self-destructive traits in his father's temperament which played such an important part in bringing about his downfall. Neither in *Lord Randolph Churchill* nor in his later endeavors in the field of biography did Sir Winston display deep interest in psychological analysis, but one must note that at the time he wrote about his father such probing did not fall within the scope of political biography, as it was then understood.

Yet if filial love can blind an author to the full truth about a parent, it can also be a fertile source of literary inspiration. Whatever his errors, Churchill believed that his father had pursued a noble and just aim—that of transforming the Conservative party from a privileged oligarchy into a party of the people. He concluded his book with this moving passage:

> There is an England which stretches far beyond the well drilled masses who are assembled by party machinery to salute with appropriate acclamation the utterances of their recognized fugelmen; an England of wise men who gaze without self-deception at the failings and follies of both political parties; of brave and earnest men who find in neither faction fair scope for the effort that is in them. . . . It was to that England that Lord Randolph Churchill appealed; it is by that England that he will be justly judged.[3]

Though Sir Winston was sometimes guilty of exaggeration on his father's behalf, *Lord Randolph Churchill* possesses a certain restraint that is lacking from some of his later works. One of Churchill's recent biographers, Peter de Mendelssohn, has remarked that in the book on his father Winston "had put aside most of the mummery borrowed from Macaulay and Gibbon, but had not yet acquired the flamboyant rhetorical style with its gilded epigrams set in a set of purple passages.[4]

Following the publication of *Lord Randolph Churchill*, preoccupation with public affairs sharply curtailed Winston's output of books for more than fifteen years. Not until after World War I did he complete his next major work, *The World Crisis*, a book combining history and autobiography that deals with the period 1911 to 1928. It covered the background and events of the Great War, the peace settlement, and major political and diplomatic developments in Europe and the Near East immediately thereafter. From the standpoint of his own

[3] Winston S. Churchill, *Lord Randolph Churchill*, II, 488–89.
[4] Peter de Mendelssohn, *The Age of Churchill: Heritage and Adventure, 1874–1911*, 265.

personal knowledge, Churchill was eminently qualified to write a history of the war. After leaving the Conservative party in 1904, he became a member of the Liberal government which declared war on Germany in 1914. Afterward he served not only as a Cabinet minister directly concerned with military affairs, but also briefly as an army officer on the Western Front.

The World Crisis was more than a personal account, for it provided a historical narrative of high quality based upon extensive research in the memoirs of Allied and enemy leaders. Yet there can be no doubt that the element of personal involvement greatly enhanced the vitality of Churchill's account. In May, 1915, he had been expelled from the Cabinet because of his initiative in launching the disastrous attack on the Dardanelles. His certainty that he had been right in the matter of the Dardanelles and his conviction that Allied commanders had been tragically mistaken in concentrating massive offensives on the Western Front gave impetus and fire to his writing. "Good, plain, straightforward attacks," he declared, "'killing Germans' while Germans killed Allies twice as often, calling out the men of forty, of fifty, and even of fifty-five, and youth of eighteen, sending the wounded soldiers three and four times over into the shambles—such were the sole manifestations reserved for the military art."

Hard-hitting as he was about the Allied leaders with whom he disagreed, Churchill tried to provide a full and fair explanation of the reasoning upon which their decisions were based, and he almost always paid tribute to their personal qualities. Writing as one who had borne the responsibility for vital decisions in the war, he manifested an instinctive and generous sympathy for those who were compelled to carry the same burden. He had no patience whatever with those postwar writers who, in reaction to the slaughter on the Western Front, dismissed Allied military leaders as fools or scoundrels.

One of the outstanding features of *The World Crisis* is the brief summing up—often with a single piercing phrase—of a man or a situation. Describing the changed atmosphere of international politics after the war he wrote, "The war of the giants has ended; the quarrels of the pygmies have begun." He asserted that, after the Communists seized power in 1918, Russia was "frozen in an indefinite winter of subhuman doctrine and superhuman tyranny." Of Britain's great war leader, David Lloyd George he wrote that he had

a power of living in the present without taking short views. Every day for him was filled with the hope and impulse of a fresh beginning. He surveyed the problems of each morning with an eye unobstructed by preconceived opinions, past utterances, or previous disappointments or defeats.

Another attraction of *The World Crisis*, as in all Churchill's books, is the clear and uninhibited way in which it reveals his personality. Repeatedly the reader feels the glow of his courage, energy, and fertile imagination, as in the story of his sudden dispatch of naval troops in an effort to save Antwerp in the autumn of 1914, and in the account of his initiative in the development of the tank. As one might expect of a practiced military historian, Churchill offered outstanding descriptions of great battles, such as those of the Marne and in Jutland. The sailor-king George V so enjoyed Churchill's accounts of the naval engagements that he spent his leisure hours working out the courses of the ships described in the narrative.

Most reviewers were enthusiastic about the literary qualities of Churchill's book. "Racy," "thrilling," "picturesque," "exciting" were among the adjectives applied to it. There were also, however, those who saw in *The World Crisis* evidence of what they regarded as Churchill's besetting weaknesses: egoism and lack of balance and objectivity. The former Conservative leader and prime minister A. J. Balfour remarked in a characteristically sardonic vein that he was "immersed in Winston's brilliant autobiography disguised as a history of the universe."

Such comments, favorable and unfavorable, contain a measure of truth, but in one sense they are superficial. Certainly Churchill's narrative is vivid and dramatic. It is also to some extent a partisan document, as he himself admitted. But together with these qualities some critics discerned an underlying judiciousness of mind and seriousness of purpose. In his book Churchill manifested an intention which overrode his desire for self-justification: that of discovering and establishing the truth in order that men might learn the bitter lessons of their errors. Above all, he showed a realization of the appalling nature of war itself. This attitude was not immediately apparent, for the reader was made constantly aware of Churchill's enjoyment of the challenge and excitement of war. Yet his recognition of its tragic cost in human suffering also became clear.

One failing that became increasingly apparent in Churchill's writing was a tendency to be overly florid. As one biographer, Philip Guedalla, stated, Churchill fell victim to the "fatal lullaby of a majestic style." Perhaps this defect was inevitable in a man who followed the model of Gibbon and Macaulay, but it also arose from his preoccupation with oratory as a politician constantly engaged in public speaking and from the fact that all his books after *Lord Randolph Churchill* were dictated, not written. Employed with proper restraint, the rhetorical style can be extremely effective in creating atmosphere and in transmitting deep and sincere emotion. Frequently Churchill used it in exactly this way, but this mode of expression sometimes led him to exaggeration and bombast.

A weakness in *The World Crisis* was the absence of perception concerning social movements. For example, the book offered little analysis of the effect of the war upon the European people. In his discussion of the Russian Revolution, he rightly condemned the deceptions and cruelties committed by the Communists but showed no understanding of corruption and incompetence in the tsarist regime, the war weariness of the ordinary Russian soldier, or the longing of the peasantry for a more just social order that opened the way for the Communist seizure of power in 1917. For Churchill, almost as in a morality play, Lenin and his followers represented the forces of evil. With a melodramatic flourish Churchill likened Lenin to a "plague bacillus" at the moment when the Communist leader was transported into Russia by the German high command in 1917. Unquestionably Churchill's tendency to portray the past in simple, highly colored terms enhanced the vitality of his style, but the failure to analyze the full complexity of events was a defect in him both as a writer and as a historian.

During the 1930's, Churchill wrote four books and more than two hundred newspaper and magazine articles and completed a draft of *The History of the English Speaking Peoples*, his last work, which was not published until after his retirement from public life in the 1950's. Someone has written that unhappiness acts as a spur to authorship.

Certainly this period, so productive from a literary point of view, was also one of deep frustration for Churchill. Following World War I, he had returned to the Conservative Party and had served in the Baldwin government from 1926 to 1929. Thereafter he spent ten years without Cabinet office as a member of the House of Commons. At that time he was regarded as a failed politician who would never regain the power he had once enjoyed. Liberals looked upon him as a deserter; the Socialists, as an enemy of the working class. By many of his fellow Conservatives he was distrusted as a former turncoat and a man whose judgment and stability were not to be relied upon. Churchill increased his isolation by attacking the foremost men of his own party for their failure to face resolutely the dangers presented by Nazi Germany and Fascist Italy. He also opposed their concessions to nationalistic movements in colonial territories. In retaliation the Conservative leaders Baldwin and Chamberlain deliberately excluded him from the government during these years.

Often in despair about the position of his country and, indeed, in regard to his own career as well, Churchill turned once more to the study of history for inspiration and consolation. The result of his labors was a four-volume biography of his ancestor John Churchill, First Duke of Marlborough. Here was a subject with whom he could identify wholeheartedly—a soldier-statesman whose genius in war, statecraft, and diplomacy raised Britain to a position of world leadership in the eighteenth century. Marlborough's life was all the more attractive to Churchill because it was such a striking confirmation of his belief in the capacity of great individuals to alter by their own actions the fate of men and nations. The further he carried his investigation into Marlborough's career the more intense his identification with him must have become. At the opening of the eighteenth century Britain and Europe had confronted the threat of a powerful France under Louis XIV, and it had been Marlborough's leadership that had preserved the liberties of both. Now Churchill was trying to alert his country to a still greater menace, the Germany of Adolf Hitler. Churchill's family background, his patriotism, his sense of drama and of history, and his growing conviction of his destiny to play Marlborough's role in his own day combined to lend impetus to his work on this book.

There was no pretense of impartiality in this biographical study. Churchill set out to demonstrate that Marlborough, who had been of great service to England, had been unjustly vilified by writers both in Marlborough's own time and afterward. With the debating skill of an experienced parliamentarian Churchill attacked his ancestor's detractors, especially the noted historian Macaulay, whose indictment of Marlborough had long held sway. He showed that Macaulay's accusations of greed and treachery were greatly exaggerated and, in one important instance, untrue. In the main Churchill's defense of Marlborough was well grounded, and, from a literary point of view, his invective added considerably to the entertainment of his narrative. However, he injured his case and weakened the credibility of his own account by overstatement. When he declared, "We can only hope that Truth will follow swiftly enough to fasten the label 'Liar' to his [Macaulay's] genteel coattails," Churchill himself was being grossly unfair. Macaulay was guilty of error, but he was not a liar.

Like Macaulay, Churchill was prone to exaggeration and overemphasis. This was unfortunate because it tended to obscure the real merit of his book, which is a work of historical scholarship based upon manuscript material in English and foreign archives and above all upon Marlborough's own correspondence at Blenheim. In spite of his frank partisanship on his ancestor's behalf, Churchill conscientiously sought to fulfill the biographer's responsibility to portray his subject in the round, his weaknesses as well as his strengths. To a considerable extent he succeeded in his objective. Marlborough emerged not as the caricature presented by Macaulay—a brilliant commander and an inspired leader of men who was also a scoundrel prepared to betray his king and his country—but as a complex and believable human being, a man who had spent his childhood in circumstances of humiliating poverty and dependence in a household where political loyalties were sharply divided. Marlborough, as Churchill showed, early acquired an ability to conceal his own opinions and feelings behind an impenetrable reserve and a determination to win freedom from material subservience by the sure agency of money.

Churchill faced up to the fact that pursuit of self-interest and financial well-being often played an important part in Marlborough's actions. What Churchill contended was that, contrary to the claims of Marlborough's detractors, he never jeopardized the well-being of his country in furthering his personal goals. Where England and the Protestant religion were concerned, his loyalty was absolute. Moreover, Churchill showed not only Marlborough's devoted efforts in the service of his country but also his kindliness and humanity in personal relationships—his love for his formidable wife, Sarah, as revealed in his letters to her, and his care for the men under his command.

In tracing Marlborough's career as supreme commander in the war against France, Churchill wove together a complex military, political, and diplomatic narrative with remarkable skill. He clearly delineated the characters of the other leading figures in the story: Marlborough's brilliant comrade-in-arms, Prince Eugene of Savoy, and leading politicians such as Robert Harley and Henry St. John. As a man who had occupied positions of high authority, Churchill could well understand the problems his ancestors faced. Still more important, he was able to comprehend and convey to the reader Marlborough's inward reaction to them. He, too, had endured disappointment in his career and obstruction from political enemies. Also like Marlborough, he suffered all his life from periods of depression.

The pictorial clarity, suspense, and action in the depiction of a battle or a military campaign is one of the most striking virtues of the book. To achieve such accuracy Churchill not only inspected all of Marlborough's battlefields but also traveled over the routes traversed by his armies. He imaginatively recaptured the violence and excitement of military action. He did not romanticize war, however; his portrayal included not only the clash of arms and the glorious victory but also the suffering and carnage. Nevertheless, in his most important works dealing with war, Churchill centered his attention on the thoughts and behavior of military leaders and on large-scale movements of troops, while the actions of the common soldiers were usually described only at moments of supreme stress in battle.

Marlborough was enlivened by Churchill's sardonic wit. Sometimes it became rather ponderous when he paused to make comparisons between the practices of warfare and international relations in the eighteenth and twentieth centuries, generally at the expense of the latter. Obviously Churchill was feeling much out of sympathy with

218

his own time. On the other hand, his humor could be sharp and effective. Of an unreliable general he remarked that Marlborough and Eugene of Savoy rated his absence from the battlefield as worth fifteen thousand men. Describing the angry reaction of the English aristocracy to the rude behavior of William of Orange toward them, Churchill observed: "The English, although submissive to the new authority of which they felt the need, were as proud as any race in Europe. No one relishes being an object of aversion and contempt."

Churchill made Marlborough intelligible both as a man and as a military and political leader—something no previous writer had done. However, the book is flawed from a biographical point of view. Churchill made an overgenerous estimate of his ancestor's statesmanship and underrated the elements of avarice and self-regard in the Duke's character. In his impetuous and warm-hearted way, Churchill allowed himself to become overly identified with Marlborough. He wrote of him almost as a contemporary and as a friend whose reputation he must defend. This attitude contributed greatly to the vitality of Churchill's work, but it was also a source of weakness, for at times it led him to almost ludicrous exaggeration.

Churchill wrote three other books of importance between 1929 and 1939: *My Early Life* (1930), *Thoughts and Adventures* (1932), and *Great Contemporaries* (1937). In the first, an autobiographical account dealing with his first twenty-eight years, he recounted in detail the various episodes of his life with characteristic vivacity, but his style was quite different from that of his earlier books. He dropped almost entirely the grand manner. His narrative was informal and conversational, and he described each stage of it in a tone suitable to his age. Of his earliest years he wrote with the simplicity and candor of a child and boy, of his youth and young manhood as a cadet and cavalry officer with humor and the sometimes slangy enthusiasm of that age. Another quality which shines in this book is his sense of humor, particularly when telling a story at his own expense. As a young man—and indeed throughout his life—he was often brash, pushing, and loquacious. However, though an egotist, he was never smug, and he was always aware of his own foibles.

Throughout the book there is a tone of mellow geniality and an especially endearing trait: an ability to convey his deep capacity for human affection. In a few touching sentences he described the death of his nanny, Mrs. Everest, and at the same time revealed something of his own lonely childhood: "Death came very easily to her. She had lived such an innocent and loving life of service to others that she had no fears at all, and did not seem to mind very much. She had been my dearest and most intimate friend during the whole twenty years I had lived." Such perceptive writing about a very ordinary person and such expression of human feeling on a simple, personal level do not often appear in Churchill's books. Far more frequently he wrote of emotion on the grand scale—as experienced by great men or by people in the mass at times of crisis. Again and again Churchill manifested his fierce zest for life and his belief that it is a man's duty to face the challenge which life offers.

In 1932, Churchill published a book of essays entitled *Thoughts and Adventures*. Though one of his minor works, it is significant because it reveals certain aspects of Churchill's mind which often escape notice. Many of the essays, of course, portray his dominant characteristics: self-confidence, optimism, and delight in activity of every kind. The book relates how, as home secretary in 1910, he personally took part in a battle with foreign anarchists who had barricaded themselves in a house in the center of London. It describes the danger and the warm comradeship which he shared with the front-line troops in France in 1915. Reading Churchill's account, one feels that he has tasted and savored every human experience except boredom.

In one of his essays Churchill told of his initiation as an artist:

Just to paint is great fun. The colors are lovely to look at and delicious to squeeze out. Matching them, however crudely, with what you see is absolutely absorbing. Try it if you have not already done so—before you die. As one slowly begins to escape the difficulties of choosing the right colors and laying them on in the right places, wider considerations come into view. One begins to see that painting a picture is like fighting a battle; and trying to paint a picture is, I suppose, like trying to fight a battle.

Churchill's vision of life had the simplicity and immediacy of a child's, and he possessed the ability to describe his personal experience with a childlike clarity that is extremely engaging. As Violet Bonham-Carter wrote:

To Winston Churchill everything under the sun was new—seen and appraised as on the first day of creation. His approach to life was full of ardor and surprise. Even eternal verities appeared to him to be an exciting personal discovery. He did not seem to be ashamed of uttering truths so simple and eternal that on another's lips they would be truisms.[5]

In addition to the naïve enthusiasm of a man who always remained young, there was also a strong vein of realism, even pessimism, that emerges in several of these essays, Churchill's confidence and optimism was not of the facile self-deluding type one finds in some successful men. Like the classical Greeks he believed that the individual's contribution to his own life was to some extent limited by an external power, which Churchill called luck, destiny, or even Providence. He believed intensely that people had the capacity to shape their own future, but he was also convinced that their power to do so was not absolute. Frequently, he said, those of his plans which had been devised with the most careful forethought and carried out with the greatest determination had resulted in failure. At other times an apparent stroke of luck or even a miscalculation had brought him undeserved success.

Normally the uncertainty of human existence did not weigh heavily upon Churchill. He accepted it with a fatalistic and somewhat rueful good humor. Occasionally, however, underneath this tone one notes in some of Churchill's books a sense of the tragic dimension of life. Savrola, Churchill's fictional hero, expressed deep uncertainty about whether his own efforts and aspirations or, indeed, those of humanity had any ultimate significance. In *Thoughts and Adventures*, Churchill revealed his pessimism about man's future even more clearly. While recognizing the material benefits conferred on man by modern advances in scientific knowledge, he feared that these advances had been dearly bought. Progress in military technology had so far outstripped human moral development that he envisaged a time when mankind might achieve its own destruction by means of bombs.

At the same time Churchill believed that contemporary conditions of life held almost equal dangers even if peace was preserved. In his view the mass organization of life threatened in the long run to destroy

[5] Violet Bonham-Carter, *Winston Churchill as I Knew Him*, 16.

freedom, initiative, and, above all, creative opportunities for men of exceptional talent. Here his imagination led him to envision still darker possibilities. Unless these tendencies toward "universal standardization" were checked, Churchill feared the day might come when despotic governments would develop scientific methods to produce human robots whose minds were wholly subject to control by their rulers. This world of the future bore a strong resemblance to that later created by George Orwell in *1984*. Churchill believed that the aristocratic England of his youthful days, when the government was still largely in the hands of a privileged minority, had offered wider opportunities for men of real ability. Writing of John Morley, he commented:

> Such men are not found today. Certainly they are not found in British politics. The tidal waves of democracy and the volcanic explosion of the war have swept the shores bare. . . . Nowadays "when one man is as good as another—or better," as John Morley once ironically said, anything will do.

Churchill concluded with one of those trenchant comments he knew how to make so effectively: "The leadership of the privileged has passed away; but it has not been succeeded by that of the eminent."[6] Very likely he was influenced in this attitude by the unwillingness of either the British public or the men they elected in the 1930's to heed his counsels about the dangers facing them.

In many of Churchill's essays we see a keen interest in human idiosyncrasies, an amused and tolerant awareness of the contradictions that so often appear in the characters of prominent men. He pointed out, for example, the contrast in George Bernard Shaw between the socialist and iconoclast who mocked the institutions and practices of his own society—private acquisition of wealth, marriage, and parliamentary government—and the man who enjoyed fully the material benefits with which that society rewarded his talents, who maintained the highest standards of bourgois respectability in his private life, and whose outspoken ridicule would have made him the first victim of the dictatorship he advocated. While Churchill obviously appreciated Shaw's irreverent gaiety and charm, he was also repelled at times by what seemed to him to be Shaw's irresponsibility.

[6] Winston S. Churchill, *Great Contemporaries*, 82–83.

Though he clearly preferred the man of action to the social critic, Churchill also recognized the same element of human contradiction in the former. He pointed out the capacity for cool ruthlessness that lay behind the urbanity and charm of Arthur Balfour and Herbert Asquith. His comments were most perceptive on men like Lord Birkenhead, for whom he felt strong affection. He related several instances of Birkenhead's savagely caustic wit, which at times did not even spare his friends. But Churchill also revealed Birkenhead's kindliness and loyalty in personal relationships. He enlivened his essays with many anecdotes about his own relations with these men which clearly brought out their personal qualities. In none of these portraits, however, are we shown the natures that lay behind the public façades which his subjects presented to the world. He made no attempt to examine the emotional drives which had shaped their lives.

Sometimes, too, Churchill's own personality intruded itself so powerfully into these sketches that it tended to obscure the men he was depicting. As Guedalla wrote of the expanded edition of *Great Contemporaries* (1938), "Mr. Churchill gleams back at us from twenty-five looking glasses, formidable, affectionate, and lovable."

During the five years he served as wartime prime minister of Great Britain, Churchill was compelled to suspend his literary activities, but the Labour victory of 1945 gave him leisure to take up his pen once more. When he received the Nobel Prize eight years later, he had published all but one of his six-volume memoirs, *The Second World War*. The first volume interweaves an account of British foreign policy and international affairs from the Versailles Treaty until the German invasion of the Low Countries in 1940 with the story of his own public career during this period. As the foremost critic of the appeasement policy pursued by the British government in the 1930's, Churchill's judgments were overwhelmingly vindicated by events. His account is made all the more compelling by his ability to convey his varying thoughts and moods as he confronted the successive crises of this period. The reader feels the depth of his frustration when men refused to heed his repeated warnings. He said that after hearing of the resignation of Sir Anthony Eden, the only opponent of appeasement in Chamberlain's cabinet, he was unable, for the only time in his life, to sleep that night: "My heart sank and for a while the dark waters of despair overwhelmed me. . . . From midnight till dawn I lay in bed consumed by doubt and fear." When one considers the bold and resolute character of the man, here indeed is a poignant confession.

Naturally it is not possible to accept as final Churchill's assessment of developments either before or during the war. He was too close to the events and too passionate a participant in them. Aware of this, he described his book not as history but as "a contribution to history which will be of service to the future." Like *The World Crisis*, Churchill's books on World War II are, to a considerable extent, a personal account. Whether judged as history or as an autobiographical narrative, *The Second World War* reveals his limitations as well as his virtues. In some respects, as we have noted, Churchill was a simple, uncomplicated man, and certain kinds of complexity eluded him. Many historians today no longer think that there was an obvious set of alternative policies by which the statesmen of the 1930's could easily have avoided what he called "the Unnecessary War." He underrated the subtle interplay of psychological and social forces which made any strong, united action against the fascist powers extremely difficult.

Nevertheless, the case he made against the appeasers in the first volume, *The Gathering Storm*, was so powerfully argued and so fully substantiated with evidence of their folly and weakness that it seems unlikely that their defenders will ever be able to make a full or convincing answer. Churchill's characterization and comparison of Baldwin and Chamberlain, the two leaders whom he held primarily responsible for the failure of the British government to hold the fascist states in check, were lucid and well drawn. Baldwin, he said, was a man with a wise, broad outlook. His supreme talent lay in his mastery of British party politics. But Churchill added: "He was largely detached from foreign and military affairs. He knew little of Europe and disliked what he knew." Churchill described Chamberlain, on the other hand, as

alert, business-like, opinionated, and self-confident in a very high degree. Unlike Baldwin, he conceived himself able to comprehend the whole field of Europe, and indeed the world. . . . His all-pervading hope was to go down in history as the Great Peacemaker; and for this he was prepared to strive continually in the teeth of facts, and face great risks for himself and for his country."[7]

These comments are the more damning by virtue of their very moderation.

The next two volumes, *Their Finest Hour* and *The Grand Alliance*, tell of the years 1940 and 1941, when Britain fought alone against Germany and the other members of the Axis until the Soviet Union and the United States entered the conflict. Here the story becomes more fully autobiographical because it deals with Churchill's experience as leader of his country at this critical moment in its history. His sense of the drama of the occasion, and of his own role in it run powerfully through the narrative. Frank pleasure in the exercise of power, the driving determination and enthusiasm that made him the indispensable leader, his impatience, his resourcefulness, and the fertility of his imagination are all clearly revealed. We easily believe him when he declares in one of his terse but memorable sentences: "This was a time when it was equally good to live or die." Especially characteristic is his account of how, immediately after Dunkirk, he began to press his generals for plans to undertake a counteroffensive and of how he unearthed a scheme which he himself had devised in 1917 for the construction of tank landing craft. Vessels of this kind were subsequently employed in the Allied landing on the French coast in 1943.

The books are moving and eloquent in the heroic aspects of the story: the valor of the R.A.F. pilots, the stoicism and humor of the civilians during the blitz. Yet there is an element of exaggeration. To understand the nervous strain and the moments of weakness experienced by ordinary people under the pressure of war, one must read other, more prosaic accounts. For example, there is no reference in Churchill's book to the fact that, while most of the troops displayed outstanding courage during the evacuation of Dunkirk, some were guilty of panic and indiscipline. Occasionally Churchill's assumption that people supporting a good cause are almost invariably moved by altruistic motives led him to a false, declamatory tone. Referring to the

[7] Winston S. Churchill, *The Gathering Storm*, Vol. VIII of *The Second World War*, 198–99.

destruction of the French fleet by the British navy in 1940, he declared: "The genius of France enabled her people to comprehend the whole significance of Oran and in her agony to draw hope from this bitter pang." Yet this streak of high-flown idealism, which not infrequently appears in Churchill's writing, should not be overstressed, for it exists side by side with a sardonic and humorous realism. After describing the tortuous means by which Franco resisted Hitler's pressure to force Spain to enter the war on the side of the Axis powers, he commented:

It is fashionable at the present time to dwell on the vices of General Franco, and I am, therefore, glad to place on record this testimony to the duplicity and ingratitude of his dealings with Hitler and Mussolini. I shall presently record even greater services which these evil qualities in General Franco rendered to the Allied cause.[8]

If Churchill's prose on occasion soared above the level of human reality, he was also capable of making effective use of episodes from ordinary life to point the moral on a major issue. He was sharply critical of Soviet leaders for their failure to heed his warnings of an attack by Germany. Describing the Nazi bombardment of Belgrade just two months before Hitler's invasion of Russia, he told of the destruction of a zoological garden: "Out of the nightmare of smoke and fire came the maddened animals released from their cages . . . a bear dazed and uncomprehending shuffled through the inferno with slow and awkward gait. He was not the only bear who did not understand."

The final three volumes of the memoirs, *The Hinge of Fate*, *Closing the Ring*, and *Triumph and Tragedy*, cover the years 1942 to the end of the war in Europe and Churchill's resignation as prime minister in July, 1945. With the same skill and assurance that he displayed in his biography of Marlborough, Churchill unfolded the vast panorama of World War II. Sometimes, however, his account of events seems rushed and his narrative crowded.

His description of foreign statesmen with whom he came in contact was of uneven quality. Roosevelt's personality, for example, does not emerge very clearly. Probably a mixture of gratitude, admiration, and discretion prevented Churchill from making a critical evaluation of

[8] Winston S. Churchill, *Their Finest Hour*, Vol. II of *The Second World War*, 452.

the American leader's capacities and achievements, although it was clear that he strongly opposed some of Roosevelt's ideas and policies. Yet following his usual practice in these memoirs with respect to other leaders, he gave his uninhibited impressions of Stalin in their several encounters during the war and provided the reader with a fascinating picture of the Russian leader in various moods. The following anecdote is an illustration. At the Teheran Conference in November, 1943, Stalin proposed that at the end of the war fifty thousand German officers, including the entire German general staff, should be shot. Churchill forcefully protested, and when Stalin persisted in his recommendation, with the joking support of President Roosevelt and his son Eliot, Churchill, who failed to see any humor in it, got up and walked out of the room. Almost immediately Stalin and Molotov followed and assured him that they were not serious. Churchill concluded:

Stalin has a very captivating manner when he chooses to use it, and I never saw him do so to such an extent as at this moment. Although I was not then, and am not now fully convinced that all was chaff and there was no serious intent behind, I consented to return, and the rest of the evening passed pleasantly.[9]

By such deft strokes as these he created the portrait of a complex and powerful personality, utterly ruthless, but enormously shrewd and able as well.

In the final three volumes of the memoirs, a chronicle of the Allied drive to victory over the Axis powers, Churchill betrayed a growing mood of frustration. The reason is not difficult to understand. With the entry of Russia and the United States into the war Great Britain and, of course, Churchill were relegated to lesser roles. Many critical decisions were made in Washington, not in London. Warm as his relationship was with the American leaders, he did not conceal his deep disagreement with them on certain matters, especially in his belief that serious errors of judgment on the part of the United States enabled Russia to fasten her grip on much of central and eastern Europe. Many outstanding critics claimed that his account was too personal and egocentric and that in some cases he twisted the facts for purposes

---

[9] Winston S. Churchill, *Closing the Ring*, Vol. VI of *The Second World War*, 319–20.

of self-justification. A more fundamental criticism was that Churchill did not stand back often enough from crowded events and point out their broad significance. He often lacked the cool detachment and the capacity for universal judgment characteristic of the greatest historians.

The appearance of the final volume of *The Second World War* in 1953, when Churchill received the Nobel Prize, marked the end of his literary career. His last work, *A History of the English-Speaking Peoples*, had been virtually completed in 1939 but was not published until the years 1956 to 1958. Although he consulted a number of leading British and American scholars, in presenting this work Churchill disclaimed any intention of rivaling the works of professional historians. It was his intention, he said, "to present a personal view of the processes whereby the English Speaking Peoples throughout the world have achieved their distinctive position and character." Churchill's style, as usual, is lucid and succinct. The narrative marches forward in clear, taut sentences, and the work is excellent in its organization and compression. He made less effort than in earlier books to embellish the story with echoing rhetoric. On the other hand, he did not manifest to quite the same degree his qualities of humor, irony, grandeur, and pathos. In fact, there is an element of restraint in this book that no doubt enhances its value as history but somewhat diminishes its merits as literature. Perhaps, as Maurice Ashley says, Churchill's natural exuberance was tempered by the advice of the scholars whom he consulted.

In judging the book, one has to keep in mind his statement that it represents his personal view of Britain's past. Considered as a historical work, it has many defects from the standpoint of the modern scholar. It centers on the two chief interests of Churchill's life—politics and war—almost to the exclusion of social, economic, and cultural factors.

Churchill's achievement in the field of oratory was even more remarkable than his accomplishments in literature. Through studying and writing about history, he gained the understanding and perspective essential to the tasks of national leadership. However, it was through mastery of the spoken word that he succeeded in winning from the British people wholehearted acceptance of his leadership and of the hardship and sacrifice which the waging of a great war required. Churchill's outstanding characteristic as a speaker, and as a writer, was his keen sensitivity to the color, sound, and rhythm of words. When still a young man, he asked a friend whether she thought "words had a language and music quite independent of their meaning." Certainly he knew how to select words and arrange them in an order that made the maximum impact on an audience.

Yet one must remember that for many years Churchill's qualities as an orator failed to gain wide recognition. Few could deny his talent for argumentation and invective. A good example of the latter was his denunciation of Stanley Baldwin in November, 1936: "The government simply cannot make up their mind, or they cannot get the Prime Minister to make up his mind. So they go on in a strange paradox, decided only to be undecided, resolved to be irresolute, adamant for drift, solid for fluidity, all powerful to be impotent." Here are the stacatto sentences and sharp antitheses characteristic of Churchill's literary style. He also had the gift for the memorable—and deadly— phrase, such as his description of Ramsey MacDonald as a "boneless wonder," or his reference to "the foul baboonery of Bolshevism."

Effective oratory, however, does not depend merely on technique. A speaker's persuasiveness depends on the willingness of listeners to accept the message he offers. It also depends on their perception of what Lord Rosebery called "the character breathing through the sentences." Unfortunately, before the Munich agreement most of Churchill's countrymen rejected his summons to resist the Fascist powers. They respected him for his brave and resolute character, but they were inclined to regard him as wanting in judgment and as an advocate of reckless courses that might plunge the country into war.

There were, moreover, those who considered his sometimes over-blown rhetoric ludicrous and old-fashioned. In his recent book *Churchill: A Study in Failure*, Robert Rhodes James quotes a letter from a woman who listened to one of Churchill's speeches in 1923. She remarked:

He [Churchill] really and truly points an accusatory finger at the crowd, and cries in sepulchral tones, "I say, that if another war is fought, civilization will perish." (Laughter. A sweeping gesture. A man laughs. Out goes the finger.) "That man dares to laugh. He dares to think the destruction of civilization a matter for humor!"

Indeed, he is such a preposterous little fellow, with his folded arms and tufted forelock and his Lyceum Theatre voice, that if one did not detest him one might love him from sheer perversity."[10]

Churchill was, in fact, deficient in some of the attributes usually considered essential for success in oratory. In the beginning he suffered from a marked speech defect, and despite his great physical courage, public speaking at times made him uneasy and fearful. He also lacked spontaneity; every speech had to be memorized and every gesture rehearsed. On one occasion early in his career he underwent the humiliation of being unable to finish a speech in Parliament because his memory suddenly failed him. Only his characteristic determination and self-discipline enabled him to surmount these difficulties and become an effective orator. And there was one problem that he could never entirely overcome: his inability to sense and respond to the mood of an audience. Churchill could only declare and defend his beliefs. If what he had to say did not conform to the feelings of his listeners, it was his, and their, misfortune.

When the truth of his assertions about the aims of Hitler and Mussolini were vindicated by events, however, a sudden change in public temper took place. Finally, and almost too late, the British people became conscious that Churchill alone was qualified to provide the inspiration and leadership which he had long offered them in vain. For Englishmen, as Churchill's Nobel award states, his oratory was a defense of human values which they held dear: love of country, love of freedom, and hatred of injustice and oppression. He had the capacity to enunciate in clear and noble phrases what ordinary people felt but could not express themselves. Moreover, they knew that his summons to valor, sacrifice, and endurance sprang from his inward qualities. James says that when Churchill told the House of Commons in May, 1940, that he had nothing to offer the people but "blood, toil, sweat, and tears," it came to the British people as a call to service and sacrifice. Less than a month later, after Dunkirk, when Churchill delivered his famous "we shall never surrender" speech, the British writer C. P. Snow recalls that

[10] Winston S. Churchill, *While England Slept, 1932–38: A Survey of World Affairs*, 153.

230

the accent was odd, not like the clipped upper class English that was already becoming fashionable; the style of oratory, like that of Lloyd-George, was obsolescent. But we noticed neither of those things as we listened that night. . . . For that voice was our hope. It was the voice of will incarnate. It was saying what we wanted to hear said.[11]

Churchill professed no formal religious belief, but his words sometimes conveyed a fervor which was religious in the deepest sense and which had great power to elevate and inspire his listeners. He also knew how to raise men's spirits by enabling them to see their own hardships and peril in the wider context of a historic past in which other peoples had been compelled to fight rather than submit to tyranny. In his first speech after becoming prime minister, Churchill referred to the struggle waged in ancient times by the Jews under the leadership of Judas Maccabaeus against their Greek oppressors.

The grasp which Churchill held on the minds of men arose in part from the way in which his words, gestures, and facial expressions combined to mirror his rich and many-sided personality. From moment to moment, as he spoke in Parliament, he might express harsh Cromwellian resolution, irony, puckish humor, deep emotion that brought tears to his own eyes and to the eyes of others, and, at times, even childish ill-temper. Harold Nicolson gives a striking example of Churchill's ability to combine humor with surprise. The speech was delivered in the autumn of 1943 at the time of the surrender of Italy:

He referred to Italy and expressed pleasure that the Italian people, "rescued from their state of servitude, could now take their rightful place among the democracies of the world." Then he raised his arm as if about to deliver the most terrific thunderbolt from his rich armory of rhetoric, but he dropped his arm and took off his spectacles . . . . "They may perhaps be allowed to work their passage home," he concluded, grinning. It is in this that one finds his mastery of the House. It is the combination of great flights of oratory with sudden swoops into the intimate and conversational. Of all his devices it is the one that never fails.[12]

[11] C. P. Snow, *Variety of Men*, 79.
[12] Harold Nicolson, *Diaries and Letters, 1939–1944*, 321.

Churchill was a man impelled from childhood by a heroic vision of life. The outbreak of war in 1939, and his elevation as prime minister transformed that vision into reality. He assumed the role of leadership in a real struggle against forces of evil personified by Nazism. Perhaps his chief claim to greatness was his capacity to arouse others by his oratory and to make them see the issue in the same heroic terms. Churchill's oratory became a factor of prime importance in creating the "spirit" of 1940 and 1941 which enabled the British people to survive and then set them on the road to victory.

In assessing Churchill as a literary figure, it is difficult to separate the author from the orator. The rhetorical quality of his literary work was both a strength and a weakness; it was effective in describing great crises in human affairs. His flamboyant word combinations were often justified by the scale and gravity of the events which they described. Moreover, Churchill varied his purple passages with simple and direct ones. There were times, however, when he almost bludgeoned the reader's mind with heavy, resounding phrases.

In 1948 Churchill wrote a little book entitled *Painting as a Pastime*, in which he described his experiences as an amateur painter and offered advice to the beginner. "I must say," he stated at one point, "that I like bright colors. I rejoice with the brilliant ones and am genuinely sorry for the poor browns." What was true of painting was also true of his writing. Churchill delighted in bright colors, sometimes to an excessive degree. On occasion his attempts to evoke emotion and his descriptions of events became glaring and extravagant.

On such vital issues as the aims of Nazi Germany or of Stalinist Russia, his understanding was keener than that of most statesmen of his time. Yet while Churchill possessed an exceptional degree of imagination and intuition, on the matter of psychological insight his capacities were limited. Certainly he was well aware of his own strengths and weaknesses. Basically, however, as an extrovert and man of action, he was not inclined to probe deeply into himself or others. On the other hand, his perception of some of the basic truths of human nature was excellent, especially when they were reflected in his own experience. Of Marlborough he made a comment which applied to himself as well: "It is said that famous men are usually the product of an unhappy childhood. The stern compression of circumstances, the twinges of adversity, the spur of slights and of taunts in early years are needed to evoke that ruthless fixity of purpose without which great actions are seldom accomplished."

Of ordinary people, unless they happened to engage his affection, he had little understanding. Churchill's perception was poor where the opposite sex was concerned. When he was still a young man, his friend Violet Bonham-Carter annoyed him by saying that he was rather innocent in his attitude toward women. The truth was that he was inclined to idealize them, as he did his mother. The few women who appear in his books—his mother; Lucille in *Savrola*; Marl-borough's wife, Sarah; Queen Anne—do not really come alive as human beings.

Churchill, in fact, paid almost no attention to the deeper psychological drives which motivate people. His approach to human personality was pre-Freudian. Describing great crises in politics and war, in which men's fortitude and resourcefulness were tested to the utmost, he wrote with eloquence and authority. When he discussed the conscious, rational motives that determined the actions of leading men in these spheres, his evaluations were usually shrewd and accurate. On the other hand, except in World War II, when he and his countrymen were at one on a single great issue, Churchill did not know or have much interest in what went on in the minds of the people. This meant that, as a writer and historian, he manifested little awareness of the underlying forces affecting human society.

Despite his shortcomings, there is no doubt that Churchill deserved the Nobel Prize. It is true that, judged only as history, his books—for all their fine qualities—fall short of the highest achievement. According to Maurice Ashley, Sir Winston did not himself usually perform the laborious task of examining and comparing sources, a fundamental part of the training and practice of the scholar. He did the writing, but the preliminary work was left to his assistants. Absorbed in public life, he had neither the time nor the inclination for such activity. History was important to him, but it remained a secondary interest. As Churchill himself said somewhat ruefully, "After all, a man's life must be nailed to the cross of thought or action." He had chosen the latter.

Partly for this reason he lacked the wide-ranging curiosity or, except in politics and war, the analytical cast of mind so essential for preeminence in the historical profession. The capacity to weigh evidence, to doubt, to suspend judgment, to question one's own assumptions are the attributes of a scholar, not of a leader of men. In these respects no one can compare Churchill with Theodor Mommsen, the only other historian to receive the Nobel Prize for Literature. Yet, despite his intensely personal approach, Churchill possessed both a sense of history and a concern for historic truth. He was sometimes wanting in detachment, but he did not write solely to justify himself or to defend a particular point of view. The works of such a man—deeply involved as he was in many of the episodes he described—frequently give a more profound insight into the past and more of the true "feel" of history than those of the objective scholar written long after the event.

Of all Churchill's books, only four are not concerned primarily with history: *My African Journey* (1908), an account of his trip to the African continent the previous year; *My Early Life, Thoughts and Adventures*; and *Painting as a Pastime*. For this reason there is some difficulty in distinguishing Churchill the writer and literary figure from Churchill the historian. To a certain extent the qualities of the two overlap. But whatever reservations one may hold about him as a historian, his excellence as a literary craftsman cannot be disputed. There is substance in the view that his last work, *The Second World War*, shows some evidence of decline. The present Lord Birkenhead the son of Churchill's friend, says of this book: "One has the impression that Sir Winston was involved in a race against time; that he was determined to present his own account of those tremendous events and to establish at last the great fortune he had so richly earned."[13]

Nevertheless, in this book, and indeed in all his writings, one finds the same overriding merits. He was a born storyteller who possessed a keen understanding of the structure of a historical narrative and the ability to make it move forward at a vigorous and unflagging pace. In addition, he had an acute sense of the structure and sound of the English language. As Churchill himself said, he had "a liking for words and for the feeling of words falling into their place like pennies in a slot." This gift enabled him to compose the clear, rhythmic sentences and the epigrammatic phrases that characterize his writing.

[13] *Report of the Royal Society of Literature, 1953, 43.*

Even more important to his effectiveness as an author were his imaginative power and the visual sense that made it possible for him to describe events with such vividness that the reader feels he is a participant. The excitement and realism of Churchill's writing was heightened, of course, by his own involvement in many of the episodes related in his books and by his personal experience in the exercise of political and military authority. He therefore depicted the way men react in such situations with an authenticity no academic historian could equal. As Siwertz remarked in presenting the Nobel Prize to Churchill: "He knows what he is talking about. He is the man who has himself been through the fire, taken risks and withstood extreme pressure."

What gives Churchill's work that real measure of greatness which merited the award of the Nobel Prize is the way in which his own character and view of human existence are stamped upon his writing. One sees in Churchill's books the expression of an intensely human and yet larger-than-life personality, a character of extraordinary vitality, range, and versatility. They reveal his generosity and courage, his humor and irony, his realism and common sense, at times his romanticism and naïveté, his impatience and ruthless drive, his alternating confidence and pessimism concerning the human condition. There was something both of the prophet and of the poet in Churchill.

It is sometimes alleged that the values embodied in Churchill's books and speeches are relics of a past without relevance to the present. Considering the age in which we live, when the antihero is held up for public admiration, one is almost inclined to agree with this pessimistic conclusion. But it is difficult to imagine any civilization, our own included, that can survive without preserving in some form those virtues of courage, resolution, honor, and magnanimity which Churchill personified as a man and writer. From the beginning he believed himself to be a man destined to greatness. Though at times afflicted with doubt, it seems clear that he believed mankind to be heir to a high destiny. His faith in the goodness of human beings (if not in their wisdom), his belief in the value of human effort, and his certainty that men are capable of raising themselves through fortitude and vigilance shines through much of his writing and oratory and gives them qualities of grandeur and nobility.

His approach to literature led him to adopt a style that seems to many people turgid and artificial. The best answer to their criticism was given by Churchill's friend the diplomat and writer Sir Isaiah Berlin:

What . . . they denounced as so much tinsel and hollow paste board was in reality solid; it was this author's natural means for the expression of his heroic, highly colored, sometimes over-simple and even naïve, but always genuine vision of life. Mr. Churchill's dominant category, the single, central organizing principle of his moral and intellectual universe is an historical imagination so strong, so comprehensive, as to encase the whole of the present and the whole of the future in the framework of a rich, multicolored past."[14]

[14] Isaiah Berlin, *Mr. Churchill in 1940*, 9.

SAMUEL BECKETT

by Sanford Sternlicht

> VLADIMIR: Well? Shall we go?
> ESTRAGON: Yes, let's go.
> *They do not move. Curtain*

THUS ENDS *Waiting for Godot,* Samuel Beckett's greatest play and one of the most important, most influential plays of twentieth-century Western drama. This work, with its nihilistic view of mankind's continuing futility, with its emphasis on the irrationality of human action, with its statement of the impossibility of communication between people, and with its ultimate despair for the human condition, is the keystone statement of the prevailing existentialist-absurdist drama of our time.

Existentialist-absurdist playwrights are concerned with the necessity of showing the theater audience and the larger literary audience that sense of isolation which is the cruelest and most essential fact of the human condition. Human communication, or the impossibility of human communication, is the core of the art of Beckett, playwright and novelist.

How central his art is to the contemporary theater may be illustrated by the fact that the prologue of the popular off-Broadway review *Oh! Calcutta!* a blatant sexual romp in which most of the actors spend much of the time in the nude, is a contribution of Beckett's. Where has the question of noncommunication led the artist? The opening of *Oh! Calcutta!* provides a possible answer. The curtain rises on a stage piled with rubbish, including various naked human beings. There is a somewhat human cry, the lights rise, the lights fall, there is another

237

cry, and then silence and curtain. The pathetic cry from the rubbish heap may indeed be the final statement on the human condition from the novelist of the nonhero and the dramatist of the cripples, the hobos, and the garbage-can dwellers.

Beckett received the Nobel Prize for Literature in 1969. The selection committee, made up of members of the Swedish Academy, cited him for introducing new forms to the novel and the drama. It was *Waiting for Godot*, of course, that was the key work influencing the decision of the judges. When the announcement of the award was made, Beckett could not be reached for comment at his Paris home, and his French publisher, Jerome Lindon, said that Beckett was out of touch in Tunisia. Beckett finally accepted the Nobel Prize for Literature but refused to go to Stockholm to receive it at the ceremonies held on December 10, 1969. In accepting the prize but avoiding the ceremonial honors, Beckett took up the position halfway to that of Jean-Paul Sartre, who in 1964 had refused the prize and the honors entirely, claiming that fame and wealth inevitably corrupted the artist. The selection of Beckett for the Nobel Prize delighted Stockholm literary circles and literary circles throughout the world. Many critics had derided the literature award in recent years as being influenced more by such factors as politics, geography, and religion than by literary merit, influence, and importance. The Academy had to do some twisting to make Beckett fit into the traditional humanitarian and optimistic mold of the Nobel award winners. Speaking on the radio about the selection of Beckett, Karl Bagnar Gierow, secretary of the Swedish Academy, probably remembering the injunction in the will of Alfred Nobel to honor "uplifting" literary works, somewhat embarrassingly equivocated: "The degradation of humanity is a recurrent theme in Beckett's writing, and to this extent his philosophy, simply accentuated by elements of the grotesque and of tragic farce, can be said to be a negativism that knows no haven." Gierow used an analogy from photography, commenting that when a negative is printed it produces "a positive, a clarification, with the black proving to be the light of day, the parts in deepest shade, those which reflect the light sources." Gierow's words may have been uttered to appease the more conservative elements of Swedish politics, which might have voiced legal and "moral" objections. To the choice of Beckett, they nevertheless state an essential truth about absurdist-existentialist writers: in that they help us to see what we are, they help us to become better than we are. If this is not their goal, it is their result.

Thus Gierow continued: "The perception of human degradation is not possible if human values are denied. This is the source of inner cleansing, the life force in spite of everything, in Beckett's pessimism." He spoke of Beckett's "love of mankind that grows in understanding as it plumbs further into the depth of abhorrence. . . . "From that position, in the realms of annihilation, the writing of Samuel Beckett rises like a *miserere* from all mankind, its muffled minor key sounding liberation to the oppressed and comfort to those in need." Thus ingeniously, and not without much truth, even Beckett, who envisions mankind on the rubbish heap of the universe, could be and was brought into the Academy and finally made welcome by the Establishment.

Beckett's "nationality" posed another problem for the Nobel officials. Was he to be considered Irish because he was born in Dublin on April 3, 1906; British because his first two novels, *Murphy* (1938) and *Watt* (1942), were composed in English; or French because he has officially lived in Paris since 1937 and his trilogy, *Molloy* (1950), *Malone Dies* (1951), and *The Unnamable* (1952), as well as the later novel *How It Is* (1961), were written in French and then translated by Beckett into English?

Perhaps at long last in the history of Western literature the question of nationality is losing its relevancy, for when we consider the portrait of the artist in this century of war, neobarbarism, and the eternal streams of refugees wandering the rubble-lined roads of the world, we find him almost always as exile. Thomas Mann fled his native Germany and the Nazis to find refuge in the United States. Bertolt Brecht did the same thing, only to return to East Germany after the war. James Joyce left his beloved Ireland to spend his life in exile on the Continent. T. S. Eliot and Ezra Pound abandoned the United States for England and for Italy, the former to become more royal and more loyal than the king and the latter to go as far as to broadcast propaganda against his native land. W. H. Auden left England for the United States at the onset of the World War II. The 1966 Nobel Prize winners Nell Sachs and S. Y. Agnon, the former a German Jew, the

239

latter a Polish Jew, lived and worked in new lands, Sweden and Israel. Ernest Hemingway lived his own almost adolescentlike exile in Spain, Cuba, and Africa. And William Faulkner saw his native countryside as an almost mythological foreign land. Graham Greene roams the earth. The itineraries of the great painters and musicians of our century, are like those of the writers. Picasso lived in France, and Stravinsky lived in the United States. Exile, perhaps even to the point of persecution, seems almost a prerequisite to great art as long as we expect the artist to be the conscience and the consciousness of our time. As the Rumanian novelist Virgil Gheorghu says in the *Twenty-fifth Hour*, "In these days anyone may suddenly be a Jew."

Samuel Barclay Beckett came of a middle-class Protestant background. He was born at Foxrock, near Dublin; attended Portora Royal School, Ulster; and went up to Trinity College, Dublin, in 1923. He was an outstanding student of English, French, and Italian literature. In 1927 he received a first-class degree in modern literature and was awarded a gold medal for exceptional merit in his studies. Beckett then received a research prize of fifty pounds, which helped him continue his studies at Trinity. He was awarded the Master of Arts degree in 1931.

Beckett first anticipated an academic career, and in 1928 he taught at Campbell College in Belfast. He then accepted a two-year lectureship in English at the École Normale Supérieure in Paris. In September, 1931, the rising young scholar-teacher was appointed lecturer in French and assistant to the professor of romance languages in Dublin. The appointment was a three-year one, but Beckett resigned in 1931, and, despite the fact that his study of Proust had been published, he abandoned his academic career because while in Paris he had met James Joyce and had become his friend. Humbly, and in great awe of the master, Beckett irrevocably decided that he must stay with Joyce in exile and attempt the lonely, difficult life of the creative writer.

It is somewhat ironic that so self-effacing and reclusive a man and artist should receive the world's highest accolade for his work. How many who deserved it less would have enjoyed it more. Beckett strove hard to avoid literary fame and the concomitant "study" by scholars and students with their inevitably tiring questions, such as, "What exactly did you mean by . . .?" To his few friends in Paris (in 1964 he fled from New York in terror after one brief visit, vowing never to return), the thin, almost cadaverous man with the sunken face, bespectacled in steel frames and thick lenses over bright-blue eyes, is affable and loquacious. To them he is a whisky-drinking, nearsighted writer named Sam. Informal in dress, Beckett's clothes are simple and neat. He frequently wears corduroy trousers, a white shirt, tie, and jacket. Despite the indigent status of so many of his characters, Beckett himself is neither bum nor Bohemian. His Paris apartment is filled with books and paintings and contains a piano, which he plays well. There is also a small country house where in the summer he prefers to stroll with the woman he loves and with whom he has shared the last twenty years of his life. Thus this *enfant terrible* of modern drama actually leads an orderly and perhaps routine life. In truth most great artists must come to accommodate a necessary routine or meteorically burn out.

Beckett has wryly remarked:

Writing was never easy for me. I never thought of myself as a writer and I don't now. I was in the wilderness for twenty years until *Godot* brought attention to my novels and short stories and poems. There was no trace of success until *Godot*, which was written in 1948, was produced in 1953. Then I received a French Government grant of 700,000 old francs that permitted a month's run in Paris.

Despite the aid of the French government, Beckett probably would not have won the Nobel Prize if T. S. Eliot had not received the award in 1948. The belated recognition of Eliot, whose "The Love Song of J. Alfred Prufrock" and "The Wasteland" made respectable the nonhero and the impoverished landscape of a mankind imprisoned in a core of empty existence, paved the way for such an anti-Establishment writer as Beckett to win the literary prize of prizes on the basis of a relatively small body of work—three plays, *Waiting for Godot, Endgame,* and *Happy Days*; six novels; short stories; poems; film and radio scripts; and the critical essay on Proust. It is as dramatist that Beckett will be remembered, and his place in twentieth-century Western drama must be clearly understood if one is to recognize his impact and importance.

Beckett is part of a movement in contemporary Western drama in

241

which playwrights like himself, Eugène Ionesco, and Jean Genet be-lieve that the theater must express in clear, valid terms the senseless-ness and the irrationality of all human actions. Life for them is a phenomenon of isolation, and the theater must offer a confrontation between the audience and this isolation. Man is encased in a void—this is the irremediable and terrible fact of the human condition. The universe itself is void, and thus communication between human beings is almost an impossibility. The strange, illogical, Dadaistic language of existentialist-absurdist dramatists illustrates that man cannot ex-press his basic thoughts and feelings.

One is immediately struck with a sense of paradox, however, for in plays like *Endgame, Waiting for Godot,* and *No Exit,* as in *Rhinoceros* or *Who's Afraid of Virginia Woolf?* the feeling of loneliness and the difficult, pathetic, and doomed gropings of human beings and para-human beings to reach each other is powerfully and clearly com-municated. This is the critical and essential paradox of contemporary drama: it communicates brilliantly the belief in noncommunicative-ness; it is vitally meaningful in its exposing of meaninglessness; it shouts a defiant, revolutionary *No* to positivist and materialistic norms, which is a significant viewpoint, a rallying point, for twentieth-century man.

Existentialism, so difficult to pin down, has been defined roughly as a descent from meaninglessness through anxiety to utter despair or to blind faith. The existentialist playwrights and other contemporary dramatists make this descent. They have rejected the old paths of naturalism, positivism, and materialism (as others, in fact, have done, most recently the symbolists), but these playwrights have also pro-fessed to have rejected the concept of the norm, the existence a priori of abstract values. However, this is not necessarily the total case. Con-temporary drama does indeed offer norms for human behavior. These values are not lightly adopted and discarded like suits of clothes when they fail to fit the size of the moment. They have a permanence, are worth defending, are being fought for, and represent through this new drama a powerful image-bearing language of dissent.

Modern Western drama—that is, social drama, naturalistic and post-naturalistic, dedicated to exposing political and social evils, and con-cerned with the psychological and physical frailties of twentieth-century human beings—began with Ibsen and led in several channels to such modern masters as Eugene O'Neill and Brecht. But the deep roots of contemporary Western existentialist-absurdist drama are also drawing nourishment from the symbolist plays of Yeats, which freed the stage from the hitherto "necessary" shackles of verisimilitude, from the subconscious memory of Alfred Jarry and his *Ubu Roi*, and from the theater of ennui, Chekhov's plays, and Luigi Pirandello's seemingly ever-contemporary, strange "romances," now almost unbelievably forty years old. Consider for a moment *The Cherry Orchard*. Here is a play which states no cause, which has no real action, in which nothing actually happens. It is the true progenitor of *Waiting for Godot*. Beckett's stark landscape is the estate of Ranevskaya transformed via Yeats's stage of symbolist history to the very essence of the experience of futile waiting for the meaningful act that can never take place.

Along with the ennui of Chekhov and the historic symbol of Yeats there is that tone of contemporary drama first struck by Pirandello, whose plays, particularly *Six Characters in Search of an Author*, anticipate the mood and techniques of today's existentialist-absurdist drama. Pirandello was the first to strike out at the "reality" of positivistic science, to ask the question, never for one moment pretending that there is an answer, "Where does reality end and art begin?" The characters of an unwritten play invading the theater where actors playing actors are rehearsing another play present what must be called the "dramatic theory of relativity." Modern drama is thus involved in a philosophical paradox. For if everything is relative, then no truth can be absolute, including the assertion of relativism. The logic is sophistic, but the disturbing fact of modern life thrust forth is that man must live with philosophical uncertainty. This uncertainty, this questioning of reality, even the questioning of the questioning, this blending of the play and life, is the precursory dramatic experience to the plays of today performed at Yale or off-off Broadway, in which the audience and the actors blend their actions. Yet this is not to say that Pirandello's world is meaningless or that he argues for the avoidance of commitment or action. On the contrary, man must strive for the communication of feeling despite the almost overwhelming difficulty.

Modern French drama was enormously influenced by Pirandello.

No other foreign playwright, with the exception of Shakespeare, has had as great an impact on French theater. Clearly Beckett's philosophy and dramaturgy are much in debt to the Italian master. Beckett's deep feelings of melancholy, his sense of futility, his despair about the disillusionment of old age, and the chronic helplessness of his characters—even the dramatic clowning—are Pirandellian in origin and outlook. Like Pirandello's, Beckett's art projects a deep sense of human isolation; it also states in very strong terms the value of human comradeship, perhaps even of the never-attainable perfection of Buber's I-Thou relationship.

As an existential dramatist, Beckett, of course, does not discuss existentialist principles. He presents an existentialist picture of life which is open to criticism, which in fact invites criticism, and which is itself pointedly critical in its negative portrayal of suffering. We the audience share this suffering, as actor, character, and viewer blur and blend into one. At the same time, and in contradiction, Brecht's famous *Verfremdungseffekt* ("alienation affect") is also operative, for we realize that, although Beckett is showing us the existential human condition, we are only beginning to approach that condition. Beckett's drama is not a drama of sympathy, as most serious drama has been, but a drama of empathy: we are bored beyond tears by life or nonlife. We suffer with Pozzo and Lucky; the slings and arrows are upon our bodies. We are exhorted to be other than Estragon and Vladimir, to truly exist. We ultimately wish to destroy frames of reference—those of the drama, of social existence, of life itself. We must revolt. There is no possibility of success, but somehow we must drive on and at least attempt to comprehend the human condition, for this knowledge, projected through Beckett's plays, can somewhat alleviate the sense of human suffering.

The existentialist-absurdist attack on the norm may be called by Beckett and other dramatists a meaningless act in that all action, even dramatic action, is meaningless. Nevertheless, the *existential* attack has an *essential* existence. The razor, waved supposedly in the neutral air and in random fashion, in fact finds the right targets as truly as a modern missile, and these targets are cruelty, indifference, and oppression. At the very same time the razor also cuts to the heart of the playwright's existential philosophy. The existential-absurdist playwright finds his work turning upon and against his *Weltanschauung*, for his artistry has meaning and function. This is the reverse side of the coin to the argument of the existential artist who insists that the work of the *essential* artist turns upon him in that it has neither meaning nor function and is therefore absurd. Thus the hand of the existentialist artist as it shaves off the beard of illusion from the face of humanity is cut by the other edge of his blade. Beckett in *Waiting for Godot* and *Endgame*, like Edward Albee in *Who's Afraid of Virginia Woolf?* (an absurdist title if there ever was one), O'Neill in *The Iceman Cometh*, Sartre in *No Exit*, and Genet in *The Blacks* and *The Balcony*, attacks human illusions as dangerous, vicious, and destructive. All these writers argue that man must see life as it is: absurd, cruel, grotesque— but as it is. If man is trapped in a world he cannot understand or control, at least he can understand that.

I am not proposing that the contemporary Western drama is totally committed to "thesis drama." That would indeed be absurd. Ionesco takes pains to point out that

> the theater is not the language of ideas. When it tries to become the vehicle of ideologies, it can only become their popularizer. It simplifies them dangerously. . . . What would be, not only its usefulness, but its proper function, if the theater were condemned to do the work of philosophy, or theology, or politics, or pedagogy? A psychological theater is insufficiently psychological. It is better to read a treatise on psychology. And ideological theater is insufficiently philosophical. Instead of going to see the dramatic illustration of such and such a political theory, I prefer to read my usual daily, or listen to a speech by the candidate of my party.

Instead of emphasizing ideas, contemporary dramatists like Beckett are thematically concerned with the deep troubles of Western man: emptiness, frustration, despair, and death. They protest against the human condition, realizing the futility of such a protest, but they also protest against the additions to the collective *angst* made by men themselves. Whereas the Ibsens, John Osbornes, Bertolt Brechts, and W. H. Audens of modern theater argue directly with ideas and words, the Becketts, Sartres, Albert Camus, and Ionescos, following Pirandello, argue by means of the play itself, the whole piece of art, for the *work is the word*, the play is itself a language—part sign language, part speech, part sound for its own sake, as spontaneous as a sigh or as wretched as a cough or as terrifying as a scream. The play *is* the idea, just as in the world of political and social action the sign carried, as well as the words on it, is the protest. The student with the sign in the street is language. The existentialist-absurdist play is an ideograph in the language of dissent.

"Farce," said Vsevolod Meyerhold, "is eternal." It is this dramatic form which is most basic in its appeal to the humanity in man, being least pretentious; in fact, it is most pointedly antipretentious. Thus it is no accident that farce is often selected by playwrights today to cast light on and comment about the pathos and problems of contemporary civilization. After all, the average modern life is really closer to Noel Coward than to Sophocles.

The grotesqueness of Beckett's drama must not be underestimated, for the "grotesque" is an extremely important factor in contemporary Western life. Jan Kott, in the chapter of his book *Shakespeare Our Contemporary* entitled "King Lear or Endgame," states that "the notion of absurdist mechanism is probably the last metaphysical conceit remaining in modern grotesque." Grotesque in contemporary drama is a criticism of the absolutes of this century and of history in the name of humanist values "and of frail human experience." Of course, grotesque is more cruel than tragedy. There is no catharsis for grotesque. Tragedy paradoxically raises and destroys the hero simultaneously against the comforting background of an a priori system, but grotesque denies the hero, raises no one and nothing, and insists that the system never existed. The absurd, the grotesque, and existentialism go hand in hand.

The themes of Beckett's work are complex and are as profound as those of Sophocles. Above all, appropriately enough, is the question of God, for Beckett has a deep negativism about the possibility of the existence of the Deity, so deep, in fact, that it almost takes on an existence akin to a positive belief. Theology, particularly Roman Catholic theology, is a frequent target of the author, especially in *Molloy*. There Moran, a lapsed Catholic, absurdly deliberates on such questions as the excommunication of vermin in the sixteenth century. Theology for Beckett is a "science" about an abstract: God is comic, pathetic, and absurd. God himself, existing or not, invention or reality, can only be hated. The oppressors in Beckett's work, such as Mr. Knott and, of course, Godot, are God figures. They and He are cruel, often indifferent, and as capricious as chance itself. Christ, who is one of us, also wonders what He has done to deserve his fate, for He, too, has been deceived by the myths of salvation and immortality which He and all mankind in their collective suffering and weariness were all too willing to embrace. Beckett's cynicism about God can be harsh. Vladimir says: "One of the thieves was saved. It's a reasonable percentage."

Man's only fate is death, says Beckett, and the efforts of mythmakers to soften this truth are wrong and dangerous. We wait around for death. It is seldom too soon and often too late. Why should it come after enormous suffering and the loss of the last shreds of human dignity? Krapp, with an image paradoxically reminiscent of conventional damnation, is "burning to be gone."

Beckett views social man as a monster. He is a brute who is concerned about only two things: his animallike pleasures and the inflicting of pain on his fellow human beings. Upholders of the Establishment, the police in particular, are especially frightening to his heroes, for they are most capable of inflicting on weaker human beings the cruelty and hatred of collective man. Man's gluttony is an abomination to Beckett, his lechery is ludicrous, his excrement pollutes everything, and the coupling of men and women is a grotesque activity. Although Beckett's attitude toward man is one of near total abhorrence, he is somewhat ambivalent in his attitude toward women. Sometimes his female characters are portrayed with a feeling near to tenderness, such as Celia in *Murphy*, Winnie in *Happy Days*, and Maddy Roony in *All That Fall*. At other times his women share all the general faults and vices of mankind, and then he attacks them with a scatalogical approach worthy of Jonathan Swift.

Underlying Beckett's pessimism is a longing for the Golden Age, for a kind and merciful humanity, for faith in mankind, and even for the possibility of hope. Ultimately Beckett's greatness as an artist is tied to the basic humanity in a sensitive, magnanimous, artistic soul. His nonheroes are heroes after all in that they struggle for their existence, painful and foolish though it may be, and, as in *The Unnamable*, they stubbornly fight on in the lost cause of life.

Samuel Beckett began his literary career as a critic, and he possibly intended to pursue such a career for the rest of his life. In 1929 at the age of twenty-two, he published an essay on James Joyce. It appeared in a collection of essays called *Our Examination*. The essay is based on Beckett's conversations with Joyce, whom he has never ceased to admire, but it is by no means a brilliant piece of work. Although he continued to publish criticism in a more or less desultory fashion for some thirty years, only one piece of Beckett criticism is really important: his essay on Proust.

The seventy-two page work, entitled simply *Proust*, was published in 1934 in English. In many ways it serves to illuminate more about what Beckett would later write than what Proust had written, although at least one critic considers the essay one of the best among the short introductions to Proust and to *Remembrance of Things Past*. The main themes of the French masterpiece are clearly presented. The concept of time lost and time regained through the agency of involuntary memory and the tragic nature of time fascinated Beckett and helped form his belief that "tragedy is the statement of an expiation, . . . of original sin, . . . the sin of having been born." Also, "there is no escape from the hours and the days." Beckett suffered through the reading and rereading of the sixteen volumes of Proust for the assignment, and he also read almost all available Proust criticism. As a result the essay is an excellent guide to the architectonics of the *Remembrance*, as well as a guide to the forming mind of an emerging young literary artist. Beckett, like Proust, would have only contempt for naturalist writing that "worships the offal of experience. . . ." Proust's adventure in memory would also help form the landscape of *Waiting for Godot*.

Beckett published his first poem in 1930. Titled "Whoroscope," it was written in blatant imitation of Eliot and Joyce. The poem came about because Beckett had heard of a poetry contest with a prize for the winner of ten pounds. The poem had to be about "time." He was reading a book by Adrien Baillet about the life of Descartes, and, being in a hurry to meet the contest deadline, he incorporated some material from the book into the poem. He won the contest, and three hundred copies of the poem were printed. Beckett was also asked to contribute verse to a forthcoming anthology. "Whoroscope" is a witty dream elaboration, with Descartes speaking in the first person. As a poem it

248

is more like a prose monologue cut up to look like verse. There is no clear language pattern, and the vocabulary is colloquially ordinary. In the poem Beckett is concerned with the generation of life and the function of the intellect. It is also laden with bad puns in a sour imitation of Joyce's use of language.

During the 1930's, Beckett followed up his limited success in poetry with various experimental pieces, some published in minor European publications and little magazines. The poems are superficial and not very witty, depending far too much upon word play for effect.

In "Alba" Beckett indicates his discomfort with poetry and foreshadows his abandonment of the medium:

> Oh I am ashamed
> of all clumsy artistry
> I am ashamed of presuming
> to arrange words

"Alba" appeared in the 1935 collection of Beckett's poetry, *Echo's Bones.* The work reveals an imitation of Yeats, Joyce, and Eliot with the settings of the poems including a "Waste Land" London, a "Dubliners" Dublin, and, rather appropriately, Dante's *Inferno.* The poems composed between 1937 and 1939 were written in French, and although they possess more clarity than his English poems, nevertheless they are elliptical, bawdy, full of poor puns, and, all in all, surprisingly immature for Beckett's age and the amount of writing he had completed to that time.

During the World War II period Beckett wrote very little verse. One poem (untitled), about his experience working for the Irish Red Cross hospital in Saint-Lô, just after the war, is beautiful and rich in language and suggestion. Indeed, this short poem may be his best. His later poems, six in all, were also written in French. They reflect the horrible European experience of total war and are preoccupied with death. The poetry of Beckett matured even as it atrophied, for his language became richer, and his imagery grew stronger and bolder, the pun falling by the wayside. He translated three of the poems, and they are equally good in English as they are in French.

Poetry for Beckett at first was a little word game he played for himself, an intelligent young man's self-amusement. As the years passed, he restrained his vulgarity, disciplined himself, developed enough self-confidence to eschew erudite exhibitionism, and mastered the trade of the poet. Ultimately what is most significant about Beckett's verse is that it permitted him to develop and express the rich irony, the lamentation, and the pity that came to fruition in his novels and, most important, in his plays.

The novels of Samuel Beckett represent a much greater achievement than his verse, and although they have not made the impact that the plays have, they nevertheless go hand in hand with Beckett's dramatic activity, sharing his dualistic philosophy of the separation between mind and matter, his concern for the nature of character, and his pessimistic outlook. Like those of his dramas the antiheroes of his novels wait in vain for God and are without hope of salvation.

Beckett's novels were born of the enormous influence which Joyce had on him. But the importance of the influence of such masters as Dante, Swift, Shakespeare, Ivan Goncharov, Proust, and Franz Kafka should not be underestimated. The themes of Beckett's prose are not dissimilar from those of his plays. There is the overriding question of man's exile and alienation, the difficulty of maintaining identity, the searing question of the flesh, the impossibility of ascertaining knowledge, and the deep longing for a return to the womb, which may in fact mask a powerful death wish within the artist. The Unnamable, the antihero of the novel of the same name, says, "First dirty, then make clean." That is Beckett's basic procedure both in the individual novels and in the totality of his prose canon. But since the process of making dirty involves the stripping away of man's strength, hope, and dignity, the process of making clean is no less than the very destruction of the human animal involved. Beckett the novelist, like Beckett the poet, is a pessimist who might well deny his pessimism, stating that he is only portraying reality, only delineating the actual human condition. Youth, good looks, health, and happiness are not the stable elements of life. Man's ultimate condition is the hopelessness of the tramp and the humiliation of the beggar. Man is, or will be, old; he will stink; he will wear his filth to the point where the excrement and the rag are inseparable; his ulcers, his hemorrhoids, his nose, his eyes, his gums—all will run with their respective rotting liquids.

Despite his disgust for the human condition, Beckett is compassionate, for he makes common cause with his cripples, ultimately saying to them: "We are brothers, we are one, our fates are hardly different." If the human outcast is Beckett's archetype, still Beckett is faithful to him and like a good nurse stays with him to the end, listening with wisdom and understanding to the halting, ignorant, common tale of woe.

Beckett's novels are best considered in chronological order. His process is that of reduction of the antihero, essentially the same figure in the stories *More Pricks Than Kicks*, *Murphy*, *Watt*, *Molloy*, *Malone Dies*, *The Unnamable*, and *How It Is*. Actually, Beckett's first novel remained unfinished. It was written in Paris in 1932 but was put aside by the author, who then cannibalized it for ten short stories published in London in 1934. The novel was to be called *Dream of Fair to Middling Women*. The stories were published under the title *More Pricks Than Kicks*. One is, of course, immediately reminded that Joyce began with the short story in *The Dubliners*. It is as though Beckett had decided to imitate literally the pattern of his mentor's career. *More Pricks Than Kicks* is out of print today, primarily because Beckett does not wish the book reissued. The stories have a recurring protagonist, Belacqua, and they offer a chronological view of a man's life about and around Dublin.

Belacqua, like Bloom, is an outsider. He is a Protestant, educated, and idle. As the individual condition of Beckett's hero deteriorates within each novel, so the collective hero deteriorates from novel to novel. Belacqua, the hero of the unpublished novel and of the published stories, starts at a higher level of human condition than any other of Beckett's protagonists, but, like the others, his exile from society grows more painful, and his suffering increases.

Belacqua shows the beginning of the physical degeneration of Beckett's collective antihero. Belacqua is fat, pale, nearly bald, wearing glasses, ill-dressed—sometimes in filthy clothes—an object of laughter. He seems to walk in a Chaplinesque manner. He is sexually discontent and maladjusted. He is prone to autoeroticism, and he is a peeping Tom who spies on love-making in the woods. Actually, sex is a horror to him, and the less sexually active a woman is the better he likes her. Thus he cannot really function as a sexual man and must remain solitary and lonely, an outsider by choice like Dostoevski's underground man. Flesh must be mortified, and ideally one might just be able to pull one's whole body up inside one's head.

After *More Pricks Than Kicks*, Beckett spent two years in London. Poor and dejected, he decided to move to Paris, finally settling there in 1937. Before leaving London, however, he visited a country mental institution and got the idea for *Murphy* (1938), his first published novel and his best comic work, which was no more commercially successful than *More Pricks Than Kicks* had been.

Murphy is a Dubliner who has gone to London and is waiting for his Irish girl friend to join him there. He has no job, no occupation, no trade, no profession. He lives off a pittance supplied by a rich uncle in the Netherlands. Murphy meets a goodhearted young Irish prostitute, and they live together for a short while. He has a rival for his first love, who comes looking for Murphy to confront him, but Murphy has meanwhile died in an accidental gas explosion in his garret. The rival identifies Murphy's charred body, which Murphy had willed to the prostitute, asking her to have his ashes

> placed in a paper bag and brought to the Abbey Theatre, Abbey Street, Dublin, and without pause into what the great and good Lord Chesterfield calls the necessary house, where their happiest hours have been spent, . . . and I desire that the chain be pulled upon them, if possible during the performance of a piece, the whole to be executed without ceremony or show of grief.

Ultimately Murphy's ashes are taken to a pub and scattered on the floor. His remains are not to have the dignity of a quick flush, for Murphy, the tragicomic Irishman, is born to failure as he quests for happiness. His prostitute love, Celia, also fails in that she loses her one love.

Murphy, like all the other Beckett novels except for *Molloy*, is a mononovel; that is, the book revolves entirely around the protagonist. Molloy differs only in that there are two sections with a different protagonist in each. Murphy is a youngish man suffering from many ailments, including a bad heart and bad feet. He cannot escape from a decaying, disgusting body. His complexion is jaundiced, his apparel without distinction. Like Belacqua he is an idle man. He was once a theology student. The initially comic situation of his life becomes more and more tragic as the novel progresses to his meaningless death, his ashes strewn among spit, vomit, cigarette butts, and filth. *Murphy*, by means of the objective correlative, reverberates with horror and disgust for the human condition.

During the years 1942 to 1944 Beckett, who had been working with a resistance group, was in hiding among French farmers in the Rhone Valley. It was then that he wrote the novel *Watt*, partly as an escape from the war around him. This novel, his last written in English, is set in Ireland. Although extracts of the book were published between 1950 and 1953, the whole work did not appear until 1953.

The novel has a somewhat complicated plot. Early in the work Watt, the protagonist, is setting out on a journey by train and foot to a Mr. Knott's house, where he will work as a servant on the ground floor. Watt serves Mr. Knott all day and most of the night. Finally he is to be replaced by another servant, and he returns to the railroad station, where he spends a night in the waiting room and is hurt in the morning when a door swings open on him. The railwaymen throw a bucket of slops on him to revive him, but they accidentally drop the bucket on him too. Nevertheless he staggers to his feet, buys a ticket to the end of the line, and departs. Thus the enigmatic story ends, and thus the Beckett protagonist has become hazier, more of a shadowy figure than Murphy, as though Beckett were saying that the more closely we scrutinize a person the more a shadow he becomes.

Watt scarcely speaks in his book. He wears an oversized greatcoat and baggy trousers. He has a boot on one foot and a shoe on the other (fortunately, both are brown). He is a big, bony middle-aged man with graying red hair. Beyond these details Beckett gives little description of his protagonist. He is mysterious and uncertain as a person, and these qualities support the theme of the alienation of the hero, or anti-hero, from his fellow human beings. However, alienation takes something of a back seat as a theme in *Watt*. The question is the difficulty, perhaps the impossibility, of real knowledge. The questions multiply. Who is Watt? What is Watt? Where is he going? Who are we? What are we? Where are we going?

Watt is an uncertain novel, experimental and transitional in nature.

It introduces us to the antisocial tramp as hero, and it points out the savagery of human indifference. And what is the meaning of Watt's quest? The meaning is that the quest is meaningless.

Lastly, *Watt* is Beckett's farewell to English as his creative language for the novel. The long prose works written after *Watt* were destined to serve as a contribution to French literature, and a great contribution they are indeed. France had become Beckett's home. He shared Joyce's great admiration—even envy—of French writers, with their highly literate and sophisticated reading public. *Watt* was followed by a group of short stories written in French, as if Beckett were trying out his new tool in short, warm-up practice pieces.

The next novel, *Molloy*, was written in French and appeared in April, 1951. It was published by an avant-garde press, which was to build its formidable reputation on the publication of Beckett's work. The author experienced the pleasant shock of at last having a book received with great critical acclaim and even some commercial success. Major French critics ungrudgingly made room for him in the pantheon of significant contemporary French writers. Sensing a good thing, the publishers issued *Malone Dies* later the same year; *Waiting for Godot* in October, 1952; and *The Unnamable* in June, 1953. These rapid publications represent one of the great publishing coups of the century, for in a two-year period Beckett's publisher published the heart of his lifework and the efforts which would result in his winning the Nobel Prize for Literature.

Molloy is part of a trilogy: *Molloy, Malone Dies,* and *The Unnamable,* written between 1946 and 1949. At the same time Beckett was also writing *Waiting for Godot.* These years were probably the most productive of his life. *Molloy* is a two-part work, each part a first-person narrative. The initial narration is by Molloy; the second half is narrated by Jacques Moran. In the first part Molloy is in his mother's room writing his story for a man who comes weekly to collect the completed work. Molloy is a cripple; one leg is stiff and he uses crutches. Nonetheless, he sets out on a bicycle journey, tying his crutches to the handlebars. At the edge of town he is arrested and questioned by the police for a supposed bicycle infraction. After being released, he runs over a dog. Lousse, the dog's owner, saves him from angry bystanders and takes him into her house, where he seems to substitute for the dog in her affections. Eventually he limps off on his crutches without his bicycle, and, after an unsuccessful attempt to take his own life, he proceeds to the seashore to replenish a supply of sucking stones which he regularly uses to cause salivation and assuage the pangs of hunger. Weakening and suffering terribly, he is no longer able to limp and must crawl until he falls into a ditch, from which he is rescued and returned to his mother's room to write the story of his life. Thus at the end of the first part we are really back at the beginning of this circular narration, for Molloy's life, and, in Beckett's view, ours, is a continuum of suffering.

Moran, the protagonist of the second part of *Molloy*, is a man of property, a practicing Catholic, who is ordered by his employer to look for a man named Molloy. It seems that Moran had been acquainted with Molloy—by which Beckett is indicating that the prosperous middle class is indeed aware of the suffering of the poor, if unwilling to do anything about them. While giving his son an enema just before departing with him on the journey to find Molloy, Moran suffers a sharp pain in one knee. On the journey the pain strikes once more, and he can no longer move the leg. His son leaves him to find a bicycle for him to ride but is away for three days. Moran finds a heavy stick and later clubs a man to death; he has become Cain. The son returns with the bicycle, and Moran says nothing of the murder. The quest is continued with both on the same bicycle until a quarrel erupts, and the son abandons the father. Moran is ordered by a messenger to return home, and he struggles to do so, hampered by increasing decrepitude and suffering. Safely home at last, Moran plans to write his report and leave again. This report is referred to at the beginning of the novel and thus the second part is also in essence a circular and cyclical narration.

The setting is again a Dublinlike town and surrounding area. Molloy and Moran are obviously to be compared. Molloy, for all his outcast imperfections, is much more a human being than the cruel, precise, bourgeois Moran. Beckett's sympathies, as ever, are clearly with the outsider.

Molloy is Beckett's first novel in which the protagonist is a writer himself, telling his own story in terms of experience and mental process. Molloy, Moran, Malone, and The Unnamable seem to be self-conscious projections of the author himself, who appears to be watching himself in a mirror as it were, fascinated by the process of literary creation. In *Molloy* the journey, or quest, is extremely important. Both men end at home, but much the worse for their efforts, like *The Pilgrim's Progress* reversed. Thus *Molloy* is a major statement of Beckett's recurring theme of exile. Man's destiny is either the absurd quixotic journey or oblivion in a little room filled to overflowing with loneliness. Life for both men is a vain quest and ultimate isolation, with the body decaying and its foolish functions exposed to ridicule. In the view of some critics *Molloy* is Beckett's finest novel, containing the most powerful statement of his major interests and themes. Modern French critics consider it a magnificent contribution to modern letters.

The second novel in the trilogy, *Malone Dies*, is somewhat lighter than its companion works. Again we have a room and a writer. Molloy writes until he dies. Awaiting death, he writes stories to himself, symbolizing the ultimate view of the existentialist artist. The events leading to his death are simple: the old woman who takes care of him stops bringing him food and emptying his chamber pot, his stick falls beyond his reach, and he is marooned in bed. Finally a man comes to watch him. Malone thinks that the visitor is an undertaker's assistant come too early. Malone must have his stick, his sight and hearing are fading, he has no teeth; his clothes are gone, and he lies naked between the blankets. He has stoically accepted the uselessness of his body and his approaching death. In his own way he is heroic, although his voyeurism as he gazes at the sexual activities of a couple opposite his room and his last desire to catch, undress, and fondle a little girl are comic, pathetic, and grotesque, and yet touchingly human.

Again the novel takes place in the Dublin area. Beckett remains true to his homeland locale, blending geographic elements of his art and his life. The primary question in *Malone Dies* is human identity, the nature of being, the question of ontology. Of course, Malone dies in *Malone Dies*, and Beckett tells us that the ontological question is meaningless in the face of death's inevitable victory.

The Unnamable, the last of the trilogy, is extremely difficult to follow—and almost unbearable to read. In the beginning The Unnamable is describing the place in which he lives and certain men who have taught him. One is named Basil, but The Unnamable soon changes his name to Mahood. We then have Mahood's story, written through the first-person narrative of the writer Unnamable.

The Unnamable's world is hardly a real place. It is more a state of mind. His body cannot move; his eyes cannot close. He has no sexual organ, no nose, no hair. He thinks of himself as a "big talking ball." In other words, Beckett has stripped his hero of all organs and extensions; Beckett the dualist has removed the body from the being. As *The Unnamable* accelerates stylistically from paragraphs through unbroken prose to one last sentence of fifteen hundred words, the reader is left sharing Beckett's and The Unnamable's intense and unmitigated loathing for life.

The pessimism of this work was so devastating for Beckett himself that he found it difficult to continue writing. In despair he felt he was repeating himself, and in the end he believed his work, like his life, would be dust. Truthfully, Beckett's latter fiction does go over old ground. Thirteen stories written between 1945 and 1950 and published in 1955 as *Texts for Nothing* seem to be devoid of human beings and reality reference points in reality. Another novel was begun and abandoned, but in 1959 and 1960, Beckett wrote *How It Is*, published in 1960. It received the International Publishers' Prize. The title is strikingly different from Beckett's usual practice of titling his novels with the names of the protagonists. However, the hero of *How It Is* is again an unnamed character, and obviously Beckett could not use "unnamable" once more. The new hero is not a writer but a "speaker" who enunciates the "latest version" of the story of Beckett's hero. He even believes in reincarnation, and we are to assume that his previous existences were as the heroes of Beckett's earlier works.

How It Is has three long parts. The first tells of the protagonist's life until he meets a man called Pim. Most of this part is devoted to descriptions of the conditions of his life and his memories. The second part is concerned with his "creature," Pim. Here the protagonist names himself Bom. Most of the time Bom is busy trying to communicate with Pim by torturing him. In a manner reminiscent of Kafka's *In the Penal Colony*, Bom "speaks" to Pim by carving out words on Pim's back with his long fingernails, even after Pim's back becomes bloody and raw. The third part continues the sadomasochistic relationship reminiscent of the relationship between Pozzo and Lucky in *Waiting for Godot* and extends the relationship to a universal symbol in which the world and time are filled with an infinite number of such couples: the eternal torturer and the eternal victim.

Thus Beckett presents the problem of human identity in an existence where all men are essentially doing the same things that they have been doing as long as there have been men. Beckett's answer here— and cumulatively—is that identity is a will-o'-the-wisp, a myth, an essence which has no existence. The delusion that man really has an individual identity may be the cruelest hoax ever played on him.

Because of its extreme typographical and syntactical innovations, *How It Is* is a difficult book to read. Furthermore, it adds little to the philosophical and artistic positions assumed and explored in Beckett's earlier novels. The world of Beckett's novels is a different world from that of everyday life. We know few derelicts; we have little to do with dying old men; and certainly we seldom share their intimate thoughts and processes. Yet, after all, the world of Beckett's novels is our world too. It projects and visualizes the underground of our existence and our inescapable fate.

Beckett's thoughts and ideas as a novelist are not always easy to comprehend, his prose is often extremely difficult, and his subjects are far from pleasant; but above all Beckett is an honest artist who insists that his audience must be willing to pay the price of admission into the world of his private and powerful vision.

Beckett's drama has had an influence on the work of younger contemporary playwrights equaled only by Brecht. The young British playwright Harold Pinter, whose lost, down-at-the-heels, sometimes underworld characters in their shabby environs are descendants of Beckett's stage and fictional heroes, said of Beckett:

The farther he goes the more good it does me. I don't want philosophies, tracts, dogmas, creeds, ways out, truths, answers, *nothing from the bargain basement.* He is the most courageous, remorseless writer going and the more he grinds my nose in the shit the more I am grateful to him. He's not fucking me about, he's not leading me up any garden, he's not slipping me any wink, he's not flogging me a remedy or a path or a revelation or a basinful of breadcrumbs, he's not selling me anything I don't want to buy, he

258

doesn't give a bollock whether I buy or not, *he hasn't got his hand over his heart.* Well, I'll buy his goods, hook, line and sinker, because he leaves no stone unturned and no maggot lonely. He brings forth a body of beauty. His work is beautiful.

One of the most widely discussed plays of the 1960's was *Rosencrantz and Guildenstern Are Dead,* by a young British playwright, Tom Stoppard. This play, which in existential terms shows the underside of heroic action seen through the eyes of the little men who are always victims of history, is another offspring of Beckett's dramaturgy. Writing in *The New Republic,* the critic Robert Brustein said: "Shakespeare provides the characters, Pirandello the technique, and Beckett the tone with which the Stoppard play proceeds." Elsewhere Brustein succinctly called the play *Waiting for Hamlet.* In an interview with *Time,* Stoppard unintentionally indicated the vast influence of Beckett on his work when he said: "Almost everybody thinks of himself as nobody. A cipher, not even a cog. In that sense, Rosencrantz and Guildenstern are everybody. I feel that I am like that." Thus Stoppard's characters and even the author himself belong to the shattered pantheon of the nonhero, the pantheon that in our time is so much the making of Beckett and other existentialist writers, particularly the dramatists.

Beckett's drama crowns his work. It brings to life and ultimately popularizes his philosophy, his world view, and his dark conception of the truth of the human condition. The play that brought Beckett international fame was his second effort, though first published and first produced, *Waiting for Godot.* (The first play was *Eleutheria,* written in 1947 and still unpublished.) As a matter of fact, *Waiting for Godot,* on which Beckett worked from 1947 through 1949, the same fertile period which produced *Molloy, Malone Dies,* and *The Unnamable,* was published before it was performed. *Godot* was published in October, 1952, but was not produced until early in 1953, thanks to a small French government grant sometimes made to first plays.

Waiting for Godot, like *Endgame,* was, of course, written in French. It is a play in which very little seems to happen. The setting consists of a place which contains only a tree and two tramps, Vladimir and

259

Estragon, waiting for someone named Godot to rescue them from their misery. Instead of Godot they are visited by a cruel master, Pozzo, and his demented slave, Lucky. The new couple stay a short while and then leave. Finally at the end of the first act a messenger arrives, purportedly from Godot, to say that he will come tomorrow.

The second act finds more waiting. Pozzo and Lucky return, but now the former has lost his sight and the latter his ability to speak. They stumble and fall, and the tramps help them along the way. The messenger enters once more, again promising that Godot will come tomorrow, and all seems as it was in the beginning. Yet small changes do take place. A carrot comes out of one tramp's pocket and is eaten by the other, the rope linking Pozzo and Lucky has been broken and between the two acts of the play, besides the loss of sight and hearing by Pozzo and Lucky, the tree acquires leaves, perhaps indicating a much longer passage of time than the one apparent night. Perhaps winter has turned to summer, perhaps years have passed, perhaps the lives of these two human beings, Vladimir and Estragon, who, despite resentment and frustration, desperately need each other's company, are reduced to a mere waiting.

For Beckett, waiting is a basic truth of the human condition. They call each other by hypercharistic terms, Gogo and Didi. The two names are made up of the letters and sounds of Godot, and if one says them fast enough together indeed the sound "Godot" seems to emerge. They are so linked together, perhaps in the eyes of Godot, that they are like a married couple. Their world is mostly a world of inertia with limited impulses, moods, impressions, and memories, none of which develop into anything substantial. They are in a limbo experiencing Thoreau's "quiet desperation." Although they are not truly living, they cannot end their lives. They are helpless, and even the faint hope of rescue from Godot can do little to alleviate their suffering.

Pozzo, Lucky's cruel master, represents vicious Hobbesian power as he shouts his orders and brutalizes his slave, who must even carry the whip with which he is beaten. Lucky's name is ironic, of course, since his fate is terrible—and yet not entirely ironic because in a mindless universe he at least has a master to think for him and order his life. Pozzo represents authoritarianism, and Lucky symbolizes all-suffering humanity, which nevertheless wishes for and needs its masters. The sadomasochistic basis between masters and men is at least as much required by slavish men as by their exploiters. Even when Pozzo has lost his sight, Lucky naturally must remain with him.

Of course, Godot is God, who to Beckett probably does not exist at all but in whose name impossible promises have been made to men so that they continue to live and suffer in hope for the impossible. If he does exist, his indifference to human suffering is either mindless or cruel.

Waiting for Godot is Beckett's chief vision of the inner universe, the mind of man in the brief interlude between the womb and the tomb expressed thus: "one day like any other." Vladimir and Estragon in their inaction symbolize the inability of man to "let go." Why cannot they let go? Probably because of the fear of dying. The act of release through suicide, which would at least bring relief, is impossible because of man's impotence and his basic inaction. The outer world of *Waiting for Godot* is strewn with the wreckage of phenomena only some of which is apparent. The outer flotsam and the inner ennui combine to offer mankind as much of a devastating nightmare as it is able to comprehend.

The one-act play *Endgame* was written in French in 1956, and the next year Beckett translated the work into English. *Waiting for Godot* had been a success, and yet no theater in Paris was willing to produce *Endgame*, probably because it seemed so lacking in action and so totally pessimistic that theater managers could not envision the play as economically viable. The first production was staged in French at the Royal Court Theatre in London on April 3, 1957. Beckett's French publisher issued the play in May, and in 1958 Beckett's translation was published.

Endgame is another play about waiting, but, as *Waiting for Godot* deals with the never-to-be-fulfilled promise of an arrival, *Endgame* is concerned with the never-to-be-fulfilled promise of departure. The "endgame" is the last part of a game of chess, during which the king is hunted down and trapped. As Martin Esslin points out in *The Theatre of the Absurd*, Beckett's *Endgame* is "the final game in the hour of death."

The setting of *Endgame* is a bare interior with two small windows high up. It is the gray inner world, for the world outside the room no longer exists. In the middle of this world, sitting in a wheelchair, is a blind old man, Hamm, paralyzed and unable to stand. He wears a dressing gown that looks like a cardinal's robe, and he has a skullcap on his head. When the curtain rises, a bloodstained handkerchief covers his face.

Standing motionless at the door is Hamm's servant Clov, who is unable to sit and can only totter. As with Pozzo and Lucky, we have a blind master and his servant, totally bound to each other. Also on stage are two ashcans standing near the wall, containing Hamm's legless parents, Nag and Nell, who only occasionally rise to be seen and heard. The four characters believe themselves to be the sole survivors of a great catastrophe; thus the play is about the end of life.

Hamm is vicious and selfish. Clov hates him and wants to leave but cannot. He does not understand why he has been irrevocably bound to a cruel master. The dramatic tension in the play centers around the question of Clov's ability to break away from Hamm. Symbolically, once more we have master and slave, lord and peasant, capitalist and worker, sadist and masochist. Hamm possesses the last food in the world, but he cannot feed himself. If Clov leaves, Hamm, the master, will die of starvation, but so will the servant. Thus there is little hope for escape from the cruel relationships of life except through a conscious commitment to death.

Hamm is a protagonist in the mold of Beckett's fiction, a writer or storyteller composing the story of a great catastrophe. Nag and Nell, who lost their legs in an accident while riding a tandem bicycle are grotesques. Their intelligence is low, and their sentimentality is sickening. Hamm hates them. Toward the end of the play Clov peers out of a window with his telescope and sees a small boy. He wonders: "A potential procreator?" Hamm sums up the play's lack of hope by replying, "If he exists he'll die there or he'll come here. And if he doesn't. . . . ." At the conclusion Hamm again covers his face, Clov remains, and all is as it was before, except that the endgame has been lost.

Endgame contains the economy and the verbal richness of a long poem. It is filled with biblical and Shakespearean parallels and illusions. There is also a plethora of multilingual puns, for Beckett has never shaken the Joycean influence. Perhaps human beings must ultimately retreat individually or collectively into their own skulls and exist in the hellish suffering of recollection. The room is the skull, and the small windows are the eyes through which—if one is interested—one might see the land and the sea and a child. *Endgame* portrays the existential end of Western values: art, God, family, and love.

Beckett's next important short play, *Krapp's Last Tape*, was written in English and was first produced at the Royal Court Theater in London on October 28, 1958. The play was published the next year. It is a monodrama whose sole character, Krapp, spends most of his time listening to the words of his younger self on his tape recordings. The ultimate writer's or storyteller's dialogue is thus an exchange with the echoes of his younger self. Nearly blind and deaf and limping painfully, old Krapp listens to a recording he made when he was thirty-nine. We hear of the death of his mother, the incident when he gives a ball to a dog, and the end of perhaps his last love affair. Krapp drinks wine and decides to record one last tape, to tell one more story. However, his mind soon wanders into the realm of vague recollections of his career as a writer and the mere parody of a love affair. He stops his recording and replays the thirty-year-old tape, allowing it to run out in silence as the play ends. Thus Beckett poignantly illustrates the necessity and the value of the work of art to the artist himself as it chronicles and structures his life. Furthermore, he shows the artist continually struggling to exist again and again, to be reborn even though existence means suffering, when one might expect that a single existence for the sensitive soul is almost more than enough.

Krapp's Last Tape is not sentimental, however. As in all of Beckett's other work its emphasis is metaphysical. Krapp is seeking knowledge and meaning and understanding. He looks for his identity in the eyes of his love, and when he asks her, "Let me in," his plea is not merely sexual but an attempt to establish reality within their relationship.

Krapp's Last Tape, like *Endgame* and *Waiting for Godot*, is as much poem as play. It is the brief epic of an artist's time and the parallel voices of his middle life and old age. In it the force of life struggles with and is wrestled down by negation, despair, and defeat.

Beckett's last important stage play was *Happy Days*, written in

English in 1961 and first produced in Greenwich Village, New York City, at the Cherry Lane Theater on September 17, 1961. It was published the same year.

Like *Waiting for Godot, Happy Days* is a two-act drama. The title is, of course, ironic; there are no happy days for Beckett's protagonists. In this case a woman named Winnie is buried up to her breasts in the earth. A happy day is one in the first act when there is slightly less pain and suffering than in the inevitably more terrible next day. Again the theme of waiting appears. This time the protagonist is not waiting for redemption or the opportunity to escape, but merely for a bell to ring, which, like Pavlov's bell and the bell of the mass, will allow her to sleep away the remainder of her life. For, next to death, sleep is the preferable condition for humankind. The happy day is the day one dies.

Winnie prays, brushes her teeth, spits, and tries unsuccessfully to communicate with her silent, invisible husband, Willie. She is running out of toothpaste, petroleum jelly, and words. Her mouth pours out "old" words in the form of quotations from Shakespeare, Milton, Herrick, Gray, Keats, and Browning.

In Act 2 Winnie is imbedded up to her neck, and her only movement is that of facial expression. Obviously things are worse. She no longer prays, and she is hardly able to understand the meaning of her own now fragmenting words. Winnie is also a storyteller, however, and the iterative artist hero of Beckett's work has taken on a feminine form. As her story ends, Willie finally crawls into sight and gropes his way to the pile of earth in which his wife is embedded. She calls out to him, but he cannot quite reach her. He does have enough energy left to mutter, "Win." Enraptured by this overwhelmingly "happy" event, Winnie, with almost unbearable dramatic irony, sings the female part of the waltz duet in the *Merry Widow* as the curtain falls on a "happy ending."

Beckett's irony in this his last important drama is devastating: suffering, sinking mankind has only its pale illusions of love and its worn-out words to go down with. However, one other aspect of life takes on importance here as it does in *Waiting for Godot*. Winnie and Willie have companionship. It is futile, absurd, grotesque; and love and hate are ambiguously entwined. Yet companionship is a distinct human value which can assuage in a small part the pain of existence. Here perhaps for Beckett is man's last a priori value, perhaps the only one that ever was meaningful. In the frozen winter of the world one suffers a little less if there is someone with him.

Beckett's innovative and important dramatic contributions come to an end with *Happy Days*, despite the publication in 1969 of *Cascando* and of other short dramatic pieces. After *Happy Days*, Beckett seems to have said all that there was for him to say in the theater. We are left with the ultimate sense of "earnest jest" which pervades the darkest tragicomedy ever written. His relatively few efforts in drama have been of utmost significance for contemporary Western theater, because Samuel Beckett is the most influential living playwright, the seminal figure in contemporary drama, and the guiding star for younger important British and American dramatists, such as Harold Pinter and Edward Albee, both of whom have expressed their admiration of Beckett and avowed their debt to him. The lean, hard, spare plays of Beckett, as sinewy as the man himself, have inspired an almost Spartan purity and purpose in contemporary existentialist-absurdist drama, which refuses to pander to sentimentality, fashion, melodramatic sensationalism, or traditional rules of dramaturgy. More so than any other living author, Samuel Beckett is the artist's artist.

No other living writer has better expressed the existential loneliness of contemporary Western man, the absurdity of the illusions by which he drags himself through his daily life, the depth of the silent suffering everywhere, and the ultimately pitiful and pitiless truth of the human condition. Assuredly Samuel Beckett was worthy of the Nobel Prize in Literature.

SELECTED BIBLIOGRAPHY

Books by Rudyard Kipling

Best Short Stories of Rudyard Kipling. Ed. by Randall Jarrell. New York, Doubleday, 1961.

Choice of Kipling's Verse. Ed. by T. S. Eliot. New York, Macmillan, 1943.

The Complete Works of Rudyard Kipling. New York, Doubleday, 1945.

Something of Myself. London, Macmillan, 1937.

Verse of Rudyard Kipling (definitive edition). New York, Doubleday, 1940.

Books About Rudyard Kipling

Bodelson, Carl. *Aspects of Kipling's Art.* New York, Barnes and Noble, 1964.

Carrington, Charles Edmund. *Rudyard Kipling: His Life and His Work.* New York, Macmillan, 1955.

Dobree, Bonamy. *Rudyard Kipling: Realist and Fabulist.* London, Oxford University Press, 1967.

Gilbert, Elliot, ed. *Kipling and the Critics.* New York, New York University Press, 1965.

Rao, Kanatur Bhaskara. *Rudyard Kipling's India.* Norman, University of Oklahoma Press, 1967.

Rutherford, Andrew, ed. *Some Aspects of Kipling's Verse.* London, British Academy Proceedings, 1965.

Shanks, Edward Buxton. *Rudyard Kipling: A Study in Literature and Political Ideas.* New York, Doubleday, 1940.

Books by William Butler Yeats

The Collected Plays of W. B. Yeats. New York, Macmillan, 1953.
Collected Poems of W. B. Yeats. New York, Macmillan, 1956.
The Letters of W. B. Yeats. Ed. by Allan Wade. New York, Macmillan, 1955.
Mythologies. New York, Macmillan, 1959.
A Vision: A Re-issue with the Author's Final Revisions. New York, Macmillan, 1956.

Books About William Butler Yeats

Adams, Hazard. *Blake and Yeats: The Contrary Vision.* Ithaca, Cornell University Press, 1955.
Bjersby, Birgit. *The Interpretation of the Cuchulain Legend in the Works of W. B. Yeats.* Uppsala, N.Y., *Uppsala Irish Studies*, No. 1, 1955.
Bloom, Harold. *Yeats.* New York, Oxford University Press, 1970.
Bowra, C. M. *The Heritage of Symbolism.* London, Macmillan, 1943.
Ellmann, Richard. *The Identity of Yeats.* New York, Oxford University Press, 1954.
Garab, Arra M. *Beyond Byzantium: The Last Phase of Yeats's Career.* De Kalb, Northern Illinois University Press, 1969.
Hall, James, and M. Steinmann. *The Permanence of Yeats.* New York, Macmillan, 1950.
Moore, Virginia. *The Unicorn: William Butler Yeats's Search for Reality.* New York, Macmillan, 1954.
Nathan, Leonard E. *The Tragic Drama of William Butler Yeats.* New York, Columbia University Press, 1965.
Robinson, Lennox. *Ireland's Abbey Theatre.* London, Sidgwick and Jackson, 1951.
Stock, Amy. *W. B. Yeats: His Poetry and Thought.* Cambridge, Cambridge University Press, 1961.
Ure, Peter. *Yeats, the Playwright: Commentary on Character and Design in the Major Plays.* New York, Barnes and Noble, 1963.
Vender, Helen Hennessy. *Yeats's "Vision" and the Later Plays.* Cambridge, Mass., Harvard University Press, 1963.

Whitaker, Thomas. *Swan and Shadow: Yeats's Dialogue with History.* Chapel Hill, University of North Carolina Press, 1964.

Books by George Bernard Shaw

Collected Letters, 1874–1897. New York, Dodd, Mead, 1965.
Complete Plays and Prefaces. New York, Dodd, Mead, 1962.
Heroes and Anti-Heroes: A Reader in Depth. Ed. by Harold Lublin. San Francisco, Chandler Publishing Company, 1968.
The Intelligent Woman's Guide to Socialism and Capitalism. New York, Brentano's, 1928.
Platform and Pulpit. New York, Hill & Wang, 1961.
Plays and Players: Essays on the Theatre. London, World's Classics, 1952.
The Quintessence of Ibsenism. New York, Brentano's, 1913.
"Shaw's Rules for Play Producers." *Strand* (London), July, 1949.
Sixteen Self-Sketches. New York, Dodd, Mead, 1949.

Books About George Bernard Shaw

Bentley, Eric. *Bernard Shaw, 1856–1950.* New York, New Directions, 1957.
Henderson, Archibald. *George Bernard Shaw: Playboy and Prophet.* New York, Appleton, 1932.
Henderson, Archibald. *George Bernard Shaw: Man of the Century.* New York, Appleton-Century-Crofts, 1956.
Irvine, William. *The Universe of G. B. S.* New York, Whittlesey House, 1949.
Kronenberger, Louis, ed. *George Bernard Shaw: A Critical Survey.* Cleveland, World Publishing Company, 1963.
Meisel, Martin. *Shaw and the Nineteenth-Century Theater.* Princeton, Princeton University Press, 1963.
Ohman, Richard M. *Shaw: The Style of the Man.* Middletown, Conn., Wesleyan University Press, 1962.
Pearson, Hesketh. *G. B. S.: A Full-Length Portrait.* Garden City, N.Y., Garden City Publishing Co., 1946.
Perry, Henry Ten Eyck. *Masters of Dramatic Comedy and Their Social Themes.* Cambridge, Mass., Harvard University Press, 1939.
Wilson, Edmund. *The Triple Thinkers.* New York, Harcourt, Brace, 1938.

Woodbridge, Homer E. *G. B. Shaw: Creative Artist.* Carbondale, Southern Illinois University Press, 1967.

Books by John Galsworthy

End of the Chapter (*Maid in Waiting* [1931], *Flowering Wilderness* [1932], *One More River* [1933]). New York, Scribner's, 1934.

The Forsyte Saga (*Man of Property* [1906], *In Chancery* [1920], *To Let* [1921]). New York, Scribner's, 1922.

Glimpses and Reflections. London, Heinemann, 1937.

A Modern Comedy (*The White Monkey* [1924], *The Silver Spoon* [1926], *Swan Song* [1928]). New York, Scribner's, 1929.

The Novels, Tales, and Plays of John Galsworthy. 22 vols. London, Devon Edition, 1926–29.

Tatterdemalion. New York, Scribner's, 1930.

The Works of John Galsworthy. 30 vols. London, Manaton Edition, 1922ff.

Books About John Galsworthy

Barker, Dudley. *The Man of Principle: A View of John Galsworthy.* London, Heinemann, 1963.

Chevrillon, André. *Three Studies in English Literature: Kipling, Galsworthy, Shakespeare.* New York, Doubleday, 1923.

Cross, Wilbur. *Four Contemporary Novelists.* New York, Macmillan, 1930.

Dupont, V. *John Galsworthy: The Dramatic Artist.* Paris, Henri Didier, 1942.

Holloway, David. *John Galsworthy.* Cranbury, N.J., A. S. Barnes, 1969.

Marrot, H. V., ed. *The Life and Letters of John Galsworthy.* London, Heinemann, 1935.

Mottram, R. H. *For Some We loved: An Intimate Portrait of Ada and John Galsworthy.* London, Hutchinson, 1956.

Sauter, Rudolf. *Galsworthy the Man: An Intimate Portrait.* London, Peter Owen, 1967.

Schalit, Leon. *John Galsworthy: A Survey.* London, Heinemann, 1929.

Smit, J. Henry. *The Short Stories of John Galsworthy.* Rotterdam, Van Sijn & Zonen, 1947.

Takahashi, Genji. *Studies in the Works of John Galsworthy with*

Special Reference to His Visions of Love and Beauty. Tokyo, Shinozaki Shorin, 1954.

Books by Bertrand Russell

The Analysis of Matter. New York, Harcourt, Brace, 1927.
The Analysis of Mind. London, Allen and Unwin, 1921.
Authority and the Individual. London, Allen and Unwin, 1950.
The Autobiography of Bertrand Russell 3 vols. New York, Simon and Schuster, 1967–69.
Freedom and Organization 1814–1914. London, Allen and Unwin, 1934.
Has Man a Future? London, Allen and Unwin, 1961.
A History of Western Philosophy. New York, Simon and Schuster, 1945.
Human Knowledge: Its Scope and Limits. New York, Simon and Schuster, 1948.
Human Society in Ethics and Politics. New York, Simon and Schuster, 1954.
The Impact of Science on Society. London, Allen and Unwin, 1952.
Introduction to Mathematical Philosophy. London, Allen and Unwin, 1919.
Our Knowledge of the External World. London, Allen and Unwin, 1914.
Principles of Social Reconstruction. London, Allen and Unwin, 1916.
Wisdom of the West. London, Rathbone Books, 1959.

Books About Bertrand Russell

Aiken, Lillian W. *Bertrand Russell's Philosophy of Morals.* New York, Humanities Press, 1963.
Ayer, A. J. *Russell and Moore: The Analytical Heritage.* Cambridge, Mass., Harvard University Press, 1971.
Crawshay-Williams, R. *Russell Remembered.* London, Oxford University Press, 1970.
Dewey, John, and H. M. Kallen. *The Bertrand Russell Case.* New York, Viking, 1941.
Eames, E. R. *Bertrand Russell's Theory of Knowledge.* New York, Braziller, 1969.

Fritz, C. A. *Bertrand Russell's Construction of the External World.* London, Routledge, Kegan-Paul, 1952.

Hardy, G. H. *Bertrand Russell and Trinity.* London, Cambridge University Press, 1970.

Lewis, John. *Bertrand Russell, Philosopher and Humanist.* New York, International Publishers, 1968.

Pears, D. F. *Bertrand Russell and the British Tradition in Philosophy.* New York, Random House, 1967.

Schoenman, R., ed. *Bertrand Russell, Philosopher of the Century.* Boston, Little, Brown, 1967.

Wood, Alan. *Bertrand Russell, the Passionate Skeptic.* London, Allen and Unwin, 1957.

Books by Winston S. Churchill

Great Contemporaries. New York, Putnam's, 1937.

A History of the English-Speaking Peoples. 4 vols. New York, Dodd, Mead, 1958.

Lord Randolph Churchill. 2 vols. London, Macmillan, 1906.

Marlborough: His Life and Times. 4 vols. London, Harrap, 1938.

My Early Life: A Roving Commission. London, Butterworth, 1930.

Savrola: A Tale of Revolution in Laurania. New York, Longmans, Green, 1930.

The Second World War. 6 vols. Boston, Houghton, Mifflin, 1948–53.

The Unwritten Alliance. London, Cassell, 1961.

The War Speeches of Winston S. Churchill. London, Cassell, 1951–52.

While England Slept, 1932–1938: A Survey of World Affairs. New York, Putnam's, 1938.

The World Crisis. 5 vols. London, Butterworth, 1931.

Books About Winston S. Churchill

Ashley, Maurice. *Churchill as a Historian.* New York, Scribner's, 1969.

Berlin, Isaiah. *Mr. Churchill in 1940.* Boston, Houghton, Mifflin, 1964.

Bonham-Carter, Violet. *Winston Churchill as I Knew Him.* London, Eyre, Spottiswoode, and Collins, 1965.

Broad, Lewis. *Winston Churchill, 1874–1951.* New York, Philosophical Library, 1952.

Churchill, Randolph S. *Winston S. Churchill.* 3 vols. Boston, Houghton, Mifflin, 1966–71.
Cowles, Virginia. *Winston Churchill: The Era and the Man.* London, Hamilton, 1953.
De Mendelssohn, Peter. *The Age of Churchill: Heritage and Adventure, 1874–1911.* London, Thames and Hudson, 1961.
Eade, Charles, ed. *Churchill and His Contemporaries.* New York, Simon and Schuster, 1953.
James, Robert Rhodes. *Churchill: A Study in Failure, 1900–1939.* London, Weidenfeld and Nicolson, 1970.
Snow, C. P. *Variety of Men.* New York, Scribner's, 1967.
Stewart, Herbert Leslie. *Winged Words: Winston Churchill as Writer.* New York, Bouregy and Curl, 1954.
Taylor, A. J. P., ed. *Churchill: Four Faces and the Man.* London, Alston Rivers, 1968.

Books by Samuel Beckett
Cascado. New York, Grove Press, 1969.
Endgame. New York, Grove Press, 1958.
Happy Days. New York, Grove Press, 1961.
Krapp's Last Tape, and Other Dramatic Pieces. New York, Grove Press, 1960.
Murphy. New York, Grove Press, 1967.
Poems in English. New York, Grove Press, 1963.
Stories and Texts for Nothing. New York, Grove Press, 1967.
Three Novels by Samuel Beckett. New York, Grove Press, 1965.
Waiting for Godot. New York, Grove Press, 1956.
Watt. New York, Grove Press, 1959.

Books About Samuel Beckett
Coe, Richard N. *Beckett.* In the series *Writers and Critics.* Edinburgh and London, Oliver and Boyd, 1964.
Cohn, Ruby. *Samuel Beckett: The Comic Gamut.* New Brunswick, Rutgers University Press, 1962.
Esslin, Martin. "Beckett," in *The Novelist as Philosopher: Studies in French Fiction, 1935–1960.* Ed. by John Cruickshank. London, Oxford University Press, 1962.

———. *The Theatre of the Absurd.* New York, Doubleday, 1961.

Fletcher, John. *The Novels of Samuel Beckett.* London, Chatto and Windus, 1964.

Grossvogel, David. *The Self-Conscious Stage in Modern French Drama.* New York, Columbia University Press, 1961.

Guicharnaud, Jacques, and June Beckelman. *Modern French Theatre from Giradoux to Beckett.* New Haven, Yale University Press, 1961.

Hoffman, Frederick J. *Samuel Beckett: The Language of the Self.* Carbondale, Southern Illinois University Press, 1962.

Kenner, Hugh. *Samuel Beckett: A Critical Study.* New York, Grove Press, 1961.

———. *Flaubert, Joyce, and Beckett: The Stoic Comedians.* London, W. H. Allen, 1964.

Pronko, Leonard Cabell. *Avant-Garde: The Experimental Theatre in France.* Berkeley, University of California Press, 1962.

Tindall, William York. *Samuel Beckett.* In the series *Columbia Essays on Modern Writers.* New York, Columbia University Press, 1964.

OTHER REFERENCES

Books

Abrams, M. H., ed. *The Norton Anthology of English Literature.* 2 vols. New York, Norton, 1962.

Block, Haskell M., and Robert A. Shedd, eds. *Masters of Modern Drama.* New York, Random House, 1962.

Cohn, Ruby, and Bernard Dukore. *Twentieth Century Drama.* New York, Random House, 1966.

Maude, Aylmer. *The Life of Tolstoy: Later Years.* Boston, Houghton, Mifflin, 1950.

Nicolson, Harold. *Diaries and Letters, 1939–1944.* New York, Putnam's, 1946.

Report of the Royal Society of Literature, 1953.

Untermeyer, Louis. *Modern British Poetry.* New York, Harcourt, Brace, 1950.

Winter, William. *Life and Art of Richard Mansfield*. New York, Doubleday, 1964.

Articles

Daiches, David. "Modern Literary Trends," *New York Times Book Review*, October 25, 1970.

Quine, W. V. "Russell's Ontological Development," *Journal of Philosophy*, November 10, 1966.

THE CONTRIBUTORS

JAMES V. BAKER, professor of English, University of Houston, was born in Reading, England. He holds the M.A. in History from Oxford and the Ph.D. in English from the University of Michigan. Besides poems, articles, and reviews in literary magazines, he has published *A Book of Songs and Meditations* (London, 1924) and *The Sacred River: Coleridge's Theory of the Imagination* (1957). He won the Hopwood Award for poetry at the University of Michigan in 1947. He was poetry editor of the University of Houston *Forum* from 1960 to 1967. He contributed the chapter on T. S. Eliot to *American Winners of the Nobel Literary Prize*, edited by Warren G. French and Walter E. Kidd.

WALTER E. KIDD, a member of Phi Beta Kappa and eight literary associations, was born near Long Creek, Oregon. He received the B.A. and M.A. degrees with highest honors from the University of Oregon and the Ph.D. from the University of Denver. Since 1950 he has been professor of English and resident writer at Stephen F. Austin State University, Nacogdoches, Texas. He was a visiting professor in the University of Michigan in 1958 and 1959 and has lectured at various universities and writers' conferences. Under the pen name of Conrad Pendleton, he is the author of four books of poetry: *Slow Fire of Time* (1956), *Time Turns West* (1961), *West: Manhattan to Oregon*

(1966), and *Oregon Wheels of Time* (1973), as well as *Adventures of Frelf* (1964), a novelette, and is co-editor of *American Winners of the Nobel Literary Prize* (1968). Besides contributing poems, stories, reviews and articles to national magazines, he has been guest editor of *Voices* and of *South and West, An International Quarterly*; editor of *PHSTA QUARTERLY*; and an editor of *Twentieth Century Literature: A Scholarly and Critical Journal*.

AMOS C. MILLER, professor of history, University of Houston, was born in Evanston, Illinois. He received the B.A. from Oberlin College, the M.A. from the University of Illinois, and the Ph.D. from the University of California at Los Angeles. Besides scholarly essays, such as "Lady Howard and Sir Richard Grenville" and "Lady Howard and Her Children" in the *Transactions of Devonshire Association*, he is the author of *Sir Henry Killigrew: Elizabethan Soldier and Diplomat* (1967) and is completing a biography of the Royalist general Sir Richard Grenville (1600–59).

FAITH G. NORRIS, professor of English, Oregon State University, was born in London, England, of an Anglo-Indian family and grew up in Japan. There she studied Kipling to learn something of India, where most of her relatives had lived for several generations. She received the B.A. from the University of British Columbia and the M.A. and Ph.D. from the University of California. In addition to a critical evaluation of Bertolt Brecht, she has centered most of her creative activity on children's fiction. She has been a member of the faculty of Oregon State University since 1947.

EDWIN B. PETTET, born in New York City, received the B.A. from Swarthmore College and the M.A. and Ph.D. from New York University. He has directed more than 125 plays for the professional and academic theater and has taught drama and lectured at several universities in the United States and abroad. He is the author of scholarly articles on drama which have appeared in literary magazines and has often appeared on television. He is president emeritus of the New York Shavians. He recently prepared an eight-week television series on the philosophy of Shaw.

IRVING I. POLONOFF, professor of philosophy, Portland State University, was born in Russia and was reared and educated in Montreal. He received the B.S. from Sir George Williams College, the M.A. from McGill University, and the Ph.D. from Yale University. He has taught logic, philosophy of science, and history of philosophy at Portland State University since 1956. He is a member of the American Philosophical Association, the History of Science Society, and the Philosophy of Science Association, and is a contributor to *Scripta Mathematica* and *Isis*. He has lectured before several learned societies. He has completed a book-length manuscript on Kant's early thought.

SANFORD STERNLICHT, professor of English, New York State University at Oswego, was born in New York City. He holds the B.S. in Education and English from New York State University College, the M.A. with distinction from Colgate University, and the Ph.D. from Syracuse University. He is listed in *Who's Who in America, Directory of American Scholars, International Who's Who in Poetry*, and *Who's Who in American Education*. In the 1960's he received a number of fellowships and research awards. His articles, stories, and poems have been published in many periodicals. He is author of *Gull's Way* (poetry), *Love in Pompeii* (poetry), *Yankee Racehorse with Sails* (history), and *Uriah Phillips Levy: The Blue Star Commodore* (biography) and is co-author of *The Black Devil of the Bayous* (history).

EARL EUGENE STEVENS, professor of English, Rhode Island College, was born in Chicago. He received the B.A. cum laude and Phi Beta Kappa membership from Indiana University, the M.A. from the University of Michigan, and the Ph.D. from the University of North Carolina. A member of the Research and Bibliography Committee for *English Literature in Transition, 1880–1920*, he helped annotate the Galsworthy checklist published in *English Fiction in Transition* (1958). He wrote "John Galsworthy: An Annotated Bibliography of Writings About Him: Supplement I" in *English Literature in Transition* (1964), and co-edited the secondary bibliography on Galsworthy for the Northern Illinois Press.

INDEX